The Complete Guide to Public Speaking

Other Books by Jeff Davidson

The One-Minute Procrastinator (Adams Media)

The Complete Idiot's Guide to Managing Your Time (Pearson Education)

101 Internet Marketing Secrets (Entrepreneur Press)

The Complete Idiot's Guide to Managing Change (Pearson Education)

The Complete Idiot's Guide to Reinventing Yourself (Pearson Education)

The Ten Minute Guide to Managing Stress (Pearson Education)

The Ten Minute Guide to Project Management (Pearson Education)

The Ten Minute Guide to Managing Time (Pearson Education)

Breathing Space (MasterMedia)

Marketing Yourself and Your Career (Adams Media)

The Complete Idiot's Guide to Managing Stress (Pearson Education)

The Joy of Simple Living (Rodale Press)

Marketing for the Home-Based Business (Adams Media)

The Complete Idiot's Guide to Reaching Your Goals (Pearson Education)

Marketing Your Consulting and Professional Services (Wiley)

The Complete Idiot's Guide to Assertiveness (Pearson Education)

Marketing on a Shoestring (Wiley)

Power and Protocol for Getting to the Top (Lifetime Books)

Getting New Clients (Wiley)

Avoiding the Pitfalls of Starting Your Own Business (Lifetime)

Selling to the Giants: Becoming a Key Supplier to Large Corporations (McGraw-Hill)

The Complete Guide to Public Speaking

Jeff Davidson

John Wiley & Sons, Inc.

Foreword

The ability to powerfully and persuasively impact audiences is an important part of your career and your life. Despite the onslaught of new communication technology, the need to develop your speaking skills seems to be greater than ever. In all sectors of business and society, the need for effective leadership is as great as ever. There is a demand for bold men and women who can rally, instruct, inspire, and entertain others.

In this exciting new book, speaker and author Jeff Davidson offers a bold, comprehensive compendium of what it takes to succeed as a public speaker. While dozens of books have been written over the years on the various aspects of public speaking, no one has ever managed to assemble a complete guide in the way that Jeff Davidson does here.

The Complete Guide to Public Speaking is a comprehensive action plan for speaking in public. It is loaded with facts, long-term perspectives, unique insights, and personal stories. These assets, combined with humor, make for a valuable, enjoyable, compelling book.

Jeff has arranged the guide into six major topic areas. They include identifying and developing a dynamite speaking topic; enlivening your presentations with humor, movement, and stories; positioning and marketing your speech; winning and negotiating speaker contracts; ground-work activities leading up to the performance; and inspiring audiences. Each of these sections contains numerous chapters, arranged chronologically as your work would unfold.

Every chapter is full of recommendations, tips, caveats, personal philosophy, and highly practical information. Jeff draws on his 19 years as a professional speaker as well as drawing on the wisdom of an enormous number of speaking professionals to provide keen insights and uncommon solutions. Jeff employs first-person observations from some of the most successful speakers in the world, along with the input of meeting planners, marketers, producers, and bureau owners. He goes straight to the experts to provide you with authoritative advice on particular speaking issues.

Jeff has delivered more than 700 presentations, ranging from keynotes and general session speeches given to large audiences, as well as breakout sessions, workshops, round tables, and executive retreats. He has spoken in large convention halls in San Francisco; Los Angeles; Las Vegas; Dallas; Nashville; Atlanta; Chicago; Washington, DC; Orlando; and nearly all domestic points in between, and foreign capitals such as Zurich, Paris, Hong Kong, and Singapore. He has made presentations in venues large and small—hotels, corporate headquarters, local meeting facilities, and even church basements. His audiences have consisted of professionals, homemakers, retirees, the military, and students.

Companies who retained Jeff as a speaker reported impressive results. Jeff has attracted clients such as America Online, NationsBank, Swissotel, IBM, American Express, Westinghouse, and more than 400 other leading organizations and associations. All told his, speaking and consulting career has taken him to more than 30 countries and 44 states. He has spoken in industries ranging from aviation to zoology and addressed individuals in administration, law, banking, education, finance, government, health care, manufacturing, retailing, and wholesaling.

Jeff Davidson has not only experienced public speaking; he has actively studied it. In *The Complete Guide to Public Speaking,* he conveys the essence of what he has gleaned, allocated into nearly four dozen major subject areas. Jeff's single goal is to offer you insightful, leading edge advice so that you have the best chance of being successful as a public speaker.

LILYAN WILDER
Speech Coach and Author
Seven Steps to Fearless Speaking

Acknowledgments

The *Complete Guide to Public Speaking* is, at its heart, the accumulation of what I have learned about the topic over more than 25 years. My knowledge has been aided by hundreds of effective role models, mentors, peers, and absolute masters of public speaking. Listed below is but a handful of the people who have made a difference in my speaking career.

Thanks to Tony Alessandra, Tom Antion, Ty Boyd, Daniel Burrus, Jim Cathcart, Roger Dawson, Joan Detz, Patricia Fripp, Jeffrey Gitomer, Mark Victor Hansen, Tony Jeary, Charles Petty, Glenna Salsbury, Brian Sturm, and David Allen Yoho.

Thanks also to subject matter experts/authors such as Emory Austin, the late Art Berg, Francine Berger, Bill Bethel, Sheila Murray Bethel, Lenora Billings-Harris, Joel Blackwell, Don Blohowiak, Terry Brock, Marjorie Brody, Bill Brooks, Brian Tracy, Bob Bly, Bob Burg, Joe Calloway, Dan Clark, Gerald Coffee, Thomas Connellan, Bert Decker, John Dolan, Mary-Ellen Drummond, Charles Dygert, Kay duPont, Gil Eagles, Joan Eisenstodt, Janet Elsea, Gerry Faust, Robert Fish, Jim Folks, Francis Friedman, Scott Friedman, Rande Gedaliah, Robert Gedaliah, Lola Gillebaard, Scott Gross, Jane Handly, Keith Harrell, Lou Heckler, James Hennig, Jane Herlong, Roger Herman, Sue Hershkowitz-Coore, Ralph Hillman, Bil Holton, Cher Holton, Don Hutson, Shep Hyken, Dale Irvin, Larry James, Elizabeth Jeffries, Peter Johnson, Willie Jolley, Danielle Kennedy, Shawn Kent, Kurt Kilpatrick, Allen Klein, and Tom Kubistant.

I also want to thank Ray Leone, Al McCree, Dennis McQuistion, Niki McQuistion, Scott McKain, David Meinz, James Melton, Rebecca Morgan, Patrick O'Dooley, Rosita Perez, Terry Paulson, Chuck Reaves, Jim Rhode, Naomi Rhode, Bill Ringle, Mary Beth Roach, Grady Jim Robinson, Edward Scannell, Juannell Teague, Richard Thieme, Dan Thurmon,

Brian Tracy, Jim Tunney, Al Walker, Dottie Walters, George Walther, and Dave Yoho.

Thanks to the array of wonderful speakers bureau owners and representatives including Nancy and Bill Lauterbach, James Bauchum, Dave Galbreath, Joanne Van Hook, Mark French, Marina Forstmann, Rainey Foster, Phil Barber, Valerie Morris, Tony Colao, Jo Cavender, Ralph Andres, Janet Pickover, Duane Ward, Porter Poole, Marilyn Montgomery, Theresa Brown, Carole Van Brocklin, Phyllis McKenzie, Esther Eagles, Lois Brown, and Julie Sloway.

Thanks to coaches, trainers, teachers, and all the other instructors in my speaking life for the inspiration and the endearing gifts you have provided. Thanks to Laura Reed, Ron Arden, Sharon Szymanski, Bonnie Raphael, Caroline Warren, Max Dixon, and Rafael Barrantes.

This book would not have happened without the wonderful folks at John Wiley & Sons including Airie Stuart who acquired my book and shaped it, Jessie Noyes, Thomas Miller, Lauren Fransen, Joe Grosso, Rosa Gonzalez, Deborah DeBlasi, John Chambers, Jason Bartholomew, Eric Holmgreen, Trudy Lindsey, Ira Tan, and Susanne Marvoka.

Thanks also to my local support staff, copy editors, reviewers, transcriber, and all-around helpers without whom this book would not be possible. They include Sharon Askew, Jessi Bromwell, and Susan Davidson. Thanks also to Valerie Davidson, now age 12, who, at age 9, demonstrated her captivating public speaking ability when to she introduced me to an audience of 150 adults in Washington, DC, and received spontaneous applause!

Contents

PART I

IDENTIFYING AND CREATING A DYNAMITE SPEAKING TOPIC

Chapter 1	A Bevy of Speech Topics	3
Chapter 2	Appealing to People's Emotions	10
Chapter 3	Why Do You Want to Speak?	18
Chapter 4	Researching Your Topic	22
Chapter 5	Tapping Your Hidden Strengths	28
Chapter 6	Dealing with Change: The All Pervasive Topic	34
Chapter 7	Meeting Types and Variations	39

PART II

DEVELOPING AND ENLIVENING YOUR PRESENTATION

Chapter 8	Get Humorous or Get Going	49
Chapter 9	Presenting the Best of You	57
Chapter 10	The High-Content Presentation	69
Chapter 11	Body and Movement	73
Chapter 12	All about Visuals	78
Chapter 13	Developing Your Signature Story	91
Chapter 14	Making Your Story Even Better	98
Chapter 15	Pauses and Silences	108

PART III

MARKETING YOUR SPEECH AND SPEAKING CAPABILITIES

Chapter 16   The Client's Mind-Set   117

Chapter 17   Positioning Is the Best Marketing   120

Chapter 18   Making Measured Progress   126

Chapter 19   Getting Paid and Selling Your Services   133

Chapter 20   Developing a Dynamite One-Sheet   141

Chapter 21   Collecting and Using Kudo Letters   155

Chapter 22   I'm Ready for My Video, Mr. DeMille   163

PART IV

PREPARING FOR AND NEGOTIATING SPEAKER CONTRACTS

Chapter 23   What Meeting Planners Seek   175

Chapter 24   Preempt the Pack and Close the Deal   184

Chapter 25   What Goes into a Speaker Agreement?   193

Chapter 26   Variations on Product Sales   199

Chapter 27   Show Me the Money   206

PART V

GROUNDWORK

Chapter 28   Responsiveness and Balance   215

Chapter 29   The Diversity Factor   222

Chapter 30   Staying in Touch All the While   226

Chapter 31   Planning for Audience Involvement   230

Chapter 32   Preparing a Seamless Presentation   235

Chapter 33   Your Introduction Is Crucial   239

Chapter 34   Have a Great Trip   245

Chapter 35   Meeting Room Layouts   249

Chapter 36   Handling Speaker Challenges   258

PART VI
CAPTIVATING AND INSPIRING YOUR AUDIENCES

Chapter 37   Pre-Speech Activities   265

Chapter 38   Open with a Flourish   269

Chapter 39   Audience Involvement   275

Chapter 40   Audience Responsiveness   281

Chapter 41   Reading (and Mis-Reading) Your Audience   288

Chapter 42   Traps and Tips   296

Chapter 43   Why Speakers Fail to Hit the Mark   301

Bibliography and Further Reading   311

About the Author   313

Index   315

PART I

IDENTIFYING AND CREATING A DYNAMITE SPEAKING TOPIC

Before you can be an effective speaker, you need to have a dynamite speaking topic. The big mistake that aspiring public speakers make is harboring a strong desire to speak while not actively pursuing the development of promising speaking topics.

The seven chapters in Part I explain precisely how to identify, test, develop, and refine a speaking topic that will interest and enthrall audiences. Public speakers whose audiences give them high ratings undertake considerable effort on their topics before anyone ever hears them. Fortunately, it is not difficult work to devise a topic; rather, it is an enjoyable, exciting, and even energizing intellectual pursuit. The chapters here will give you the fundamentals of succeeding in the vital area of topic development.

Throughout the book, I will heavily refer to other professional speakers, and to the tips and techniques that they offer. For consistency, I will draw largely upon artifacts and examples from my own speaking career. By referring to my own marketing materials, preprinted forms, and approaches, and you will be able to follow a path of sorts that offers a fuller, holistic sense of successful strategies for both public speaking and professional speaking.

1

A Bevy of
Speech Topics

When I was younger, I worked for three different firms in management consulting over a total of nine years. With my second firm, in my fourth year in the profession, 16 of the 24 staff consultants were fired. I was among the "lucky" eight. That experience taught me to develop *career advancement skills.* As a part of this development process, I spoke to groups outside of work (at breakfast meetings, during lunch, and after work). I wrote articles. I took steps that would make me indispensable on the job.

I developed a personal set of behaviors and strategies for success. I had no idea that I was going to be a speaker, nor did I have any idea that I was going to be an author. Unknowingly, I was living my future material.

I had been developing career advancement strategies for myself, and I realized that if the strategies had helped me overcome obstacles, then surely they'd be of benefit to someone else. This experience prepared me for writing a book many years later on career advancement strategies.

The following is a list of some of the chapters in the book that I wrote. As you read, you might envision speech topics from your own experiences emerging:

- Your Personal Marketing Plan
- Time Management and Career Marketing

- Finding a Career Counselor or Mentor
- Becoming Indispensable
- When Your Boss Is a Roadblock

Every one of these chapters could be a topic for a speech. In many instances, the problems we face are exactly what others want to hear about, particularly if we were good at overcoming these roadblocks. There are some topics that we've become experts in, without even realizing it.

IS YOUR TOPIC SEASONAL?

Another type of speaking topic is what I call a *seasonal* topic. For example, if, during the holidays, you were to lead a management seminar on stress, you could include a message that would fit the appropriate holiday.

For example, I'm hired a couple of times a year by groups to deliver a variation of my overall theme of breathing space and shape it to fit the seasonal topic of having breathing space for the holidays. My primary message is that you don't have to have stress during the holidays; you can have breathing space.

To capitalize on the seasonal topics, look at your calendar, identify events, and perhaps develop some kind of expertise. You may not be hired for a seasonal topic throughout the year, but you may be able to get two or three engagements annually, and you may be hired months in advance.

CYCLICAL, PARADIGM SHIFT, AND LONG-TERM TOPICS

There are also examples of speakers who capitalize on "hot topics." For example, Dr. Ken Dychtwald, author of *Age Ware,* a book that looks at trends within life expectancy and aging, has become a sought-after speaker as Baby Boomers hit their fifties. He commands enormous sums because he is an expert on this hot topic. In addition to hot topics and seasonal topics, there are *cyclical* topics. These are subjects that come around again and again. It might be once a year; it might be every couple of years.

A cyclical topic may arise when a business is going through major changes and consultant speakers are brought in. The business may even out for a while, shift, and eventually, changes will again occur and the corporation will want the speaker back again.

The fourth type of topic for speeches is what I call the *one time,* or *paradigm shift.* This refers to a shift that is not going to return to where it was, for example, downsizing as we know it. This topic is neither seasonal nor cyclical; it is lasting because of technology and the way people compete. Corporations will continue to maintain a core staff and use more supplemental staff (people who are not full-time, but who can provide specific services). If you have expertise in this area, you will be among those who get hired.

Ten Ways to Spot a Trend before Everyone Else

Increasingly, many professionals speak about change. Being able to spot trends ahead of everyone else can prove to be a valuable skill.

- Read magazines such as *The Futurist.*
- Listen to lectures or review books and cassettes from leading forecasters.
- Visit the Web sites of top opinion pollsters and survey research firms.
- Cross fertilize your thinking by reading alternative magazines.
- Attend meetings and expositions that you normally would not attend.
- Take a college or adult education course on forecasting or futurism.
- Examine longitudinal trends (such as those published by the U.S. Census Bureau) to make reasonable predictions as to where those trends will head in the future.
- Learn to develop and trust your intuition.
- Read *Advertising Age, Variety,* and other publications that discuss the themes and campaigns designed by Madison Avenue and Hollywood moguls.
- Read books by Bill Gates, Jack Welch, Andy Grove, and other industry leaders.

THE BUZZWORD APPROACH

Buzzwords permeate business, industry, health care, and government. Dr. Charles Digart, based in Columbus, Ohio, observes, "The avalanche of buzzwords is never-ending and growing in size and complexity. The frequency of change is compressing at an alarming rate."

One way public speakers can stay abreast of this phenomenon while honing their skills in making effective, timely, presentations is to learn the buzzwords in their industry. If you want to be successful in speaking to bankers, then immerse yourself in the issues and affairs of bankers. Learn the jargon. Subscribe to the magazines that they read. Expose yourself to the broad array of traditional and emerging terms that bankers know and use or will have to know and use in the future.

Likewise, if you choose to speak to manufacturers, club managers, accountants, or yacht captains, you need to know the latest buzzwords in those areas. Once you become familiar with the terminology, an array of topic ideas presents itself.

In the past few years, Dr. Digart notes, a variety of business buzzwords have emerged, each of which carries the seeds of a potential presentation topic. A brief listing of such words includes:

- Groupware
- Netiquette
- Telecommunicating
- Benchmarking
- Self-directed teams
- Scenario thinking
- Learner-friendly
- Open architecture
- Core staff
- Team orientation
- Reeingineering

- Virtual teams
- Multimedia
- Cross-training
- User-based
- Diversity training
- Multitasking
- Global market
- Gain sharing
- Right sizing
- Knowledge worker
- Shareholder value

- Micro-technology
- Chief operating officer
- Learning organizations
- Virtual manufacturing
- Relationship assets
- Career coach
- Transferable skills
- Matrix management

Similarly, in these and other arenas, a host of new terms representing new concepts or variations on old themes continually appears. Each of them carries the seeds of potential speaker topic development. Sometimes simply by reviewing such a list for any given industry or drawing up a list of the buzzwords with which you are already familiar, you develop new ideas for presentation topics.

DEVELOPING TOPICS WITH LONG SHELF LIVES

If you're going to take the time and energy to develop a topic that you can successfully present to an audience, why undercut yourself by choosing a topic with a short shelf life? Be on the lookout for topics that are in demand today and, with minimal updating, will continue to be in demand in the future. (Chapter 4 discusses how to continually stay in touch with developments in your field and on your topics.)

As professional speaker Bruce Wilkinson says, "Most speakers today look for a single topic that they can sell to a specific market or audience. Tomorrow's speakers are looking for specific topics that they can sell to multiple markets and audiences." Wilkinson suggests considering the following criteria when developing a multiple market topic:

1. Is there a need for this topic in associations and corporations? This is an important consideration because most successful speakers develop a blend of association and corporation business; furthermore, speaking to associations actually enhances your corporate business and vice versa. When you speak to local, state, regional, national, or even international associations, audiences are comprised of individuals who come from different organizations, even if they all happen to be in the same industry. As such, a sterling speech to a large association could result in your being scheduled to speak within the corporations of audience members. For the same reason, you increase the chances of developing more association business when you speak to corporate groups. The best way to ensure that you benefit from this cross-exposure is to develop a topic that will work within both associations and corporate markets with minimum modifications. The same logic applies for speaking at partner's programs during a convention. The larger the audience, the greater the potential for spin-off business.

2. Use several titles for the same subject to attract multiple markets. Sometimes merely changing the wording of your presentation titles makes them more attractive to entirely different markets. For example, my presentation on managing information and communication overload is worded so as to attract corporate markets. Essentially the same presentation, re-titled "Managing the Pace with Grace," is attractive to local groups, cruise ship audiences, and even as breakout sessions for a spouse's or partner's program at association conventions.

3. Create both a serious and a humorous version of the same topic. This is a bit arduous for the aspiring public speaker. If you have been making presentations for a while, however, devising serious and humorous versions won't be too difficult.

Consider the topics offered by speaker Joel Blackwell. He speaks on grassroots lobbying and is effective in serving associations that call on members of Congress to get their points across. He can deliver a highly serious presentation on this topic as a keynote address, a breakout session, an executive roundtable, or a half-day or full-day seminar. He is also creative and witty enough to offer this session as a humorous keynote presentation or as a short after-lunch or after-dinner presentation. As a result, he is not limited to fixed slots within an organization's conference agenda.

4. Present this topic with and without a handout or audience participant packet. Many public speakers do an adequate job of making a presentation armed with printed materials. Giving a presentation without such aids is harder, but developing that capacity increases the range of venues at which you could be successful. If, for example, a meeting planner requests your services for a luncheon gathering of 1,800 people, a handout, workbook, or audience participant packet may not be practical. Moreover, the levels of enthusiasm, energy, and humor required for such a presentation necessitate that it be markedly different from its counterpart in front of a smaller audience. These issues are discussed in much greater detail, but for now, the point is that flexibility can go a long way in your being hired for speaking at vastly different events, while still addressing essentially the same topic.

IDENTIFYING SECONDARY AUDIENCES

Wilkinson says, "To be successful in selling today's topics for tomorrow's profits, speakers need to identify each secondary audience before they step onto the platform." Hence, at the same convention, you might deliver a keynote presentation to the members of an association and, at a different point in the day, deliver a presentation for nonmembers who are in attendance.

The public speaker who is on the lookout for topics that he or she can use for presentations to multiple markets and multiple audiences is always cognizant of the value of employing stories, anecdotes, and references that will appeal to diverse elements of society.

You know that you have a topic that has broad appeal when it can interest a wide range of groups such as those in government, education, military, and health care. Is the topic in the news? Is it in professional journals, the Internet, and magazines? In addition, it is not unprofessional to attend a presentation, workshop, or training session on the topic you have in mind to see if it is something you wish to further develop and pursue on your own.

To maintain an ethical stance, you would not engage in any lifting of another presenter's material, and you certainly would not violate any copyright, trademark, or other intellectual property rights. Instead, your quest is to gather ideas, from any source, reflect on them, expand on them, and arrange them in some type of sequence. The next chapters help you develop your own stellar, engaging presentation. In Chapter 2, we begin to develop your topic by selecting a subject that appeals to people's emotions.

Appealing to People's Emotions

That which motivates people lends itself to topic exploration. Motivators could include money, survival, fear of failure, fun and enjoyment, recognition, boredom, deadlines, participation with and by others, and avoidance of pain.

Some people regard "pain management" as the greatest single motivator for people to achieve what they want. Proponents maintain that unless you associate sufficient amounts of pain with your current situation, in a week, a month, or a year from now, you will find yourself right where you started. You'll likely be surrounded by all of the unpleasant aspects of your current situation because you won't muster sufficient impetus to break through the transition state getting you en route to your desired end result.

A public speaker who recognizes and understands a group's pain can be highly influential in addressing that group. Success guru Tony Robbins says that "how you define pain and pleasure shapes your destiny." He asserts that people do more to avoid pain than to seek pleasure. As a public speaker, your challenge is to ask, "What are my audience members facing—what is it that they absolutely cannot do without? What is it that they continue to lack?" Address those issues and you will have everyone in the room hanging on your every word.

One of Robbins' recommendations is to convert the pain that your audiences may be experiencing to a form of pleasure by showing them a safe path.

You want to create an *emotional* path for audiences, not an intellectual path. Feeling in control and experiencing less frustration are examples of emotional payoffs that audiences can relate to. By focusing on people's pain, you can offer audiences inspirational or motivational presentations.

INSPIRATIONAL PRESENTATIONS

An inspirational presentation is one that stirs emotion. It contains a message that has deep and potentially long-lasting impact. It is delivered from the heart and often stokes the empathy and creative imagination of all audience members. While an inspirational presentation can draw on religious or spiritual themes, such an approach is not necessary.

The common denominator to an inspirational presentation is that it leaves the audience on a high note. While there may be elements of sadness and sorrow interspersed within the presentation, ultimately, the uplifting elements win out. The audience leaves feeling that tomorrow can be better than today.

MOTIVATIONAL PRESENTATIONS

A motivational presentation shares characteristics with an inspirational presentation, but it is more action-oriented. It is designed to induce audience members to want to leave their seats and accomplish urgent tasks. To be effective, the speaker needs to understand some specific challenges faced by audience members. As with all effective presentations, a good motivational speech requires homework on the part of the presenter.

When the presentation hones in on the specific activities and mind-set that audience participants need to accomplish a goal, all the better. Therefore, an effective motivational presentation offers specific advice and often detailed information as to how participants can succeed. The presenter fashions such information in a forceful, positive, and highly supportive way. He or she enlightens people about his or her point of view and suggests a plan for taking action.

THE SEVEN SUBTLE UNCONSCIOUS DESIRES

Tony Jeary, author of *How to Inspire Any Audience,* believes that audiences have seven subtle unconscious desires (not unrelated to the concept of alleviating pain, that I just discussed), and that if you appeal to these desires during your presentation, you can't help but win participants over. Here is a brief description of each of the seven desires as identified by Jeary:

1. *To belong*—Everyone wants to feel that they are part of something. Obviously, each participant is a member of the audience that happens to be gathered for your presentation. More than that, how can you appeal to them as professionals, parents, or citizens?

In my presentation on "Having More Breathing Space in Your Life," I often unify my audiences by telling them, "You are part of the most time-pressed generation in history." People instantly understand what this means. To be alive today and to hold any position of responsibility all but ensures that you face significant time-related challenges.

2. *To be respected*—Paying respects to your audience members only takes a sentence or two but yields great dividends. Let the audience know that you appreciate the opportunity to give your presentation to them. Let them know that you understand, at least in part, some of the challenges that they face. Let them know anything that signifies that you respect them as individuals, as professionals, and as a group.

3. *To be appreciated*—Appreciation is closely tied to respect. At various junctures throughout your presentation, let the audience members know that you appreciate them by using words of praise or thanks. Conclude by letting the audience know that you greatly enjoyed speaking to them. I tell my audiences, when it is true, "You have been a wonderful audience."

4. *To find romance*—This may not be an issue that you'll address directly in your speech, but in a large gathering, nearly all people will have an ongoing need to maintain strong connections with others, particularly a significant other.

5. *To be liked*—Along with finding romance, Jeary contends that people have a deep-seated desire to be liked. In the work place, in associations and clubs, at leisure activities, and among friends, we all want to be liked—and well liked at that.

6. *To be safe*—Safety comes in many forms: physical, financial, and emotional, to name a few. Within a meeting environment, people want to feel safe to participate, laugh, cry, agree, or disagree. As a speaker, it's your responsibility to help audience participants feel safe during your presentation.

7. *To be enthusiastic*—This seventh unconscious desire may seem less likely to belong on the list, but when you examine it further, it makes sense. People want to champion a cause and to be on a winning team.

In the movie *Jerry McGuire,* Dorothy Boyd says to Jerry, "What I really want is to be inspired." The best way to ensure that you appeal to the subtle unconscious desire of members of your audience to be enthusiastic is to convey enthusiasm yourself. (More on this in Part VI.)

TOPICS BASED ON WHAT PEOPLE TRADITIONALLY WANT

Drawing on human nature and the knowledge of what people traditionally want and need is one way of discerning potential popular speech topics. I am always encountering lists of what people want or need, and I find such rosters intriguing. For example, a study entitled "Ten Triggers That Satisfy Human Desire," based on research from the University of Minnesota, cites the following:

- Making money
- Being popular
- Being in style
- Protecting one's family
- Saving time
- Saving money
- Being healthy
- Avoiding pain
- Living comfortably
- Attracting attention, attracting the opposite sex

Other such lists point to more basic needs. One list, for which the source is unknown, cites "Ten Things There Is Always a Need For":

- Love
- Variety and novelty
- Sleep
- Food, shelter, and clothing
- Exercise and fresh air
- Nutrition

- Sex
- Sense of Belonging
- Sense of Accomplishment
- Sense of Ownership

Many items presented on such lists overlap and, in some cases, are divergent! It all depends on what the researchers are looking for, how they conduct their studies, whom they sample, and how they interpret the results.

Any presentation you develop that incorporates some of these basic themes has a high probability of being of interest to audiences.

GETTING INTO THE ACT

I've generated some of my own lists, usually on planes when I'm headed home from a speech. One of my lists is called "Items People Always Need," and it contains six elements:

- A safe residence
- To avoid injury
- Money
- To appear in public
- Recognition
- Partners

You may debate the importance of some elements on the list; but the probability is that most of your audiences can relate to several, if not all, of these factors.

I generated another list called "Eight Lectures I Would Pay a Small Fortune to Hear" as an exercise in stimulating my own thinking when it comes to grabber topics. I came up with the following:

- How to think twice as effectively.
- How to relate to and with anyone.
- How to work half as much with double the effectiveness.
- How to become sexually irresistible.
- How to get a $100,000 book advance.
- How to never be bored.
- How to maintain 100 percent self-confidence.
- How to stay in love forever.

OBSTACLES AND IRRITATIONS

I've found that if you notice as few as two people experiencing a problem in their personal lives, careers, or organizations, you have enough preliminary evidence to begin exploration of the topic. Many ideas for topics spring from obstacles and irritations. You may personally be confronting an obstacle or irritation that is a topic worth exploring:

- If you face a roadblock.
- If there's a situation wherein you could leap over the hurdle if only you could get the right information.
- If there is an issue that is too big for you.

Before I wrote a book on careers, I looked at the career books already in print and found that most of them focused on things in which I had little interest. Most career books talk about how to get a raise, how to get a promotion, how to deal with/survive office politics, or how to fend for your turf. I wasn't looking to do any of these things—I wanted to know how to get more visibility in my current position.

> Look closely at every quest, irritation, obstacle, or roadblock in your life. The things that you encounter each day may turn into a speaking topic for you.

THE DEFICIENCIES APPROACH

Related to the irritations approach, another way to address the wants and needs of audience members is to uncover "deficiencies"—unfilled wants and needs. Here are some questions that will help you identify other presentation topics that will readily resonate with audiences:

- What do people want to have or possess that they don't have?
- What do they want to resolve but thus far have not resolved?
- What do people easily begin but then not finish?

- What would they like to change (within their power) but so far haven't been able to?
- What are the routines they would like to break out of?
- What do they want to say but haven't said or perhaps don't know how to say?
- What are the activities they would like to do but can't get started on?
- What are they retaining that they would prefer to let go?
- How would they like to feel but haven't been able to feel?
- In what directions would they like to grow?

EXERCISES TO STIMULATE THOUGHT

While the issue of topics is firmly in your mind, some simple exercises will help you identify, dislodge, and recognize potential presentation topics.

First, take a piece of paper and title it, "Irritations, Roadblocks," followed by three blank lines.

Now fill in the blanks. Come up with three irritations or roadblocks you encounter when pursuing information in a given area. Often these relate to something you want to accomplish, a problem you want to solve, or a challenge that arises. Then do the same for "deficiencies."

Next, on the same page, write the word "gap" with three blank lines. In the books, articles, and lectures to which you were recently exposed, what parts prompted you to think there was something missing? Write those gaps on these lines. At work, if there are some new procedures, programs, instructions, or operating guidelines that have an obvious gap, write them down. If you notice gaps in topics, chances are good that other people have made the same observations. Therefore, they represent potentially fertile ground for future presentation topics.

Now set up another sheet titled "Horses to Ride." This represents any significant trend that has emerged or is looming on the horizon. The trend could be related to your career, personal life, or something that is more widely observable among career professionals or society in general.

For what kind of training do people in your industry routinely sign up? What types of skills are currently in high demand and will likely be so for the foreseeable future? Leadership? Time management? Customer service? Adapting to technology?

"Horses to ride," that is, popular topics that are well within your expertise and comfort zone are worth further exploration as future presentation topics.

Finally, set up another sheet to list "Other Topics." Think about topics that are already hot, such as those reflected in current books and lectures. What are the big topics in the news right now? What special insights do you have into these topics, based on your experiences?

As you continue to mull over these issues, turn to the question of why you want to speak. This important consideration is another way to uncover your perfect speaking topic.

3

Why Do You
Want to Speak?

Sometimes simply recognizing why you want to speak is important for your overall development as a speaker. Some speakers want to get free trips to great places, stay in nice hotels or resorts, eat good meals, and deliver their presentations in magnificent meeting rooms in festive atmospheres surrounded by enthusiastic participants. Many people want to be public speakers because they, either knowingly or not, need a large dose of approval. How else do you get people to applaud when you finish saying something? Certainly not at home! Audience approval can be highly stimulating, even intoxicating. I'd guess that nearly 50 percent of professional speakers were drawn to the profession in large part because of the psychological payoff they get from the audiences.

Other speakers want to be held in high esteem by their peers—coworkers, friends, relatives, or other public speakers. Since public speaking traditionally makes the top 10 lists of things people would prefer to avoid, being a confident public speaker clearly could engender the admiration and esteem of others. Some speakers seek the challenge of encountering people they've never met and quickly convincing them that what they have to present can change their lives for the better. A speaker who flies to a city, makes his way to the convention hall, steps up to the lectern, and in the next 45 minutes argues persuasively enough about some way to accomplish some great thing to convince virtually everyone in the room performs a small act of magic.

Some, and hopefully you fall into this camp, have a burning desire to serve their audiences. They are motivated by a passion for their topic and compassion for helping others. Some want to help right wrongs, expose injustices, and some empower their listeners, or create advocates—people who will go out and carry the message further.

TOPICS OF PASSION

Conducting an audit of your own driving forces is a surprisingly simple and highly effective way to identify your "topics of passion." When you are passionate about a topic, you are more likely to become an excellent presenter on that topic. What motivates you? What inspires you?

The list that follows presents a wide range of characteristics that may describe your ideal topic:

- *The need to be creative*—This presentation might cover problem solving, reducing costs, or how to be more creative.
- *Using time productively*—If the use of time is a driving force in your life, you might gravitate toward these issues: time management, overcoming procrastination, project management, change management, or life balance.
- *Experiencing inner harmony*—These presentation topics might include life balance, meditation, travel, or self-discovery.
- *Improving your intellect*—Topics for those who value having fine minds could include increasing your brain power, developing a personal philosophy, lifelong education, and improving your IQ.
- *Generating wealth*—Subjects in this arena include building your net worth, choosing a financial planner, strategies for increasing your savings, earning and retaining more, starting your own business, and how to protect your assets.
- *Gaining recognition*—This includes topics on the need for acknowledgment and praise, self-esteem, self-worth, promoting yourself or your business, getting interviewed by the media, and developing charisma.

- *Family unity*—Related topics abound, including developing a strong family; putting your family first; achieving a stronger marriage, family, and faith; raising happy, healthy children; handling divorce.
- *Personal power*—All people need some degree of personal power in their lives. Related issues include increasing your personal power, influencing others, expressing yourself, assertiveness, and, of course, how to be a public speaker!
- *Spirituality*—Topics include understanding your faith, the world's great religions, religion and the family, defining Christianity (or any other religion), and finding God within.
- *Compete for success*—Many people feel the need to be in the game and to do well in it, and a range of business, sports, and personal topics can be derived from this drive, such as succeeding in your own business, getting a raise, beating the competition, learning secrets of top competitors, and achieving peak performance.
- *Getting or staying organized*—Related issues include getting organized, simplicity, time management, stress management, eliminating waste, and controlling your environment.
- *Staying healthy*—The list of subjects related to personal health and safety is nearly endless, but may include nutrition and health, a healthier you, how to be your own doctor, avoiding sports injuries, and safe travel.
- *Serving others*—Volunteering is on the rise and related topics include how charity begins at home, effective gift giving, being a better listener, customer service, running for public office, and supporting a cause.

Other personal drives related or unrelated to these may be responsible for the initial breakthrough that leads to your interest in a particular topic area. Think about the issues that inspire or frustrate you. In addition, what is your personal mantra or belief system? If you own a company, what is your mission statement?

To speak on a topic with any kind of passion, you need to do more than move into that space. The topic has to be a part of you. It needs to be something that you would be willing to speak about for free. The best topics develop out of the great and not so great individual experiences in our lives and the lives of people we observe.

JEFF DAVIDSON'S PRESENTATION TOPICS

My most successful speeches are based on my audiences' needs. A few of these speeches are discussed next. Use this discussion to stimulate ideas about your own unique speeches.

"Staying Prosperous in a World of Rapid Change"

Everywhere you look there are managers who are concerned about what it takes to stay competitive in our rapidly changing society. In this presentation, I address this concern by laying out high-probability scenarios of the future and what people can do to achieve or maintain leadership positions in their markets and specialty areas, despite the frequency of change to which they're exposed.

"The Learning Organization"

The Information Age can overwhelm any company and its managers and increase their workload, or it can help speed their work and increase their free time. In this speech, I prepare organizations to handle the pace of competing in a future that perpetually comes too fast. Once audiences understand the futility of attempting to access more than a tiny slice of the information available to them, they'll actually be happy about what they're missing—intentionally. Moreover, they'll learn to make the most of what they choose to keep pace with.

Researching
Your Topic

There are a number of ways to find information on a particular topic—from talking with meeting planners and industry leaders to keeping up with the latest industry trends.

TAP MEETING PLANNERS

An excellent way to determine your best topic is to study the issues faced by the actual meeting planners (and the organizations that employ them). Some can speak at length about the topics that would interest their members. Many a successful topic has sprung from a meeting planner's request to a speaker to provide a certain type of program. In addition, periodically some of the leading organizations in the meeting planning industry, among them Meeting Professionals International, survey their members to ascertain what types of challenges they are facing.

If you're a little reticent to tap a meeting planner, an easy way to find out what's of interest to the members of an organization is to ask for their brochure, data, or a flyer from the previous year's convention. Alternatively, you could find information on the organization's Web site. The content doesn't change so quickly as to make this year's interests completely different from last year's. You can also request:

- A quarterly report, annual report, or 10K report. To obtain these, write to an organization's information department.
- A video or cassette. If they're part of a company, they may have a promotional video or cassette that they send to their customers or potential shareholders.
- A membership directory. These are generally available in any association.
- Monthly publications, newsletters, legislative updates, key memos, and faxes.

All of these help you get to know an industry, client, association, or company. If I receive three or four of these items, I have enough information to show up at the convention or meeting knowing something about my audience. If you want to develop a topic, often all you need to do is run through the information that you can gather on any group.

CURRENT CHALLENGES

I contacted a number of meeting planners I know to ask about their pressing concerns. Briefly summarized, here is a long list of current challenges for meeting planners primarily from the ranks of business and industry and professional and trade associations:

- *Intense competition*—"How does our organization stay competitive and profitable in the face of new companies entering the marketplace, some of which use cutthroat pricing?"
- *Reducing costs*—"The ability to profitably produce and deliver our products is as great as it has ever been. We can't continually raise prices, so reducing operational costs has become the way to go."
- *Surviving*—"Our industry is in a downturn; right now simply staying afloat is our greatest organizational challenge."
- *Industry consolidation*—"Everywhere you look, the larger firms are buying up the smaller ones. With bigger budgets, bigger marketing campaigns, and an extended reach, the industry giants are making it hard for us to maintain our market share. If we don't merge with somebody, we might go under."

- *Employee recruitment*—"Identifying, attracting, and retaining the right people for the right positions have gotten incredibly difficult. It seems as if there are many organizations vying for the same few key job candidates."
- *Employee turnover*—"When we lose a good staff person, the impact can be devastating. There is considerable down time during the search, loss of morale, sometimes among the departed coworkers, and the feeling that often we're simply spinning our wheels."
- *Restricted budgets*—"We have to operate with less funding than last year, and far less than the year before that. Meanwhile, job responsibilities have increased, not decreased, or even held constant."
- *Government regulations*—"Despite everything you read about this being an era of 'deregulation,' in our industry every other month some new regulation comes down the pike causing us to devote countless staff hours and a sizable chunk of our budget to comply."
- *Dealing with change*—"Our people report feeling overwhelmed with everything they've had to endure, and yet, it seems as if the pace of change is coming even faster. New procedures, equipment, technology—when does it end?" (See Chapter 6.)
- *Continuing education*—"We need to keep providing high quality education for our members and assist them in compiling sufficient continuing education units (CEUs) on their path to certification, promotion, and advancement."
- *More programs to plan*—"I'm managing 50 percent more meetings this year than I did two years ago. Meanwhile, the lead-time for meetings is shrinking, and I was already working as hard as I could."

FINDING OPINION LEADERS

Richard Connor, my co-author for *Marketing Your Consulting and Professional Services,* says, "Those who serve, influence, and regulate members of a selected niche are able to identify hot industry topics and those destined to become hot." By meeting such industry influentials and establishing relationships with them, you can find today's hot buttons—key issues affecting your target industry. These issues are good speaking topics.

In addition, every industry has people who are influential—people who give primary information as to what is plaguing their industry.

Examples are CEOs of corporations, columnists, and stock analysts. There are several ways to meet or speak with these individuals:

- Call them directly and identify a topic of great interest to them. Later in the conversation, you can transition to your interests.
- Attend meetings, conventions, trade shows, and civic, charitable, and social functions at which industry influentials will be present.
- Through a third party, arrange to meet them at lunch. This form of leveraging your existing relationships can double, or even triple, the number of industry influentials you personally contact and the understanding you gain of emerging issues.

OTHER SOURCES FOR TOPICS

The challenges that meeting planners face aren't necessarily the same topics that their members would like to hear about at a convention. The opinion columns of editors do, however, contain seeds, nuggets, and ideas that are there for the taking.

Another reliable source for discovering topics is in the commentary section of every newspaper or the opinion page of the Sunday newspaper. As you read the editorials, often the author is expressing an opinion or an idea that taps a nerve. What the editor says is what many people are thinking. You may have been affected by it because it fits what you have been working on, who you are, or what you are moving toward. Examine *United States Today,* the *New York Times,* the *Wall Street Journal* and other trend-identifying publications. If you beat most of the rest of the pack on a particular emerging topic, you may be able to carve out a niche for yourself for many years.

How many times have you opened up a magazine to see that someone has written a letter to the editor or a rebuttal to a letter, and it is filled with topic gems? In *Atlantic Monthly, Harper's,* or other similar publications, the letters always appear to be written by smart people who had their postsecondary education at Ivy League universities. Many times, topics are right there for the taking, and no other reader is aware of the opportunities. Even old magazine issues contain universally ignored topic gems buried in the letters to the editor.

Association executives are also opinion leaders. They influence industry because they tell you what their members need. Do you belong to the state or national association or society? You can join as an associate member if you are not an executive or an association official. You don't have to be an association member to receive its publication. You can still read the monthly magazine and see what issues the association comes up against. The clues are there in abundance.

Once you uncover some interesting speaking topics, you need to select those that match where you're already headed. The topics need to coincide with who you are and what you face in life, because this is where your passion is going to be. Because of your excitement in your chosen direction, people will pay to hear you over and over again.

FOLLOW THE GURUS

Each industry has gurus. These individuals set off chain reactions that can be used for subject matter. Two authors, Tom Peters and Robert Waterman, wrote a book on excellence that was a best-seller. The authors, Peters in particular, became widely quoted managment gurus. It is inevitable that for the next several years, there will be sessions within conventions and meetings among salespeople, engineers, and other corporate departments that will involve the topic of excellence.

How do you know when the book is big enough and enduring enough? The sales figures say so. It is an oddity for a business book to be a *New York Times* best-seller for a year or more. While the Peters and Waterman book sold six million copies worldwide, authors Silva and Hickman sold 400,000 copies of their book, *Managing Excellence.* Not bad. Another book, *Creating Excellence,* sold several hundred thousand copies. These authors and speakers were able to feed off a guru's hot topic, and through their well-presented contribution, they made a good living on those topics.

TAKE A LIBRARIAN TO LUNCH

Librarians can prove to be beneficial sources of good speaking topics. I realized the value of tapping a librarian's knowledge years ago when I first started writing books, primarily on small business.

Margaret Hickey was the head librarian at the U.S. Small Business Administration in Washington, DC. She knew about every new book on small business. She cataloged each item, knew the articles, and, in many instances, she knew the authors. She knew the special reports, think tank, university, and the government-based publications.

One day, I asked Hickey if she had a list of the most frequently requested topics by those who come into the library or those who call. She went over to her desk and whipped out a list of 15 topics. The list represented several years and several hundred inquiries of what people were looking for. It was right there!

I went to another librarian, a city librarian, and asked if she had such a list. The librarian in the municipal library also had a list. And it then struck me—librarians know what isn't being covered!

Business librarians and meeting planners seem like such obvious sources of great information—and yet perhaps it hadn't occurred to you to ask them. In this next chapter, I'll explore your own intrinsic skills and strengths that you might also have overlooked.

5

Tapping Your Hidden Strengths

nother strategy for finding winning presentation topics is to consider your "throwaways" that others would pay a fortune to hear.

SAVE YOUR THROWAWAYS

What is a throwaway? It is something that you're so good at, so fully immersed and so proficient in, that you would never imagine that anyone would want to hear it as a presentation! For you, the topic is so simple that it is below your radar screen.

This being my thirty-second book, you could make the observation that a great presentation topic for me would be how to get a book published, how to write a book, or how to handle some other aspect of developing book topics, proposals, chapters and so on. (It would be a great topic for me to deliver, but I have *no* interest in addressing it as a presentation.)

The challenge for you is to uncover your own throwaways and begin to seriously explore them as presentation topics. Here are some key statements you can use to help unearth those topics that lie within you:

- *"If I do it, others want to know about it."*—Are you an opinion leader among your peer group? Do you have activities or hobbies that routinely seem to enamor others? Do you have any skills or abilities that others envy? If so, these areas are ripe for further exploration.

- *"If I'm thinking about it others want to know."*—Have you written any articles, letters to the editor, or online replies to a question posed in a forum? Review what you've written. There are insights and potentially fresh perspectives buried within them.

CREATE A MODEL

Years ago, I hit upon the notion that (1) regardless of what happens in the future, the world population will continue to increase; (2) media growth that transmits and disseminates all the information generated by the 6.5 billion people will continue; (3) for the foreseeable future, paper will continue to amass; and thus (4) the overabundance of choices each person faces each day will continue.

For the last 14 years, I've gathered every shred of information I've encountered in a newspaper or a magazine, on a Web site, or during conversations that fits into one of my four mega-realities. These ideas have become my model, which I've built up over the years as I've added more and more information. Happily, the longer you stick with your model, the more your topic deepens, growing in a positive way. You remain forever on the "cutting edge" without even seeming to work.

EXPAND ON WHAT YOU'RE ALREADY SAYING

What can be expanded among the topics you're already presenting? When I give my presentation on "Breathing Space®," I have a component on creative procrastination techniques. It occurred to me that with a little time and effort, I could expand the five to eight minutes I had on creative procrastination into a one-hour program. Now, whenever I'm booked to speak at a major convention for a keynote, I also suggest to the meeting planner that my presentation on creative procrastination would make a wonderful breakout session. Often, I get booked for this session as well.

Once you start actively speaking, remember to listen to your audience. If you give a presentation and get a laugh, maybe you have struck a nerve. You may have something that merits more conversation or even a whole speech. When you get a gasp or a groan from your audience, you have either told a bad joke or have received a great clue to other topics.

Beyond paying attention to their reactions during your presentation, listen to audience comments during breaks and afterwards, in person and in letters. Many times audience remarks provide valuable hints as to which topics they are interested in and would like for you to expand. You might also poll audiences about what would interest them—you might be surprised by their desires.

In addition, have you ever been interviewed by newspaper reporters? Often they ask questions that lead us in different directions than what we expected to be interviewed about and, in some instances, particularly when the conversation gets lively, the seeds of another topic lie within. For example, I was interviewed by *USA Today* on the topic of how people can have more breathing space in their lives. During our interview, the reporter asked me about an issue I hadn't considered as a speaking topic. As it turned out, this issue made for a good breakout session, and I have since added it to my repertoire. Here is a list of some more of my topics. Notice that each subtopic supports the overall topic in a small way:

1. Overworked or Overwhelmed?
   - The Root Causes of the Pressure You Feel
   - Recapturing Your Day, Week, Year, Career, and Life
2. Creating More Time and Space in Your Life
   - What They Don't Teach You at Time Management Seminars
   - Harnessing Creative Procrastination
3. Choosing When It's Confusing: Better Decision Making
   - Which Decisions Are Worth Making
   - When to Trust Your Intuition and How to Test Your Proficiency

For any topic that you derive, as you give the issue more thought, and perhaps more research, four, six, and eight topics or more emerge, almost naturally. Once you become immersed, you rarely have to work at it.

WHAT'S MISSING IN OTHER PEOPLE'S PRESENTATIONS

When you look at business practices, educational institutions, government, or human interaction in general, keep a keen eye out for what's missing. Often, great speaking topics develop because someone was astute enough to conclude that, for example, business executives were sufficiently deficient in some skill area or leadership technique such that a speech could be developed to fill the gap.

For example, most sales training programs concentrate mostly on the opening and closing parts of a sale, despite the fact that the most important point in landing a sale is the follow-up. It is the strategic, properly timed follow-up that brings the person along a particular path to the point where he or she is ready, and yet I see little said about follow-up. If anybody came out with a great presentation on the follow-up to a sales call, he or she would be in demand overnight.

GO WITH THE INTRIGUE

Think back to the last time you saw a provocative television show, listened to a captivating radio program, or read something in a book or magazine that intrigued you. In 1963, Jessica Mitford gave a successful lecture on the funeral industry in America and how people approach their deaths, the deaths of loved ones, and the whole prospect of choosing a final resting place.

Her book, *The American Way of Death,* was an exposé of mortuary malpractice as well as an anthropological study of a peculiar strata of American culture. Mitford uncovered the secret language of morticians. For example, funeral directors referred to cremated ashes as "cremains." As you might imagine, Mitford's lectures caused quite a stir. Ms. Mitford was not initially an expert in this field, yet she carved out a niche for herself because the topic intrigued her personally.

If a topic intrigues you, it's bound to intrigue others. Ask yourself, "Why does this intrigue me? Why does it intrigue others?" These questions will allow you to find some explanations. The answers themselves may merit further exploration.

To accelerate your awareness of topics within you, work with a friend. Ask someone who knows you well to help you identify your own driving forces, how these play out in your daily affairs, and what potentially related public speaking topics might be worth developing.

CONVERSE, RECORD, AND WIN

Some of your best presentation topics can originate from telephone conversations. It's not expensive to acquire two-way recording capabilities. The next time you are speaking to a friend or confidant about some topic vital to one or both of you, pause for a moment and say, "Let me get this on tape." Once you have turned on your machine, let the conversation rip.

FROM BRAINSTORM TO SPEAKING TOPIC

To tap further into the rich vein of intellectual thought, brainstorm with a friend or small group of people who know you well. Simply pose this question to the group: "What topics could I effectively speak on?" Then, let the brainstorming process ensue.

Brainstorming is a mental technique that offers a valuable way of exploring new ideas, in this case speech topics, or of supporting ideas you've already established. When brainstorming, give free flight to your topic ideas. Let ideas flow without judging them, and you will generate many times the ideas produced through the normal reasoning process. After you've generated many ideas, you can go back to evaluate their viability.

Here are some quick guidelines for brainstorming:

1. *Suspend all judgment.* This is a time to remove your internal censor. No topic is too silly or too wild to include when brainstorming.
2. *Think quantity, not quality.* The more topic ideas you generate, the better the chances are of hitting upon something new and intriguing.
3. *Extrapolate and cross-fertilize.* No matter how silly it may seem, take your ideas to the nth degree. Combine ideas in unusual ways to stimulate yet more ideas.
4. *Evaluate later.* Do not close your mind to any suggestions. A topic idea that seemed ridiculous yesterday may seem more palatable tomorrow.

For the most effective brainstorming, eliminate distractions. Sit comfortably with a pencil and paper or a pocket dictator. Then form a question or a problem to be handled. Make your question specific, such as, "What represents a high-demand speaking topic that I could develop?" Once you've aired the question, immediately begin jotting down or recording your ideas.

Record the first thing that comes to your mind. Do not judge your responses or you'll short-change the process. You can fill in the details of your notes later. If you're writing, make notes in brief phrases to save time. If you're dictating, allow yourself full sentences, but then return to your brainstorming mode so that other ideas may follow.

After you've finished, review your notes. Examine the possibilities. Discard unusable ideas only at the end. Continue to suspend all judgment during this exercise. Often, wild and crazy topics, when combined or altered slightly, prove to be your most novel, effective ideas. Remember that your imagination is one of your best tools. So let yourself go.

LET YOUR CREATIVITY UNFOLD

I know people who get their ideas in the shower, while jogging, while listening to tapes, or while eating or driving. Take advantage of those places that for whatever reason seem to stimulate your creative energies. Have a pen or pocket dictator nearby so that you can capture your thoughts. The late Earl Nightingale once said, "Ideas are like slippery fish." If you let them get away, you probably won't get them back. Don't let this happen to you.

Finally, never underestimate the power and potential of a topic. Try out new topics or topic segments. Donate several minutes of a presentation to a new topic, a wrinkle on a topic, or at least a wrinkle on a subtopic. Devote three-, six-, or nine-minute segments of your presentation to being absolutely experimental. Regardless of what happens, you'll gain valuable information.

Perhaps during your brainstorming, you'll select the topic of mitigating change. As I discuss in the next chapter, change is an evergreen subject, especially in today's tumultuous economy.

6

Dealing with Change: The All Pervasive Topic

All groups and individuals confront change in one form or another. If you speak to organizations, associations, or businesses (and that covers considerable territory), it's useful to understand some of the fundamental issues common to all organizations and change managers and highlight a number of change situations that audiences may be encountering.

SUCCESSFUL CHANGE CAMPAIGNS

The most successful change campaigns, ideally, are comprehensive—no stones are left unturned; all of the steps, interim goals, and final outcomes are achieved. By many estimates, less than one-third of actual change campaigns proceed according to plan and generate the intended results.

Change campaigns may affect a small part of an organization or the entire organization. In any case, something is irrevocably altered. The organization, department, or division can't go back to what came before, how people used to do things, or "standard operating procedures."

In *Change Is an Unnatural Act*, Andrew Grove, the much-quoted chairman of Intel Corporation, observes that many changes hit organizations "in such a way that those of us in senior management are among the last to notice." Hence, there can be a pressing need to bring in outside speakers, trainers, and consultants. Michael Porter, PhD, a professor at Harvard University, and the author of *Competitive Advantage,* adds that large-scale change within an organization represents an unnatural act. "The behavior required to sustain advantage, then, is in many respects an unnatural act for established firms." Porter says, "Few companies make significant improvements in strategy changes voluntarily. Most are forced to. The management of companies that sustain competitive advantage always runs a little scared."

Therefore, if you're asked to address a group that's undertaking any type of change campaign, recognize that many people may disguise the fact that they are a little scared. Such feelings are par for the course. There are a realm of professionals who need to commit to behaviors that "constitute an unnatural act" while being leery about the change campaign in general.

CULTURAL CHANGE

Many organizations today are seeking some variation of cultural change, such as increasing the diversity of the workforce, converting to a flatter organizational structure, helping professional staff balance work and family life, altering and extending the lines of communication, or even developing a new operating philosophy and corporate image. If you address any of these issues, your presentation could be in demand.

Speakers whose presentations are based on change can help managers decide on strategic alternatives. When faced with three possible paths that an organization can take, for example, it's not uncommon to commission someone from within or hire an outside speaker-expert or consultant. The greater the departure the paths represent from the organization's operating history, the more crucial the need for an outside expert's viewpoint.

In the rest of the chapter, I'll discuss some of the pervasive change issues (and hence potent speaking topics) facing many of your potential audiences.

RESTRUCTURING, DOWNSIZING

Over the years, articles in publications such as the *Wall Street Journal* and *Business Week* have discussed how companies' efforts to downsize often result in too much purging; hence, the term "rightsizing" became popular. It means determining the appropriate staffing levels within an organization based on both a short- and a long-term perspective. Speakers who touted downsizing as a panacea to all company ills have fallen out of favor.

A variety of other widely used terms, such as "restructuring," "reorganizing," "rationalizing," and "de-layering" emerged recently. In such change situations, the elimination of staff must be done for the express purpose of meeting specific objectives and/or fostering growth, and not as an expedient, cost-cutting reflex.

As a result of downsizing or other organization-shaking initiatives, you may find yourself addressing a group that needs to rebuild trust or confidence.

Those surviving downsizing often take on a guarded posture—they don't share information freely with others, they are less likely to be effective team members, and they are reluctant to make sacrifices for the organization. The challenge of addressing groups comprised of such individuals may be considerable. As I'll discuss in later chapters, it's critical when you sign on as a speaker to ask the event organizer what pertinent issues the company is facing and what sensitive topics to avoid.

CAPITALIZING ON CONSTITUENCIES

Many companies find themselves facing diversity issues when they have not creatively approached the situation (see Chapter 29, "The Diversity Factor"). By failing to address immediate challenges, such companies may find they have internal morale problems with employees, as well as problems in the marketplace. As a speaker on diversity issues, you may be assigned the challenge of helping managers and staff incorporate the best and most effective elements of diversity into their organizations, departments, or divisions. Again, gathering information prior to the presentation is crucial for shaping this type of talk.

Find the Trailblazer

When the process a company seeks to install does not represent a first for its industry, the company often looks for a trailblazer. Who else in the industry has made such an installation or has knowledge of the change dynamics? As a speaker, you can help audiences understand how the changes they embark on will impact them and thus, how to best approach them.

In Virgin Territory

Clients who tread in completely new territory, that is, no one else has incorporated a given process and the change will position them as industry leaders, understandably incur high risk and commensurate high reward. Speakers who can address issues related to risk and reward, and overcoming specific challenges, are in demand among these organizations.

Incorporating New Technology

Perhaps an organization is installing new hardware or software that offers tremendous operating advantages, and it's ultimately to everyone's benefit to have this new technology incorporated as soon as possible. This would necessitate the development of a training schedule and often the retention of speakers, trainers, and consultants with applicable technical expertise.

Many organizations have long-standing departments whose missions are to provide such training, as the benefits of adopting new technology become apparent. Some organizations, however, outsource this function. Smaller companies often don't have the means internally, and hence may be even more likely to seek outside help.

INSTILLING A SENSE OF OWNERSHIP

Employee stock operating plans (ESOPs) give staffs the opportunity to participate in the ownership of their organizations. This is in contrast to the sense of ownership that speakers are called in to address: This is psychological ownership, not financial. Employees need and want to believe that their efforts will be instrumental in the future success of the organization. This sounds like Management 101, but unless employees have a sense of ownership regarding the work that they do, their goals, and the overall success of the company, they're merely putting in time. Speakers effective at helping to instill a sense of ownership among organization members are often in high demand.

Vital Companies, Vital Involvement

Vital organizations find ways to get employees involved in the work and affairs of the organization on many levels, often bringing in outside speakers to plant the seeds of involvement and initiative. Some organizations draw on speakers to help with interorganizational campaigns that raise levels of employee pride, encouraging greater participation among employees in company-sponsored community involvement volunteering situations, or as facilitators for tapping the insights and opinions of employees through focus groups, forums, and roundtable sessions.

OTHER CHANGE MANAGEMENT SITUATIONS

Beyond what has been discussed thus far, is the company expanding, adding branches, or relocating its headquarters? Moves often merit the wisdom of outside experts. Other types of changes might include adopting a new quality management system; revising a mission or mission statement; restructuring a specific operation; or reorienting the way an organization, department, or division operates.

7

Meeting Types and Variations

Once you have a list of various speaking topics, it's important to find out what kinds of audiences will hear your presentations. The descriptors that groups use when announcing and conducting their meetings yield valuable clues as to what a speaker can expect at such gatherings. By understanding the various types of meetings, you can create speeches that fit their schedules, audiences, and time frames.

A summary of the most common types of meetings follows. Recognize, however, that a particular group may classify its meeting one way but actually have the operating characteristics of another type. For instance, a group may call its annual meeting a conference when it operates far more like a convention. Recognize as well that any particular group's meeting might encompass elements of two or more of the meeting categories.

CONVENTION

A convention is usually driven by a theme. Ideally, all of the presentations and programs offered at the convention in some way tie in to the overall theme. Conventions can last anywhere from two to more than seven days and, during this time, there may be one or more keynote or general session presentations and many educational or workshop-type sessions, often called breakout sessions. Such sessions provide detailed information and support of general session presentations while offering participants a full range of other topics relevant to their careers or personal lives.

The annual convention of most groups is synonymous with their "annual meeting." At such a gathering, the board of directors and officers may have pre- and postconvention sessions apart from the typical breakout sessions. Some officers and directors heavily involved with committee meetings and behind-the-scenes affairs will actually attend few or none of the general or breakout sessions.

One of the strong attractions of a convention or annual meeting for many participants is the opportunity to network with fellow participants. However, the networking generally occurs between the speeches. Virtually all of the presentations and sessions scheduled at a convention represent one-way information dissemination. While there may be panels, forums, and question-and-answer opportunities for audience members in particular sessions, participants are generally there to listen and learn.

CONFERENCE

A conference can run for many days, but it may also be held on a single day; in fact, half-day conferences have become popular. Like conventions, conferences are frequently based on an overall theme. Whereas a convention is likely to be an annual event, a conference may or may not be held on a regular basis.

There is no hard rule as to how many people need to attend for a meeting to be deemed a conference. Conference participants, unlike convention participants, may find themselves involved in presentations and discussions to a great degree. Again, panels, forums, and question-and-answer sessions offer participants a variety of interaction. There may also be scheduled sessions for consultations, group problem solving, table topic discussions, fact-finding or formal inquiry panels, and so on. The meeting location for a scheduled conference could be on the premises of the host organization, elsewhere in the same city, or at a meeting facility or resort of regional or national attraction.

SYMPOSIUM

Symposiums are formal proceedings that focus on a particular discussion topic. The gathering has a specific focus and/or is taking a unique or special approach to a current or emerging issue. People in health care or education attend them regularly.

Symposiums can be as brief as a couple of hours or they can span several days. There may be fewer than 10 participants or a large number equal to that of á conference or even convention. Symposiums can take many forms, such as a series of presentations, often called "delivering a paper," panel discussions with qualified experts and significant audience participation, or panel discussions.

FORUM

Public forums are the stock and trade of local governments, commissions, counties, wards, and other political or legal jurisdictions. Subject matter experts are often invited to discuss various aspects of a public issue, and sometimes a panel of experts with both pro and con opinions is assembled. Audience members often have free-ranging opportunities to question forum participants; however, audience participation is not necessarily an element of every forum.

Forums tend to be held on a single day, usually for periods between 45 minutes and 3 hours. The meeting location is easily accessible to a majority of constituents. It is publicly announced, anyone may attend, and there is no charge. Finally, as a result of the issues raised, action on the topic in discussion is usually forthcoming in the days or weeks following the forum.

SEMINAR

The term *seminar* originated in academia, when a professor or teacher working closely with a small group of students would meet to cover a specific topic. Over the years, the term has broadened to encompass a meeting of at least 10 to 100 people. Seminars often take place in a quiet, out-of-the-way location.

A seminar instructor, leader, or facilitator may make an opening presentation and other presentations throughout the duration of the meeting, often punctuated by group discussions and team meetings. There is a significant amount of give and take between attendees.

Seminars can be for either a specific or a general audience including the public. Participants can thoroughly benefit without doing any preseminar work or postseminar follow-up. In that sense, the information imparted during a seminar is designed to be a distinct, complete, comprehensive unit in and of itself.

Each participant in a seminar is usually there because he or she wants to be or, at the least, has been directed to be. The time away from routine activities is regarded as valuable. Detailed, comprehensive materials, such as audiovisuals and participant packets, are produced to ensure optimal benefit and participation.

WORKSHOP

Workshops share many of the same characteristics of seminars. The size of the group, the location, the orientation, and the audiovisual materials and participant packets are similar to those used in a seminar. The fundamental difference is that a workshop implies that the group meets on at least a semi-regular basis or as part of a convention or conference.

The content of the information provided in a workshop is specific to the group in attendance and may concentrate on a narrow topic area. Unlike a seminar, workshop participants may be required to do work in advance and/or may be required to do follow-up work once the workshop is completed.

Workshop participants are encouraged to communicate with the instructor, facilitator, or workshop leader and with one another. The idea is to create a "hands-on" experience in some key job or skill-related area that you can implement immediately.

TRAINING

Training is a term that is widely used in the meeting industry. Training may take place at a client's location or at an off-site facility. Generally, the content of such a presentation is tailored, if not customized for the audience, and designed to meet specific learning objectives that the host organization has agreed on with the meeting planner and presenter.

Training session participants are often required to do work in advance, in the form of reading, exercise, or experimentation. Following a training session, there may be assessment, follow-up, and additional sessions. Professional speaker Phil Wexler makes a nice distinction between training and other forms of public speaking: "Training is when you *are* the agenda; speaking is when you are *on* the agenda."

In a training session, participants are assembled to develop a particular skill or set of skills. The hands-on environment lets them practice during the session. At the end of the session, new goals may be set for subsequent sessions, depending on assessments from feedback.

LECTURE

A lecture is usually regarded as a one-time presentation to a unique audience. Lectures can be given annually, and usually, a different speaker is sought each year. Universities, as well as health care organizations and libraries, will often sponsor lecture series, and lectures typically last no longer than two hours.

RETREAT

A retreat refers to any type of learning environment where a presenter (or instructor) and participants are convened at a location apart from the routine distractions and disturbances that otherwise would hamper learning. Retreats are often held at locations with meeting facilities designed specifically to host such gatherings. An executive retreat may consist of a handful of top executives in a department. An outside facilitator or presenter may or may not be employed.

Retreats generally last at least half a day and multiple-day retreats are not uncommon. The presumption at the conclusion of a retreat is that the participants will resolve specific topics and develop some type of action plan or some agreed on new, collective behavior to be implemented immediately.

Most retreats are designed to enhance participants' abilities to focus on the issue at hand in a supportive, pleasant environment. Business casual or casual dress is the norm, as are ample break times, snacks, refreshments, and opportunities to mingle.

If you're asked to make a presentation at a convention, conference, symposium, forum, seminar, workshop, or lecture, make sure that you understand exactly what the meeting planner means by such terminology, and structure your speech accordingly.

TYPES OF HOST ORGANIZATIONS

The type of organization to which you speak may also affect the nature of your topic. By becoming familiar with the types, you can adjust your presentations to fit their needs. Descriptions of the key types of host organizations follow:

- *Large corporations:* These hosts represent any companies in the Fortune 500 or Service 500, multinational corporations, and foreign corporations. Such groups often have their own meeting facilities, but they may opt to rent a hotel or conference space for particular meetings. Large corporations have narrower time frames in terms of planning.
- *Mid-sized companies:* This category represents the largest area of host organizations. Such companies are not household names, but they often have a strong local or regional presence. A bank is not likely to be a Fortune 500 or Service 500 company, but it may not be a small business either, particularly if it has several branches.
- *Small businesses:* Most small businesses in America have less than 10 employees. However, there are still nearly 1,500,000 businesses with 50 employees or more. For a public speaker, that fact translates to presentation opportunities. Such businesses may have regularly scheduled, annual, quarterly, or monthly staff meetings that may or may not include the services of an outside speaker.
- *Professional societies:* This includes groups such as Toastmasters International and American Society of Association Executives, both of which are composed of individuals who have common interests. In the case of Toastmasters, for example, public speaking is

the interest. Their annual meetings can be huge affairs. Such groups also have many regional, local, or district meetings.

- *Trade associations:* There are thousands of these types of associations just within the United States alone. Members of such groups tend to be owners or managers of businesses offering a service or engaging in some type of trade. They often welcome speakers who offer vital information about their trades.

- *Professional associations:* Professional associations abound in every field. From American Trial Attorneys to the National Association of Realtors to the American Society of Associations, executives in every conceivable profession are represented by at least one association. Speakers are often beneficial to them.

- *Government agencies:* Federal, state, and local government agencies hold meetings for their staffs and bring in outside speakers primarily for some aspect of skill development. Whether it is the U.S. Treasury, the State of California, or Suffolk County, staff members in government organizations need to continually update their job skills just like people in the private sector.

- *Educational institutions:* Universities, schools, and other institutions of learning can also hold opportunities for outside speakers. Many universities have visiting lecture series and other annually and seasonally based events in which nonstaff personnel are asked to make presentations. Specific departments within an educational institution sometimes look for opportunities to bring in outside speakers.

- *Local groups:* Within communities with at least 50,000 or more people, you can count on the existence of a variety of local groups, including political groups, men's or women's groups, and local chapters of civic and fraternal organizations, such as the Citizens, Lyons, Rotarians, and Elks Club. The opportunities to address such groups are virtually endless, and many meet on a weekly, biweekly, or monthly basis.

KEEPING YOUR MATERIAL FRESH

No matter how interesting your topic is originally, when you deliver it too often, a problem can occur—it falls into a somewhat mechanical routine. Slowly, subtly, in ways that the speaker doesn't perceive, his or her presentation starts to go flat and comes across as a "canned" speech. Some speakers half-heartedly inject new elements into the presentation to help enliven it, but the fix is only temporary.

When your speeches start boring your audiences, return to square one. Before you give another presentation, revisit every element of your speech. If you have an audio- or videotape of yourself, closely watch or listen to it. Take notes as to where and when you can improve the timing and delivery of your presentation. Does it need fresh data or new anecdotes?

Maintaining a clipping file is a good start in meeting the challenge of continually improving your presentation. Many professional speakers routinely refer to them. Such files include any relevant articles from magazines, newspapers, or Web sites. On a long-term basis, clipping, saving, and reviewing articles related to your presentations may confirm what you've been saying all along. Occasionally you find something that prompts you to rethink what you've been telling audiences. Is it time to change your view? Perhaps a minor point in your presentation should gain more recognition, or vice versa.

THE FAST TRACK TO A FLAT PRESENTATION

If you don't routinely clip and file articles, watch out—it's only a matter of time before your presentations go stale. Changes in society, technology, your marketplace, business, and the world at large occur too frequently for any speech to remain intact over the long haul, no matter how well you can deliver it.

You need to go the extra mile to stay in the forefront of your topic's presenters. Take your own surveys and attend conventions. Be an opinion leader by deciding that you'll write a letter to the editor. When you go that extra mile, it will seem easy because you are working on something that is a part of you; furthermore, soon, you'll be the one who starts to shake the industry.

Now, we'll focus on how to make your topic come alive by using humor, gestures, visuals, stories, pauses, and silence!

PART II

DEVELOPING AND ENLIVENING YOUR PRESENTATION

Audiences today are overwhelmed by too much competition for their time and attention. Each audience member is more distracted, has more on his or her mind, and has a harder time maintaining concentration than people of prior generations. The chapters in Part II focus on gaining listeners' attention, honing and refining your timing and delivery, using humor, "owning" the stage, and using stories to connect with your audiences on a higher level. Developing these skills will make your speeches memorable. Audience members have been subjected to many speakers who lack appropriate humor, gestures, and stories. Thus, when someone steps up to the podium and effectively offers humor, they can't help but be drawn in.

Get Humorous or Get Going

Far too often speakers are satisfied with simply offering an interesting presentation. They ignore the role that humor plays in contributing to the effectiveness of their presentation.

KEEP IT ALL IN PERSPECTIVE

Few events in life are so serious that humor cannot be injected into them. Do you remember when Ronald Reagan was shot? Although he was seriously injured, he reportedly said to his doctors: "Please assure me you are all Republicans." Reagan put everyone else at ease by infusing some humor in what was undoubtedly a very tense situation. That humor at the pivotal moment made a difference in how some people viewed him and his administration for the rest of his presidency.

HUMOR IN A TENSE WORLD

Why use humor at all? We've grown up in a world in which everyone has the ability to take the remote control, click it, and surf through the channels. People's attention spans are decreasing to all-time lows. If you're in front of a group and you don't have something humorous to say at least once every seven minutes, you are going to have a tough time.

If it helps, think of yourself as a television show, with a humorous commercial break every seven minutes to give your audience a chance to digest what you have been saying. You're competing today with all media, not just the speaker in the next room, MTV, or CDs, but all media from which your audience expects a good mix of entertainment and information.

HUMOROUS INTRODUCTIONS

Starting at the beginning of your time on stage, should your introduction be humorous? It should if your entire speech is going to be humorous. You don't want to lead the audience to believe that they're getting one type of speech when you plan on delivering another.

Begin by stating in your introduction (delivered by someone else) what you do and then make a joke about it. As such, you can begin to entertain your audience before you say a word. For example, my introduction states: "Jeff has spoken on three continents to organizations such as America Online, American Express, Nation's Bank, Swissotel, and Uncle Joe's Eat and Run."

Sometimes, the audience or some other outsider adds humor to your speech. Once, a woman who introduced me added, "You can look it up," regarding the frequency of my book sales. I didn't think the line made sense—however, it got a laugh, so thereafter I included it in my introductions.

Opening Lines

You can use a funny opener even if you don't have a funny introduction. There are cases when you should assess the audience before proceeding with your jokes. Professional speaker Dale Irvin warns against the dangers of attempting to be humorous with a "cold" audience. As he says, "The audience has to have laughed a little bit about something before they will laugh a lot about anything," he says. "Hence, your entré to humor can be a warm-up story that brings a smile," he advises, "but is not outright funny."

GETTING STARTED

If you haven't employed humor before, don't be reticent; there are easy ways to get started. Lola Gillebaard recommends being "yourself on the edge." Gillebaard, on the Web at www.laughandlearn.org, is one of my favorite humorists. A veteran speaker with a keen sense of mirth and a twinkle in her eye, Gillebaard has delighted audiences all over the world. She advises using humor based "on your own universal experience. Be original."

As with many humorists, she feels it's vital to let the audience have "enough time to laugh. Deliver your line, give them a few moments, then enhance whatever gets a laugh." Seek added opportunities to inject a second and third punch line.

Gillebaard is not averse to including a dash of impropriety in her humor while ensuring that it doesn't offend particular groups or individuals. She believes that "the key to staying funny is to be a little scared." Even if you're not a humorist, she advises offering something humorous about every five minutes during your presentation.

Too many public speakers who attempt to add humor to their presentations take too long to build up. "Be brief," Gillebaard says. "The longer the audience has to wait before you reach the punch line, the funnier it better be."

For speakers committed to improving their on-stage humor, Gillebaard suggests, "taking a stand-up comic course via a local college or going to an open microphone session. Today's conflict with pain is tomorrow's humor," she says. "If you've lived it, you can be humorous about it."

For practice, speak to a small, friendly group. Begin with a story that you know will work. Also, don't be afraid to try new things, like limericks or poems. In other words, attempt to generate humor that accents the absurd.

READING JOKES

Some speakers say that you should not read a joke aloud during a speech. But this depends on the situation. You can determine whether or not to read a joke depending on the audience, how long you've been speaking to them, and what the atmosphere is like. There is no hard and fast rule, and you have to do what fits for you.

Sometimes, you can use a joke based on the audience to whom you are speaking. If you're speaking to a group of lawyers or small business entrepreneurs, you could get away with a joke that's related to their own industry. This depends on the time, the place, how long you have been with the audience, the atmosphere, the repertoire, and the dynamics of the situation.

You can also take the little occurrences that may happen during a speech or presentation and make them humorous. Scott Friedman uses such humor. If Scott is speaking to a group and a beeper goes off, he says, "Oh, time to take my pills." If you're speaking to an audience when an ambulance goes by, and the siren distracts your audience, then you bring their attention back to you with a line like, "There's my ride, got to go."

INTERACTIVE HUMOR

Humor can occur in conversations between you and your audience members. While speaking to the International Management Council of the YMCA on the topic of confidence, I offered books and tapes as bonuses to audience participants. A young man in the audience answered a question I posed, so I handed him a CD on having a better relationship with your spouse. He announced to the whole room, "But I'm not married."

I then said to him, "Well, now you've got incentive."

This remark prompted a huge laugh from the audience. The off-the-cuff exchange could have been a dead spot, but he played along, and through our exchange, I was able to get closer to my audience.

USE YOUR EVERYDAY EXPERIENCE

Take jokes from everyday life and use them when you can. You can develop a complete arsenal of funny stories. One speaker I know maintains a log or a journal of all the funny things that happen in his life at the train station, airport, or wherever. He works them into his routines if he can. Take my advice: Write down those anecdotes.

I started doing this about four or five years ago and now I've got 88 anecdotes on my hard drive. Of those 88, I routinely use about 10 or 12. Although the anecdotes may not have seemed funny at the time, you never know how they may affect an audience.

KNOW THE AUDIENCE

Research your audience to see if there is something that unites them. Suppose you're speaking to a corporation and everyone must complete reporting forms, which they all hate. Use their animosity toward that form as a way of breaking the ice with the audience. If you know more about the group and what is on their minds at the time, your probability of making a great joke out of it increases.

Suppose that you're speaking to General Electric and the lights in the meeting room flutter off and on. What is your comeback line? "Those darn Sylvania bulbs."

Kurt Kilpatrick, a humorist from Birmingham, Alabama, is a big believer in doing your homework when it comes to customized humor. He says, "In reviewing a group's literature seek common themes that the whole audience can relate to." Kilpatrick will often arrive hours early so he has a chance to "talk to hotel and facility people to find out some of the unique aspects of the meeting, how the group has interacted with the facility, and even such things as have they met there before?

GONE ASTRAY?

Speaker Tom Antion has a whole repertoire of comeback lines. If only one person laughs following a joke, he'll say, "Will you be kind enough to run around the room as if everyone is having fun?" If he delivers a joke and nobody laughs, he will look at the audience directly and say, "You've got marvelous self-control."

HUMORISTS ARE PUBLIC SPEAKERS

Not all public speakers are humorists, but all humorists are public speakers. Scott Friedman is one such speaker. His tips on how to enliven your presentation with more humor are so on target that any public speaker can benefit from them.

- When something funny happens during a presentation, scheduled or not, make a note of it. Thereafter, employ the scenario with the next audience and the ones that follow. If it continues to get a laugh, it's well worth the inclusion.
- Something that gets a laugh at the start of a speech can be used a few more times in a sort of "running gag" fashion. This is particularly true if something amusing happens as a result of audience interaction. Perhaps a participant says something funny, and, later in the presentation, you can refer to that person with a humorous, good-natured sling.
- When searching for funny material, consider that it could be sitting in your own files. I once wrote an article on the dangers of "multitasking" and sent it to an editor. She wrote back and told me that, while reading it, she was so amused that she almost choked on her apple. She must have known that her own letter would be amusing, and it certainly has gotten a laugh every time I have brought it up to audiences.

ABBREVIATED HUMOR

Creating and using your own abbreviations within your presentations can also add humor. Years ago I heard reference to the BFI method. I was told that it meant pursuing a challenge with "Brute Force and Ignorance." I thought it was funny, and I have used the acronym periodically in my presentations.

Author Dennis Hensley refers to what he calls the IDIOS syndrome. While some people think it refers to a lack of intelligence, it actually stands for "I'll do it on Saturday." Hensley says IDIOS is a trap to ensure that you're forever grappling for parking spaces with other people who also ignore handling errands until the weekend.

SPEAKING AS A DUO

Although it isn't a common occurrence, some public speakers, particularly humorists, present their presentations as part of a duo. Duos come in the form of a husband and wife team, partners in a business, joint venturers for a one-time project, or other combinations. Duos can represent a nice break or major enhancement on a conference program. However, speaking in tandem can be very difficult, and I personally advise against it.

If you do want to perform as a duo, proceed without thinking of your own ego, and make things work on the fly. Otherwise, your chance of being successful as a duo is relatively small. If you're willing to initiate measures, start the same way as a solo speaker.

First, practice without anyone else around, using mirrors, audio- and videotape, and then each other. Move on to small groups. Get your timing down perfectly. Do you want to begin and end based on the clock? It hardly ever works out that way. It's better to have a verbal cue, such as, "When I finish saying 'office building,' that is when you pick up on your next line."

It's unlikely that you will have equal presentation capabilities. One person is going to outshine the other, possibly by a wide margin. Play to each other's strengths. If one person is good at holding up charts or explaining complex material, assign that person such chores. If one is good with humor, ad hoc repartee, or fielding questions, allocate responsibilities accordingly.

Resist the temptation to be equal partners in the presentation. One person is going to be dominate. High-ego-type individuals are not good candidates for speaking duos.

Dual presenters have an advantage over single presenters—it is often more interesting to view two people on stage, no matter how talented one may be. The combined dynamism of two people, the conversational interplay, the humor, and the depth of knowledge they have can be far more interesting than watching a single speaker.

If you're a veteran speaker and you are teamed with another veteran speaker, don't believe you can wing it and everything will work out. As with any dual presenters, you have important preparations to undertake if you want to accomplish the objective of partnering in the first place. When two veteran or otherwise effective speakers are in sync, however, it can be a true pleasure to watch!

A PARTING OBSERVATION

Chances are that your audience will not remember your name following the presentation. They may not even remember your material. They will remember how they felt; they will remember the laughs. You want your audience to have a good time and feel as though they learned something.

Connect with your audience members through humor, and they will remember you!

9

Presenting the
Best of You

What is the key to successful communication? Roger Ailes, Chairman of Fox News Channel, suggests identifying three times in your life when you know you communicated successfully. What made them work? "You were committed to what you were saying, you knew your topic, and you were so wrapped up in the moment that you lost all feelings of self-consciousness," he suggests. According to Ailes, once you reach that comfortable, successful level of communication, you *never* have to change it. He holds that whether you're speaking to one person or a thousand people the essential principles hold true. The key element, he says, is that you *not* change or adapt your essential "self" to different audiences or media. Ailes preaches that *you are the message.* Once you can "play yourself" successfully, he assures that you'll never have to worry again.

Before you can "play yourself" in front of an audience, you need to get into character—first, you need to establish your image. As you practice "playing yourself," you'll also need to work on diction and delivery. The use of outside professionals in all of these areas will help you present the very best of you.

WARDROBE AND THE PUBLIC SPEAKER

Whether or not your wardrobe and comportment is important to you, it is important to your audience. The moment you appear before any member of the audience both knowingly and unknowingly they make a series of instantaneous observations and assumptions regarding every aspect of your being. They will make assumptions about your heritage, values, education, and even level of sophistication. Based on your posture, stride, and vocal characteristics once they are exposed to them, they will add to the assumptions they have already made and modify, correct, or drop some of the earlier ones. It may seem unfair, it may seem rude. After all, haven't we all been drilled for years to not make judgments about others? Nevertheless, these processes occur day in and day out as people initially encounter one another.

The wardrobe "thing" was always a hurdle for me. I figured as long as I was great on stage, why would anybody care what I was wearing? Fellow speakers however, convinced me that *my* views on wardrobe were not important. It was the views of the people who would be hiring me and listening to me that counted.

One of the first people I sought when I decided to heed the advice of fellow speakers was a wardrobe consultant. Judy Turisi offered courses through a local adult education program on shaping your image through wardrobe. I hired her to come look at my closet.

At our first meeting, I opened up my closet doors. I was aware that several of my shirts were old, the collars frayed, and perhaps some of them didn't go with my coloring. Nevertheless, I was sure that at least one-half or so were salvageable. I thought I could round out my wardrobe by purchasing new ones as she recommended.

Less than 30 seconds after I opened the closet doors, she said in a clear, authoritative tone, "Throw them all out." I was aghast! *"All of them?"* I asked.

Turisi turned toward me and slowly and carefully said, "Read my lips—all of them." For the balance of the afternoon, we discussed what I would need to buy, including what colors, what materials, and from which stores.

From top to bottom, it was clear. What I wanted to project to others and what I was projecting were not in sync. It was futile to continue to wear what I was wearing because my clothes were simply functional. Publishers, large conference meeting planners, and others whom I wanted to influence needed to feel "right" about me in their own ways. The only way to ensure that others would feel "right," at least from a wardrobe standpoint, was to dress impeccably.

Hire someone, if only for a one-hour assessment, to view your professional wardrobe. Maybe you're fine as is, or maybe you need remedial help as I did. Either way, you need to know and "redress" the situation before your next speaking engagement.

IMPROVING YOUR DICTION

How often do you consider how you sound to others? Being an effective speaker ought to be an ongoing goal for everyone. For public speakers, however, it needs to be a top priority. When you become the center of attention, audience members tune in to your language and diction, so you want to ensure they appreciate your pronunciation and clarity. Here are several ways to quickly and easily improve your diction.

Listen to the Best

Any time you are at a conference or convention, visit the sessions of other presenters. It's particularly helpful to attend opening or general sessions. Notice the diction of the keynote speaker. Take notes.

You don't have to be at a conference or convention, however, to listen to good public speakers. You only have to turn on your television or radio. Each night, the major network anchors and other news anchors, broadcast journalists, talk show hosts, and actors speak to audiences. Pay attention to how these people form words. You do not need to be an expert to determine what's pleasing to your own ear.

What elements of other speech patterns could you adopt or, more precisely, adapt to your own speech pattern? If you add only one or two tips each day, you will be making significant progress.

Make a Word List

While working with your coach or taping yourself, some words will continue to be problematic. Make a list of problem words. You'll need at least

10 words on it to get started. If you use these words often while speaking, your presentations will improve.

Practice Aloud

Armed with your word list, pronounce your problem words several times daily. When you're alone in your car, you have a great opportunity to practice. You could write your words on a Post-it note and stick it to your dashboard. Then, work on one word at a time as you drive.

When flying to a speaking engagement, the sound of the plane's engine will ensure that any words you say to yourself can't be heard by other passengers. Also, after you land, your hotel room represents a viable practice area.

It's not enough to merely contemplate a word and how you prefer to say it; you have to develop the habit of saying it aloud. Pronouncing a word over and over again may seem boring, but your audience will appreciate your efforts.

Put It into Practice

The proof of your enhanced speech skills will show up in your presentations. For your next speech, seek to improve the pronunciation of a few words on your list. (If you attempt too many, you may not do as well.) Tape yourself and then review the tape carefully, noting the words on your list whenever you hear them. Monitor your improvement.

Play a tape of a recent speech and compare it to a tape from months or years ago. Do you notice a difference? You will if you work on your diction.

Audience members don't grade your diction with checklists; they won't even be outwardly conscious of it. Nevertheless, good speech is noticeable, and it prompts more invitations to speaking engagements.

The topic of maintaining and caring for your voice is beyond the scope of this book. Fortunately, several excellent texts adequately cover this topic including:

- *Seven Steps to Fearless Speaking* by Lilian Wilder.
- *Change Your Voice, Change Your Life* by Lyle Mayer.
- *How to Write and Give a Speech* by Joan Detz.
- *How to Inspire Any Audience,* by Tony Jeary.

EMPLOYING TRILOGISTIC SPEECH

The cadence and natural rhythm of lists containing three items—trilogies—is a tried and true audience pleaser and an effective attention grabber: "Blood, sweat, and tears" is an example. Here are some more:

"We came, we saw, we conquered."

"Of the people, by the people, for the people."

"Earth, wind, and fire."

With a little practice, you can begin crafting your own trilogistic phrases. Suppose you're discussing a labor group that has been economically shortchanged. You could say, "They've earned it, they deserve it, and they're going to receive it." Or, in facing some adversity you could say, "We were tired, we were confused, and we felt defeated."

DEEP-SEATED APPEAL

Enthralling use of language also generates high audience attention. Audiences respond well to statements that resonate, such as these classics:

"The only things worth talking about are the things you can't easily talk about."

"A problem well-stated is a problem half-solved."

Such linguistic twists naturally pique the interest of audience members who, too often, have been subjected to mundane presentations.

Curiously, use of such language ultimately stimulates intellect. Behind such inventive and majestic words is a theme or concept, a belief or wish that merits further reflection. When I hear the phrase, "All the world is a stage," I can't help but momentarily reflect on how true that statement is and how I periodically see demonstrations of it.

USING A SPEECH COACH

Olympic athletes aren't the only professionals who have coaches. Top professionals in almost every arena recognize the value of working with coaches. A speech coach can make the difference between speakers who are booked often and paid well, and those stuck at the same fee level with few engagements.

Coaches range from the high-priced, one-day, super-session types to graduate students in speech departments at your local university who are thrilled to make $20 to $25 an hour and will gladly travel to their clients' offices or homes.

The mere act of hiring a coach already puts you ahead. You become more conscious of your diction and gain a qualified listener who catches what you might not notice.

- Do you say "yer" instead of your?
- Do you say "manage" with a flat "a"?
- Are your word-endings crisp?

A speech coach will help you notice things like these, and people will begin to notice that you sound better. To record your progress, tape your speeches and conversations (whether over the phone or in person). Any time you can play the tape for at least five minutes, you have the chance to learn and improve. Phone conversations work particularly well, because you're often not conscious of your diction. The playback is valuable because you have the chance to hear the words that you may be incorrectly pronouncing. From that standpoint, you have a fabulous opportunity to improve.

Here are nine tips for working with a coach that will help ensure that your overall experience is career-enhancing, worthwhile, and productive:

1. Determine Your Objectives

Speech coaches come in many varieties, with all sorts of experience. Not every coach can help you in every facet of your speaking career, but most of them can help you with the majority of the improvements you want to make.

Prior to actually getting in touch with prospective coaches, draw up a comprehensive list of everything that you would like to achieve. This will help with selecting a coach, deciding how much time to spend with your coach, and the rate at which you attain your goals.

2. Find a Speaking Coach

With the help of the Internet, this can often be a simple task—simply log onto the World Wide Web and type the words "speech coach" into any one of the popular search engines. In refining your search, you could put the name of your state or closest major city. One organization in particular, Voice and Speech Trainers Association (VASTA), contains a bevy of professionals listed on its Web site (www.vasta.org), many of whom can be of great value to you. Vasta members consist of professors and graduate students from nearby colleges in the drama, speech, or music departments. There are a number of good coaches in the directory, many of whom have a national clientele. While these coaches tend to charge more, many clients swear by their results.

Another method for selecting a coach is to simply ask fellow speakers whom they use. Also, if you live in a metro area, use the Yellow Pages of your phone book. You'll be surprised at who might be located within close proximity. Local coaches tend to charge slightly less, if conserving expenses is important to you, and you can meet with them more frequently.

3. Your Office, Not Theirs

It is to your extreme advantage if you can have your speech coach come to your office. This is more than simply a logistical and time-saving convenience. At your office, you have your computer, audio and videotapes, speech notes, handouts, and articles—all of your intellectual property is at your fingertips.

Understandably, many speech coaches may not agree to such an arrangement. This doesn't rule them out. It does mean that your sessions with them will be limited, unless you are willing to bring your items (tapes, outlines, notes, etc.) with you. I've found it worth the cost to pay a little more to have the speech coach visit my office.

4. Consider Both Agendas—the Coach's and Yours

Once you acquire a coach, both of your agendas are important. You can diagnose the areas in which you need instruction, and you know how you would like the time to be spent. The speech coach's agenda is important, too, because he or she will have some definite ideas on how to help you. He or she will form goals based on your discussions, your speech patterns, and his or her experience in working with other speakers.

Compare agendas, and find points of commonality. Your speech coach may have a mini-curriculum that takes you down a path you may not have contemplated that will provide great benefit. In addition, the speech coach can open up new vistas for you that you simply would not have otherwise noticed. He or she can point out speech impediments and common mistakes that you are making and simply haven't noticed on your own.

5. Plot a Course of Action

Next, consider logistics:

- How often will you meet?
- How long will the sessions be?
- Will there be homework practices for you to complete?

These are important considerations. I find homework practices during the week to be quite tedious. I tend not to do them, even when I know I should. To get around this problem, my speech coach created a tape for me so that I can get in practice at times I hadn't considered, like when I'm driving. By pointing certain situations out prior to your sessions, you and your coach can devise solutions to problem areas.

6. Tape the Session

It is a good idea to have a video camera, tape recorder, or handheld pocket dictator available during your sessions. You at least want to capture the highs and lows of your sessions because the new techniques you learn are worth reviewing. You may have to engage in various warm-up exercises, and if you want to recapture any of these instructions and techniques after the coach leaves, you need to have taping equipment in place during your sessions.

Some speakers report tremendous benefits from simply taping entire coaching sessions. In the playback, they gain many observations and insights that weren't fully formed during the actual session. Listening to the tapes is like getting double your money's worth. I have tapes from a session conducted more than two years ago that still yield benefits to me.

7. Schedule Many Timely Sessions

As you begin working with your coach, strange and marvelous insights develop. No matter how far along you are in your speaking career, more areas of improvement emerge. Not only can you improve your diction, you can also work on a multitude of other areas, like your breathing, eye contact, pauses, openings and closings, and anecdotes. The best speakers continue training with their coaches for their entire careers.

Because it takes time to recognize these keys for continuous improvement, in the beginning you need to schedule at least 10 sessions with your speech coach. As your schedule permits, it makes sense to devote some of your sessions to upcoming speaking engagements.

Given the particular venue and considering the audience, the objectives of the organization and meeting planner, and everything else that goes into making a successful presentation, plan ahead and train with your coach on the areas that need the most work. This way you will be even more effective in giving your forthcoming speech. When you have a particular presentation in mind, this may make you concentrate more during your coaching session, because your objectives become highly definite and your focus is keen. Invariably, when you get out in front of that group, you will find that things go more smoothly. You'll have command. Most of all, you'll be glad that you were coached.

8. Establish Benchmarks

As you progress in your relationship with your speech coach, establishing benchmarks of performance becomes almost a natural byproduct. These benchmarks are different for every speaker, but here are some that you may wish to adapt:

- The ability to sustain several dramatic pauses throughout your presentation.
- Consistent high-energy openings and closings.

- Improved use of your gestures.
- Improved eye contact.
- Maintenance of your vocal strength throughout the presentation.
- Development of a more humorous presentation.
- Efficient manipulation of audiovisual materials.
- Improved aspects of diction.

Your speech coach will undoubtedly have some goals to suggest as well. Take these as valuable contributions. In many cases, he or she will improve your overall presentation skills in ways that you have not considered.

9. Constantly Assess Your Progress

Beyond mere goal-setting, periodically assess your overall progress with your coach. Do you feel different? Can you tell that your effectiveness has improved? Do you look forward to the sessions? What might both of you do to mutually improve the value of the session?

After six months or more, it's difficult for your coach to avoid experiencing some tedium. He or she has heard most of your presentations, stories, anecdotes, and verbal asides. To keep the relationship vibrant, consult with your coach about what he or she would like to work on and how your sessions ought to be conducted.

On some occasions, you can review an audio- or videotape together. Occasionally skip a session with your coach, substituting instead his or her review of your most recent presentation. All the while, keep taking steps to ensure that you both derive optimal benefit from your relationship.

THE SECRET TO EFFECTIVE SPEAKING

If hiring a coach is too big a move for you right now, focus on what you can do on your own. If you can master one rarely cited ingredient to effective speaking that all but ensures your success, than you'll have made great progress indeed—enjoying yourself.

If you enjoy yourself when you give a presentation, regardless of your level of professionalism, the place, and the setting, you're likely to be successful. Think of unprepared, uneasy speakers that get up in front of groups. The nervousness they convey to the audience detracts from their effectiveness on several levels—they are not as persuasive, the audience is not as receptive, and the points they make don't have the proper impact. Overall, the message isn't usually memorable.

By contrast, a speaker who enjoys himself or herself in front of a group can conceivably get away with less preparation, less focus, less clarity, and less coherence, while still being highly effective. Julia Roberts' acceptance speech at the 2001 Academy Awards is an example of a successful speech. Roberts had strong suspicions in advance that she would win the Oscar, since she had won several other awards leading up to the Oscar telecast. Nevertheless, her acceptance speech had spark, vitality, and even elements of spontaneity that enthralled the audience.

When she made it onto the stage, she let out a cheer and gave her wide, $20 million grin, which quickly drew in the audience. Then, weaving left and right, citing this person and that person, she beseeched the orchestra conductor not to wave her off the stage. She expressed her thanks, her glee, and her amazement in a way that made the audience, and television viewers, hang on her every word.

CONVEY ENJOYMENT TO YOUR AUDIENCE

Whether they're giving 45-minute keynotes or half-day training seminars, if professional speakers enjoy themselves and openly convey those feelings to their audiences, given that it's not done in a haughty or condescending way, they will be successful. What is the key to being able to enjoy yourself in front of a group? Practice, practice, practice. Although practice may seem the antithesis of spontaneity, the more experience you have in making presentations, the more at ease you can be in front of your audience, and case translates into enjoyment.

In the case of Julia Roberts, she made preparations in the event that she won. She had the names of cast and crew members, executives, and producers, and she was ready to use them in her acceptance speech. She also incorporated what was occurring in the auditorium, made reference to a joke made earlier in the evening, looked directly at the people she saluted, and still managed to include those in the distant seats and the home viewing audience.

Enjoying yourself includes being open to what is happening in the room. When you first step up to the lectern or stage and say, "I'm happy to be here," does anyone believe you? If you are happy, it doesn't have to be announced. Feel and convey the emotion, and you will be spared having to offer mundane preliminaries.

A Natural Energy Inducer

The ability to enjoy yourself in front of a group magically and automatically raises your level of energy. In many cases, you can sustain it for the duration of your presentation. That level of energy permeates the audience. Your listeners receive the gift of your energy and gain a higher level of it themselves. Hence, the entire interaction proceeds on a more dynamic, vibrant, interactive level. Your enjoyment in front of a group opens up dialogue, even if members of the audience have no actual words to say.

Enjoying yourself while presenting is a mind-set. As mentioned, giving many presentations, getting adept in front of groups, and knowing your material all greatly facilitate your ability to enjoy yourself. In the end, however, being able to get to that hallowed state of enjoyment is based on a series of choices you make about yourself, your audience, and your speaking ability.

The High-Content Presentation

DEFINING OR DEALING WITH HIGH CONTENT

Speakers who offer presentations that motivate, offer a specific message, or provide how-to information often state that their presentations are "high content." In recent years, however, the term "high content" has been overused and, consequently, its meaning has become unclear.

If a meeting planner asks you what you mean when you say high content, have a specific response ready. Use the terminology in your speaker literature or on your Web site so you'll be able to clarify what your presentations offer and the value they hold for your target audiences.

GEARED TO NEEDS

A high-content presentation is one geared to the needs of audience participants. That implies that you've done critical homework in terms of the vital issues audience members are facing and have provided innovative solutions to such challenges. High-content speeches benefit enormously from humor, effective use of language, and stories.

A key indicator of whether or not you are providing timely, relevant content is the willingness and enthusiasm audience participants have for ingesting your information. Specifically with a how-to presentation, you can gain some indication on site, but the real proof is what participants do with the information you provided. In 99.9 percent of the cases, a presenter simply isn't directly privy to such information. (See Chapter 18 about how to gauge results.)

If you're a motivational speaker, or simply one with an important message, the payoff may be reflected on the spot based on the way audiences members react to your presentation and the thoughts and the feelings that they have as a result of listening to it.

LEADING EDGE IS NOT NECESSARY

High content doesn't necessarily mean that your material is original. Most speakers don't have the wherewithal to conduct comprehensive surveys or undertake longitudinal research that they can then fashion into a highly credible, high-content presentation. All speakers, however, can draw insights and develop compelling conclusions from primary data published in newspapers, magazines, and scientific and academic journals by think tanks and government experts. The speaker who is able to extract data from a diverse array of primary sources and intersperse his or her findings within a coherent, compelling presentation can be among the most *successful and sought after speakers in the field.*

A LOGICAL SEQUENCE AT THE RIGHT TIME

High content implies that the audience does not have to make inordinate efforts to ingest and understand the information. Audiences do not need to be spoon-fed sentence after sentence, paragraph after paragraph; nor do speakers have to "dumb down" to be understood. To be deemed effective, however, speakers have to consider the impediments to understanding and following the presentation based on time, date, place, room, atmosphere and a host of other factors. The most brilliant high-content performance delivered at 7 A.M. may not go over as effectively as the same presentation offered at 10 A.M. To be a high-content speaker means that you have to be keenly attuned to what is required to ensure that the audience can effectively receive your presentation.

STIMULATE OR ENERVATE

High-content presentations need to stimulate the audience in one way or another. The stimulation can come in the form of high energy, entertainment, or strong appeal to the emotions. Simply delivering meaty material will never cut it if the connection to the audience is lacking and the speaker's style is far less than dynamic. This is a paradox—any seemingly high-content presentation can succeed or fail based on factors unrelated to the actual presentation material. Automatons, stuffed shirts, and other robot-like presenters, beware. It doesn't matter how good your material is if you can't present it in a way that somehow uplifts, inspires, or otherwise nurtures audience members.

ASSIGNMENT EXPECTATIONS

What's expected in a high-content presentation varies somewhat based on the speaker's assignment. A high-content keynote speaker certainly would have to have sufficient topic expertise and depth of knowledge to immediately convince everyone in the lecture hall that he or she was a good choice to deliver this keynote presentation. Such a speaker would need a dynamic delivery and would be somewhat provocative to retain the attention of everyone in the room. Since a keynote presentation implies the absence of participant packets, the presentation would need to proceed along a clear path that virtually everyone in the room could follow.

The general session presentation, which has many similarities to a keynote, also requires significant topic expertise and depth of knowledge.

More pointedly, the high-content presentation needs to be customized especially for this audience. A general session presenter might offer a participant packet to the audience.

What would a high-content breakout session encompass? Once again, significant depth of knowledge presented in an interactive, give-and-take type of style. A high-content breakout requires a significant body of "how-to" information bolstered by printed materials and/or audiovisual materials.

PERCEIVED VALUE IS UP TO THEM

The value that you offer to audiences is based on their perceptions, not yours. Speaker Dan Clark contends that speakers need to be continually training and pushing themselves to their ultimate potential as human beings so that when it is time for them to make a presentation, they are the best they can be. Referring to specifically professional speakers, Clark says, "We are not paid by the hour, we are paid for the value we bring to that hour." Whether you speak for fee or for free, if you wish to be deemed a high-content speaker, your ever-present goal is to bring great value to all of your presentations regardless of their length and despite any impediments based on day, time, room, and atmospheric conditions.

When you demonstrate the capacity to consistently offer audiences high-content presentations, go ahead and make that claim on your literature, but not before then.

Body and Movement

Aspiring public speakers often fall into the trap of believing that if their words are effective their presentations will be convincing. The truth is that audiences believe body language before they believe words. If you're not convincing with your movements, no matter how eloquent your words, you are not likely to be convincing.

EXPAND AND WIN

One way to win audiences over is to make your motions expand. Think upward and outward. Most speakers restrict themselves. They get "smaller." They hold their heads down. They don't act as if they own the spaces in which they speak.

When you hold your head down, you actually restrict your lungs from working at an optimal capacity. As a result, other body movements may seem forced, stilted. A variety of exercises can help you extend the space of your body naturally and easily. First, imagine your chest expanding for an inch or two. Olympic swimmers often envision their fingers as being 3 or 4 inches longer than they truly are. Thus, when they envision themselves grabbing the water for each successive strokes, they are propelled forward at a faster pace with greater ease. Similarly, visualizing chest expansion may enable you to draw deeper, stronger breaths.

MIXED VOLUMES AND TONES

The natural inclination of anyone who engages in conversation with another person or a group is to begin at a relatively low volume and tone. As the speech continues, higher volumes, higher tones, and higher energy seem to follow. This type of progression is a mistake when speaking in front of a group. You want to begin as if you are already in midspeech. This enables you to convey a sufficient level of opening presentation energy to capture the attention of audience participants.

Beginning in midstride means that you have already summoned a sizable amount of energy and that your speech is animated, not monotonous or dull. Gestures follow directly from animated speech. Therefore, your body language becomes more interesting to the audience.

FREEZING THE MOMENT

Kevin Lohan and Alistair Rylatt, authors of *Creating Training Miracles,* contend that presenters need to find "ways of engaging learners physically, intellectually, or emotionally." Lohan says that offering opportunities for audience participation will help maintain the audience's attention. Midsession stretching exercises can also liven up audiences if you can work them into your routine.

The more often audience members attend meetings, however, the more likely it is that they have participated in all manner of techniques designed to keep them involved. For some audience members, especially late in the day, "shake 'em up" routines could be seen as unnecessary. Lohan says there are innovative ways of keeping the audience involved without "creating the perception that the session is frivolous."

Keeping them engaged mentally, physically, and emotionally in the content of the day is key. Lohan has had success with energizing activities that are also closely linked to the content. At various times, he has had his audience members listen to the theme songs of old familiar sitcoms. He then asks them to write new verses using the material they have learned during his presentation.

Many audience members recall their verses months after the presentation. Considering the rate at which audience members forget presentations, recalling a self-penned jingle months later is quite a feat. Since the lyrics are based on material from the presentation, audience members retain the information they learned.

Lohan and Rylatt's observations have been backed by scientific research. Researchers have found that presenters "freeze the moment" for their audience.

Such findings are not a prescription for public speakers to wantonly initiate outrageous acts during conferences unless they have *thought through the point, the appropriateness of the act, the link between the point and the act,* and its *overall suitability for the conference theme and presentation objective.* That said, any presenter has the opportunity to create such moments.

I know of speakers who have asked audience members in advance to pose humorous, ridiculous, or outrageous questions. Then the speakers answer in ways that bring rooms to a standstill. Some law professors are known for recruiting students to stand up in the middle of class, perform a particular act, and then run out the door so as to engender a lively discussion.

The professors can then launch discussions, such as the perils of relying on eyewitnesses in criminal trials. The students in such sessions may take home a lesson that stays with them for years.

The Rare, Sheer Power

Sometimes, the sheer power of a sentence or phrase helps to freeze the moment for the listeners. Ronald Reagan's admonition to Mikhail Gorbachev to "tear down that wall," remains one of the best examples. Perhaps because it was prefaced with the words, "Mr. Gorbachev," Reagan's stirring presentation somehow struck all listeners, those who experienced it live and those who watched it on television or listened to it on the radio.

Realistically, a fine public speaker simply can't count on the power of a phrase as freeze-the-moment material. The setting often has as much to do with the speaker's ability to freeze the moment as anything. However, the combination of a potent statement and setting can be highly memorable, such as when Rudy Giuliani calmed the nation following September 11, 2001.

Props can also be useful in creating a memorable freeze-the-moment situation. Robert Bookman once used a technique that involved simply blowing up a balloon. To prove a point about setting goals and being totally committed to achieving them, Bookman began blowing up the balloon and let people know that he could make it burst within 25 seconds. The task looked impossible but he did it (usually in around 23 seconds).

Everyone would watch intently. As he began blowing up a balloon, when it had a diameter of more than a foot, the would audience bade him to stop. He continued. At 15 inches, can you picture the audience urging him to halt? Unbeknownst to his audiences, Bookman had procured balloons that could be blown up to at least a 20-inch diameter. Audience interest intensified. People watched with heightened awareness knowing that at any second there would be a loud pop. As he continued on to a volume that no one in the room had anticipated, the balloon finally did burst.

LET'S GET PHYSICAL

If you have any type of athletic skill that you can use in your presentation, it may help lead to a frozen moment. For example, Dan Thurmon combines an upbeat speaking style with his acrobatic abilities to supercharge his audiences. I first saw Thurmon some years ago speaking to a room of about 100 people. When he was introduced, rather than walk to the front of the room, Thurmon cartwheeled the whole way, dressed in his suit and tie. When he "landed" in the front of the room, the whole audience was in an uproar. Few members had ever seen anything like it. Thurmon proceeded to talk about being your best and maintaining high energy. His remarks were peppered by various physical gestures and audience exercises, such as learning how to juggle.

You don't need to learn to do somersaults, juggle, and operate a unicycle in a crowded room to be effective, however. Drawing on lessons from Thurmon's performance, what can you do that is novel or innovative? Do you have a great memory? Can you speak at a rapid pace? Do you sing? Anything that you are capable of doing merits consideration in terms of enlivening your presentations. Depending on the group, theme of the meeting, and why you were hired, you may find that some skill you had as a child, a hobby you engage in, or some current pastime can be used to enhance your presentation and make it memorable.

Get physical, get dramatic, get poetic, get melodious—get innovative so that your audiences simply can't forget you. As I discuss in the next chapter, visual effects can also go a long way in making your presentation a success.

All about Visuals

S tudies vary widely as to how much information people retain. Nevertheless, all research shows that humans do have limited attention spans and, therefore, retain limited amounts of information.

VISUALS ADD POWER

When you use an audio or visual aid in making a presentation, audience members are inclined to be impacted more than they would if you didn't use such materials. As a result:

1. You tend to be perceived as more organized.
2. There seems to be less resistance to your presentation.
3. Overall, people are likely to judge you as more professional.

Visuals are not needed for every presentation; however, because they can be effective, you'll want to make an informed choice as to whether or not to use visuals, what types to use, and what level of use is appropriate for the types of presentations you make. Speakers sometimes over-rely on overheads or slides to the degree that they're essentially presenting a narrated slide show as opposed to giving a speech. Given that you understand the importance of making an interpersonal connection with audience members, it behooves you to use visuals only where and when they're appropriate.

If you are speaking for, say, 40 minutes, and you have no visuals, the audience's collective experience is somewhat different than if you put something up on a screen even as infrequently as once every 7 to 10 minutes. The visuals become anchors or hooks around which people can focus their attention. Visuals might also be helpful in clarifying your points. On the other hand, storytellers may not want to use visuals because they paint mental pictures for their listeners.

If your visuals are crafted appropriately, you may actually help audience members understand and retain your information. A visual may also foster higher levels of agreement among audience participants. Speakers who use visuals effectively make meeting times seem to fly by, leaving audience members wanting more.

KEY CONSIDERATIONS

Sharon Adcock, a speaker and trainer, is an authority on the use of visuals. Adcock says that the key considerations for any speaker when deciding to use particular types of visuals in a presentation include the following:

- What is the size of the audience?
- How will the audience be seated?
- What is the objective of the presentation?
- Will audience members be taking notes?

She classifies visuals into six basic categories, including printed materials, viewcharts, overhead transparencies, slides, videos, and multimedia.

PRINTED MATERIALS

Printed materials encompass anything you can put on paper and distribute to audience members. Many speakers refer to them as handouts; I prefer to use the term "participant packets." Participant packets can be appropriate for any audience. However, the larger the audience, the smaller the packet needs to be because it is unwieldy to have a huge audience dealing with large stacks of paper. For smaller groups and longer training sessions, on the other hand, a large packet can be appropriate.

The pages you distribute, whether one at a time or preassembled, help to supplement your presentation. As with any document, certain fundamentals need to be heeded when making prints. You never want to load up pages so that there is no room for people to write notes. Consistent margins, legibility, page numbering, clean lines, clear reprints, and all the other niceties that you would employ in a professionally produced report or document are applicable here.

Some speakers advocate intentionally offering the audience more than they can absorb in one sitting believing that such an approach conveys a strong message about your capabilities. Supposedly, if you have far more information than you could present in the time allotted, the group might be more inclined to have you back. I believe that people hold on to packets based on how well they have been assembled, the effectiveness of the presentation, and the link between the presentation and the packet. Because I speak on topics such as "managing information and communication overload," I offer participation packets with no excess.

Audience members are already beleaguered by too much information and communication in their professional and personal lives. I want audience members to feel like they've received everything I had to offer for that presentation and to experience a sense of closure. If appropriate, in one way or another, I convey that I know far more than I'm presenting today and that I have other presentations.

The compromise to overly long participant materials is to offer a right-sized packet and have optional information available such as article reprints, self-scoring quizzes, and charts that could be stationed at tables within the room or as an appendix to your packet. If the latter, explain that the appendix will not be covered during your session but represents a bonus. I've found that audience members like that.

VIEWCHARTS

By their nature, viewcharts or flipcharts can only be used with small audiences, not exceeding 40 to 60 members. Some presenters prepare flipchart presentations in advance—long before the audiences assemble.

By doing so, little writing and drawing needs to occur once the presentation begins.

Adcock says that flipcharts allow for flexibility and high levels of interactivity with the audience. You can use different colors to accent certain points and to make the charts more visually pleasing. One of the biggest drawbacks to flipcharts, however, is that they can get sloppy in a hurry. In addition, some presenters write on them and flip to the next page before the audience has a chance to absorb the information. Sometimes speakers also over-rely on the flipchart as a presentation crutch as opposed to simply using it as a tool to facilitate understanding.

When speakers wisely use every page of a flipchart, it makes for greater readability—the underlying text of pages does not diminish the audience's ability to see and read the front page. This is particularly useful if you go back and forth between pages on your flipchart. Many speakers remove pages from the chart and tape them to the walls, particularly in training sessions in which the charts will be used throughout the day.

OVERHEAD TRANSPARENCIES

In many respects, overhead transparencies are like flipcharts. They can be used with slightly larger audiences, however, since their contents are projected onto a large screen. Like flipcharts, they afford quite a bit of flexibility and promote a fair degree of audience activity. They can be used with the house lights, which is an advantage over other electronic media.

If you are using predesigned visuals (which is highly recommended), acquire cardboard frames for them. This is helpful to both you and your audiences. You get the opportunity to write margin notes on the frames. They also offer visual barriers for audiences that help them better view and understand what is within the frame itself.

Some speakers create overheads during their presentation. This is not recommended, as few speakers can do so neatly and without disrupting the presentation. Your hands also make shadows on the screen, distracting audiences further. Working on overheads during your presentation can ultimately represent the low point of your speech.

Even among speakers who only use carefully crafted, professionally designed overheads, they tend to rely too much on them. As mentioned earlier, you never want to be in a situation in which you simply moderate a slide show. Go back through your overheads as if you are an audience member. How appropriate are they? Do you have too many? Then, find someone else who is willing to give you a critical assessment. You don't necessarily have to find another public speaker, although it could be to your benefit.

For any given 30-minute presentation, I may use as many as five or six overheads. I have 60 all together, and I draw on them based on my audience's objectives. Don't fall in love with your visuals; there might be some simple ways to make them even better.

SLIDES

Slides have long been a fixture among presenters and could conceivably represent the preferred choice of associations and corporate meeting planners. Slides offer many apparent advantages including the fact that they are easy to organize, store, pack, carry, and use. Slides in any format, like Corel or PowerPoint, should be relatively simple in design, because they should be shown for no more than 30 to 60 seconds. They can be divided up so that two or more build off of each other.

Slides are best viewed when house lights are dimmed. Reducing the level of lighting in a presentation, however, puts the speaker in a bind. Human beings are poised to go to sleep when sunlight or artificial lights dim. Even among those who don't doze, many participants go into a lower energy mode.

The possible exception to the dim lights phenomenon occurs in large gatherings in which I-Mag projection systems (see next section), generally on both sides of the stage, offer movie screen size images of you so that the people way in the back of the room can more easily see and hear. Even in relatively dark rooms, big, bold, brilliant I-Mag projection systems tend to have a neutralizing effect on the dim lights.

IMAGE MAGNIFICATION TECHNOLOGY

I-Mag screens are effective due to their sheer size. If you are using slides during your presentation, they can be inserted where and when you want them. As such, your slides will supersede your own image.

The overwhelming benefit of I-Mag screens is that virtually everyone in the room has an enhanced opportunity to see and hear you. Theoretically, people in the back row get the same view as if they were sitting three or four feet in front of the speaker. There is something about seeing the full range of facial expressions and nonverbal cues that can be substituted. The color and sound technology is magnificent. I have observed audiences giving rapt attention to emcees, introducers, and people coming up to the stage momentarily for awards simply because their images are so captivating, and even poor presenters have audience members' attention more of the time.

With I-Mag, you are the visual. Therefore, many of the recommendations for using gestures need to be slightly altered. In a large lecture hall, where it is okay to make grand sweeping gestures for the throngs of people in attendance, once you are on the I-Mag screen, it is preferable to return to tighter, more controlled gestures; otherwise, the screen tends to magnify your exaggerated movements, resulting in the appearance of an unprofessional, overly animated presenter.

The cardinal rule for speaking with I-Mag screens to the left and right of you is to forget about them. As always, focus on your presentation and on the audience. If you are adequately prepared, everything should run smoothly.

VIDEOS

Using videos in presentations offers distinct advantages, but the screen size is your first consideration: If you are limited to sticking a video cartridge into a television-size monitor, then, of course, your audience is limited to no more than 60 to 80 people. If your video can be played on the wide screen through the house system—emulating the effects of at least an in-flight airline movie—it can be appropriate for large audiences.

As with any electronic technology, glitches may occur. The wrong sequences may be shown. The tape may get damaged. Be prepared with a back-up plan.

The best use of video is to enhance your core messages. I saw a speaker air an eight-minute video segment that enabled the audience to have a quick, full understanding of situations he was addressing in his presentation. In this case, the video supported, but didn't compete with, the direct verbal aspects of his presentation. He remained the "star" and the focus of attention. After the presentation, people commented on his performance, not the relevance and poignancy of his videos.

MULTIMEDIA

Multimedia involves using a combination of visuals, such as videos, slides, and music. When used properly, it can be highly effective for audiences of any size, but only speakers who have high levels of experience in using such visuals should employ them—multimedia are not for aspiring public speakers or those who feel anything less than totally confident in them.

The potential for equipment failure or some other glitches in the overall presentation is obviously higher the more elaborate your equipment. The use of multimedia requires an audiovisual professional with whom the speaker consults long before his or her presentation.

GENERAL PRINCIPLES FOR USING VISUALS

When using visuals in any presentation, the cardinal and primary rule is to be organized and clear. Adcock says, "You want to move smoothly from point to point," so she advises using one point per visual. "It helps to have data available to back you," she says. "Often, you can establish credibility by including a quote or a simple reference at the bottom of the visual." She also recommends incorporating your logo in your visuals, usually in a corner or employed as a textured background.

The text for your visuals needs to be legible so that audience members in the back row are able to read them. Ray Fujioka, director of USC-Television in Los Angeles, adheres to the "Six-Three-Six Rule," which states that the best visuals contain no more than six lines with three to six words per line. Any more, and you risk crowding the visual, increasing the chance that it will be difficult for all people in the room to view, read, and comprehend. You are far better off going on to a second visual, and a third if necessary, in "build-up" fashion than to attempt to jam-pack a single visual.

When an audience gazes at a graphic, they are first attracted to large simple shapes such as a square, rectangle, circle, or triangle. Text is among the last things that the audience focuses on; however, putting text within a simple geometric figure such as a square or circle helps the audience to more easily see and understand your message. It also promotes order and helps audience members decide in which direction they should view a graphic.

A word on font: Don't fall into the trap of using all caps, which comes across as too overbearing. Use both caps and lower case letters for most of your text. It is okay to use all capital letters for a title, key word, or something you want to emphasize, but don't go overboard. Although serif fonts, which have tiny tails on the end of printed letters and numbers, are appropriate for your presentation packets, for projected visuals, sans-serif fonts are best.

Many presenters go wild when it comes to employing fonts and point sizes, but Adcock recommends adhering to the 10 Percent Rule—no more than 10 percent of your visuals should be different, that is, bold, underlined, or italicized. She advises using the same typeface within each visual and within your overall presentation.

COLOR COMBINATIONS

Audiences routinely deem color slides to be more effective than simple black and white ones. Presenters, however, often need to limit the amount of colors and the range of colors they use in their visuals. When using audiovisuals, particularly overheads or slides, keep in mind that many people have color-perception deficiencies and particular combinations of colors may pose problems. For example, bright red and bright green clash with one another for many audience participants.

Also, it is too easy to craft a series of visuals that have little connection to one another and lack overall consistency. Hence, you're better off limiting the number of theme colors to a chosen few. While black represents a viable background color, since it conveys authority, be wary of using it with a dark blue, a purple or brown foreground color, as they will easily get lost. Dark blue background with yellow titles and white text is among the most readable and palatable combinations.

Many shades of blue used as a background color with white or light print have a calming effect on some audience participants. Green represents another useful background color and is often overlooked. White or yellow lettering on a traffic light green or forest green background color can be invigorating to audiences. White or yellow on a black background often conveys a sense of finality—you can count on what's on the screen. Finally, bright red background with light text conveys energy, passion, spirit, or competition.

Suppose you are using several colors in close proximity to one another, such as showing revenues based on four categories over three years. Each bar might contain four different colors each representing one of the revenue areas. In such cases, proceed in a sky down to earth fashion—lighter colors such as sky blue would appear on top and darker colors such as brown or black would appear at the bottom of each bar. This makes for easier reading and understanding of the information you're offering.

Adcock advises matching the backgrounds of slides with the background of the room in which you will be presenting. She further advises using medium backgrounds for overheads shown in partially lit rooms, and light backgrounds only for fully lit meeting rooms.

Finally, prior to each speaking engagement, review your visuals to determine if each one is appropriate for the forthcoming audience. Don't fall into the trap of using the same sequence of visuals for each audience because demographics and characteristics vary widely. Choose your visual aids based on your audience, topic, and location. If you're in doubt as to whether a visual should be included, it probably should not. By using only the visuals you know are appropriate, you'll feel more comfortable with your presentation, and so will your audience members.

WORKING WITH THE
HOTEL AUDIOVISUAL STAFF

Any speaker may unexpectedly experience a bulb burning out, a plug coming loose, interference noise, or some other technological mishap. In advance of your speech, it pays to know the staff person assigned to your room and how this person can be quickly reached in an emergency.

Often the AV specialist will introduce himself or herself to you prior to your presentation. He or she will do a run though of all the equipment in the room to ensure it is in sound working order. But too many speakers scarcely greet this person and quickly forget his name, face, and how to get in touch, all of which you need to know in the event that something goes wrong during your presentation.

If something does go wrong, unless you are well versed in various types of equipment, don't attempt to deal directly with the matter your-self—you may make it worse! Here are some alternatives:

- If the noise is intrusive and apparently will not stop, think quickly. Can you call a short recess in your program during which time the situation will be corrected? Having an unplanned break can cause more problems than it's worth, so be careful. When people exit the meeting room, you will be unable to reconvene in under five min-utes, so plan accordingly.
- Sometimes, in the face of distracting noise, move from where you are speaking to someplace else in the room so as to redirect the au-dience's attention. With some rooms and some layouts this is not an option, but if so it is, worth considering.
- The larger the gathering, the greater the probability that someone in the audience will have a technical background and can tend to the offending equipment. In such cases, you might ask, "Is there anyone familiar with this equipment who can help out here?"
- If there are no takers, then ask someone in the far rows or nearest the exit to go on the aforementioned reconnaissance mission for you.
- If the equipment glitch was particularly onerous, at the close of your presentation profusely thank the audience for their patience and professionalism. Often, this simple acknowledgment will win back many who otherwise felt somewhat irritated as a result of what tran-spired during the session.
- If your session is being taped, sometimes the tape can be altered so as to minimize the disruption. Ask about this, because you may sal-vage an otherwise good presentation on tape.

Whatever you do, do not visibly show frustration or irritation either at the equipment, the setting, the meeting planner, or the audiovisual staff. In cases where your presentation was badly disrupted, you win empathy points from members of your audience if you are gracious under fire. If you succumb to feeling rankled as a result of having your presentation disrupted, you tend to be rated less favorably. As with other distractions, no matter how long and loud this disruption, if you handle it skillfully and there is sufficient time left in your presentation, most members of your audience will all but forget what transpired.

EFFECTIVE ONLINE PRESENTATIONS

Sooner or later, you may find yourself making presentations disseminated via Web or long distance connections. In such cases, the entire presentation represents a visual of sorts. Over the Web, you have to be even more dramatic and emotional to keep potentially distracted listeners online and alert. Here are 10 tips for inspiring your cyberspace audience and making your online presentations stand out from all the rest.

1. *Barricade yourself.* Ensure that absolutely nobody can intrude into your space while you're giving a presentation. This privacy is necessary for two reasons. The first, of course, is that sounds could make their way onto the program itself. The second and perhaps more important reason is that you'll be more confident if you know that you can proceed for the duration of your presentation without interruption.

2. *Use a telephone headset.* Headsets ensure that you have fluid motion, reduced potential for fatigue, and freedom to shift positions. If you can't use a headset, make sure that you have a highly comfortable chair, plenty of desk space, and room to maneuver. Your ability to quickly and easily convey information is the make-or-break factor in determining whether online viewers will stay glued to their screens, wander off, or click off altogether.

3. *Be at your best.* You need to get a good night's sleep and eat a balanced meal before you give a presentation. Also, prepare a cup of tea or water to keep your throat clear. Listeners can tell when your energy is down, when you are rushing, and when your voice is getting fatigued.

4. *Have all your materials arranged in advance.* You don't want to be shuffling through papers or other documents when you need to give your complete attention to listeners.

5. *Mentally rehearse your entire presentation.* No matter how many times you have given a presentation, the dynamics of a Web-based presentation are different than those of other media. Whether or not you're working with a host or interviewer, you want to be prepared to deliver your presentation from A to Z without a hitch, so that your listeners get the best.

6. *Visualize your audience members.* As with a live audience, your mission is to find out as much about the audience members as possible (well before your Web cast). What kind of environment do they work in? What are their challenges? What are they hoping to get from your session? If you don't know the answer to these questions, you'll have your work cut out for you.

7. *Orchestrate your presentation.* What are the highs and lows? Where do you want to enthrall your audience? Where will you make dramatic pauses? What parts of your speech will you stress? Your goal at all times is to be as informative and as entertaining as possible.

8. *Prepare for questions in advance.* Live online programs increasingly allow for participants' questions. You can't always anticipate what is going to be asked, but you can be prepared. Welcome and encourage questions, recalling at all times that answering a participant's questions may prove to be a valuable service.

9. *Prepare for your closing.* Even if you have slated a question-and-answer session near the end of your presentation, take back the reins and have at least a two- or three-minute closing prepared. As with an onsite audience, people need a sense of closure, and the best way to ensure one is through preparation.

10. *End on time.* Participants and providers remember those presenters who go over the allotted time and appreciate those who don't.

LONG-DISTANCE LEARNING

If you're making a presentation via closed circuit television, satellite uplink, video, or television, there are other subtleties for inspiring audiences who can see you when you can't see them. Over many years of presenting long-distance learning programs, I've learned that there are some things worth doing differently in this medium. Here are the highlights:

1. It's okay to gesture frequently, but it's important to keep the movements tight. Chances are the camera can't follow you as well as a live audience would.
2. Smile frequently. The audience only has you to go on, and they need visual cues throughout the broadcast.
3. Use your face as a medium for gestures. If you can raise an eyebrow, grimace, act surprised, look excited, or make some other gesture, all of these help keep the audience focused.
4. Vary your rate of speech and amplitude. Sometimes, lean in toward the camera and speak softly. Other times, say something loud or twice for emphasis.
5. Don't be afraid to pause, especially if you've just said something you'd like the audience to reflect upon. As with traditional audiences, a pause, offered correctly, can be a moment of high drama.
6. Have your visuals and graphics ready, and in order. On camera is no time to be bumbling around.
7. If you have no live audience, pretend the audience is everyone. If it helps, tape a picture of people near the camera so that you can easily see it. Conversely, pretend you're talking to a live group you just met with. A lot of the dynamics will still be in mind.
8. If it's a mixed live and long-distance audience, draw your energy from the people before you, but intermittently, give your attention to those out in TV land. You might say "for those viewing via satellite," or something of that nature. Sometimes, simply pose a question to the remote viewing audience, even though you can't hear them answer.

Don't be afraid to come across as authoritative as long you keep it friendly. Feel free to say you don't know about a particular issue, or "that's not an area we'll explore today." People want information from an expert, but they also want the truth. You're not expected to know everything. Most important, have fun while you're presenting. After all, that's why you're a speaker, isn't it?

In the next chapter, I'll speak about developing your signature story. In my opinion, telling a great story is a sure-fire way to have fun on stage.

Developing Your Signature Story

Through sounds, pantomimes, or gestures, people have always communicated with each other through stories. Storytelling is essentially relating a tale to one or more people using tools such as voices, props, movements, and whatever else helps convey meaning.

Storytelling is different from acting, reciting verse or prose, reading, or other forms of communication, although all communication shares some common characteristics. In conveying a story, the teller shares a part of himself or herself. Good storytellers envision and replicate essential images. Good tellers relive the story in a manner that enables audience members to feel as if they are actually part of it.

BRINGING THE AUDIENCE ALONG

Many students of storytelling have observed that the exploration involved in telling a story helps both the teller and members of the audience explore themselves. While each audience member may be formulating a somewhat unique body of images based on his or her imagination, as well as the meaning that he or she attaches to various phrases, movements, sounds, and gestures, everyone shares the experience. Audience members report that these experiences can be profound—some are moved to tears, some to exaltation. Some are ready to take action as a result of hearing a stirring tale.

Some storytelling experts liken the storytelling process to a dance. The teller knows the steps. The audience takes on the part of the follower, indicating the pace. Good tellers are not necessarily performing for an audience as much as they are including them in an experience.

When storytellers "lose" audiences, the cause might be that:

1. The teller is not familiar enough with the story to make it engaging. He or she labors to get through it, gets bogged down in unnecessary details, or otherwise does not keep the audience in mind. At such times, audience members are prone to be fidgety, bored, frustrated, and ready to move on.

2. The teller is not reading the audience as the story unfolds. Even gifted tellers who get too wrapped up in telling the story can lose otherwise potentially receptive audiences. The audience members will tell you the appropriate rate and level of detail that seems most suitable through their movements, eye contact, and nonverbal cues.

3. Sometimes a story will prove to be less effective than it could otherwise be, based on conditions of the moment. Are you speaking before lunch? If so, shorter is better. Are you speaking at the end of what has been a busy day for audience members? Again, shorter and peppier is better than longer and drawn out. Are you competing with noise from outside the room? Are there other factors that have conspired to diminish or detract from the audience's capability to follow along? Speaking outdoors, for example, requires a much higher level of energy and higher volume than the same presentation would merit indoors.

A DIFFERENT KIND OF STORY

A signature story, by definition, is one that is unique to you. You are the only one who can tell it. A great signature is a true story that requires little or no embellishment because it is a story that the teller experienced first-hand. The teller's own experience adds an element to the story that cannot otherwise be emulated. He or she doesn't have to attempt to take on a larger role. If anything, his or her actual role is more than sufficient. Hence, a fable or folk legend passed down though the years cannot serve as a signature story.

While professional storytellers can simply tell stories to entertain and amuse, the public speaker has to have an ulterior motive in delivering a story, especially a signature story. Ideally, your signature story will convey the major lesson or point of your overall message. You deliver it in such a way that it perfectly links up with your message.

Many speakers believe that the best signature stories are delivered so that the audience senses the vulnerability of the teller; that is, the audience can tell that the experience had a deep impact on the speaker, and the speaker is willing to take a chance with the audience.

Professional speaker Emory Austin believes that the best closes to signature stories are those that relate to something that was imparted to the audience earlier in the overall presentation. If the signature story is profoundly moving, audience members may leave with the thought, "I am now ready to take action." You make your story both personal and applicable to others. You touch upon universal themes such as love, loyalty, amazement, sacrifice, sadness, or exaltation. Many of the most memorable signature stories span the emotional spectrum. Audience participants feel great joy, deep sadness, and everything in between.

As with storytelling in general, a great signature story is memorable. People sometimes quote lines and phrases from it. They enthusiastically share it with others. There is something about the story that puts audience members into a trance.

LEARNING FROM OTHERS

Fortunately, there are many opportunities to develop storytelling ideas. You can find stories through television performers, teachers, dancers, musicians, and even members of your own household. Everyone has stories to tell. Most public libraries contain stories on cassette, often in the children's section, that you can listen to at home or while driving.

The local events section of your newspaper often lists times, dates, and locations of storytelling performances. (Most of these events are free.)

Even local, amateur storytellers with little experience may prove enlightening to you as you seek out your own signature story. As you begin to attend such sessions, take note of audience reactions in ways that you may not have done before. By listening to other people's stories, you may gain insight into which of your own stories to tell.

SEARCHING THE PAST

How do you identify your signature story? Reflect upon those stories that you have already presented to audiences. Which one do you want most eagerly to impart? Which one gets the biggest rise? Which one, if not told, would make your presentation seem incomplete? If you can identify such a story, that may well be your signature story.

To begin finding your stories, you need look no further than your own past. You can start by walking yourself through the memories of your earliest days. Look at pictures, yearbooks, and old school notebooks; there are stories in them all. Don't worry about how they'll fit in your speech or what point they could assist you in making. You will find that a good story fits into several different contexts and can be used in a variety of circumstances. The important thing is to begin to collect your stories. Consider the following:

- *Sports and hobbies.* Did something happen on an athletic field that impacted you in an enduring way? What about hobbies, favorite pastimes, or games you used to play?
- *Your family and relatives.* Is there a character (or two!) among your family that imparted some lesson or bit of wisdom that has stayed with you all these years? Are there heroes or villains among them, or simply everyday people acting in extraordinary ways?
- *Achievements or failures.* Among your accomplishments, is there something that stands out? Something that is so compelling that you want to share it again and again with others? What about your failures? Is there something that upon reflection ultimately served to impart an important lesson? While you don't want to make the mistake

of using an audience for therapy, such as telling stories that are emotionally painful for you in hopes of achieving a catharsis, some of your greatest disappointments, heartbreaks, and failures may carry the seeds of a great signature story. Don't overlook them.

- *Your most memorable character. Reader's Digest* and other magazines through the years have long noted the power and impact of publishing stories by authors who cite the most memorable characters in their lives. The traits and circumstances that make such characters memorable often contain universal elements that quite possibly could add up to a fine signature story.
- *Embarrassments.* Veteran speakers know that everything that happens to them in life is potential fodder for the podium. As emotionally painful or embarrassing as a situation might be, the passage of time invariable makes it less so, and as embarrassing situations "age," they often get funnier in the retelling.
- *Life's gambles.* Did you ever take a great risk to accomplish something in your career or personal life? You don't necessarily want to brag about foolish risk taking; still, each of us has taken foolish risks at one time or another, perhaps jeopardizing personal safety, financial security, or a relationship. Which of your gambles might contain the seeds that will produce a wonderful signature story?

Professional speaker and storyteller Grady Jim Robinson, based in San Francisco, says, "It is highly possible that the most profound, moving, inspiring, or thought-provoking story you have to offer is still inside you, buried beneath layers of ego, fear, timidity, and over-developed concerns about what 'they' might think." "It would be a shame," he says "if you allowed a story buried deep within you to stay submerged when it could have so much value for your audiences and enhance your public speaking capabilities and reputation. Once you allow one of these long submerged stories to see the light of day, often you find that in the telling, much of your own reticence and inhibition about the event evaporates."

Real-Life Examples

Dave Yoho tells stories of a personal nature that lend insight into the lessons he has learned. Yoho shows his audience a life filled with emotional extremes. From his unloving father and childhood speech impediment, to becoming a millionaire by age 28, to his own failures as a father, Yoho gives of himself completely to keep his audience riveted.

Dan Clark uses a similar approach by taking his audience through his battle with cancer. He relies on evoking certain emotions in the audience members to open them up to an understanding of his particular point. Like Yoho, Clark uses his tale of hardships to grab his audience's attention.

Evoking a feeling of empathy among your audience doesn't need to be so heavy, however. Many speakers take a lighter approach, just as effective in bringing the audience to a sympathetic and understanding mind-set. Mary Jane Mapes and Bruce Wilkenson talk about teenagers. This is effective because it is a topic to which everyone can relate. Whether audience members are now parents or simply recall their own teenage years, every one of them will feel a natural affinity between these stories and their personal experiences.

All of these speakers present stories in different manners. Some are funny, some are sad, and some are personal, while others may be little quirks of life. What they have in common, though, is that they all help make an entertaining and effective speech.

Live, Observe, and Record

On my hard drive, in a folder called "speaker," in a subfolder called "anecdotes," I have more than 80 vignettes ranging from one paragraph to two pages. The file has steadily grown over the years.

Whenever I am waiting in lines, finishing the dictation of a chapter for another book, or if the spirit moves me, I record into my pocket dictator whatever story happens to come to mind. It is amazing how some of the most distant memories often come to the forefront at times you least expect them. Don't let those fleeting memories get away.

Jean Robertson also has an ingenious way to keep track of what stories and vignettes she used with what groups. Using a grid, she lists the names of her stories and vignettes down the left side of the page. Across the top she lists the names of the groups to whom she has spoken. Directly following her presentations she revisits her grid and checks off each vignette or story that she presented to the latest group. She keeps the chart fully up to date at all times. It is a rather simple system yet has great potency. When Jean is rebooked to speak to a group a second or third time, she merely has to consult her chart to determine what she has already told that group. Now, she makes choices related to what she will say on second, third, and subsequent visits. As a matter of policy, she will avoid giving the vignette or story that she has already presented, unless of course she is specifically asked to "tell that story again."

Now, while the idea is fresh in your mind, take out a piece of paper or go over to your computer and write or type in any key words or phrases that relate to 10 possible vignettes or stories that you could tell. Don't worry about fleshing them out at this time. For now, you simply want to have a core of 10 possibilities you will be developing in the coming weeks and months.

As the opportunities present themselves or as your energy dictates, pick the vignette or story that seems easiest to tell, is the most meaty, or registers the greatest emotional impact with you. No matter how you find your signature story, make sure it's one that's interesting and personal to you. By doing so, you ensure that you'll present the story with an enthusiasm that will enliven your audiences.

Making Your Story Even Better

O nce you develop a signature story, or group of stories, what can you do to make your presentation even more effective? By diagnosing what you tell and why you tell it, you unlock the potential to be more effective. If you have a special story in mind, reflect on it as you proceed through the following pages.

DISCOVERING YOUR MOTIVES

There are many reasons that people tell particular stories. Among them are the following:

- *To captivate listeners.* A good story can keep audience members hanging on every word.
- *To evoke emotion.* A poignant story is an efficient vehicle for moving audience members in one direction or another.
- *To reveal deep truths.* It's often easier to convey a message about the human condition to audiences through stories rather than factual assertions.
- *To stimulate the audience to think in new ways, explore new ideas, and be open to new possibilities.* My own signature story is about

Katharine Hepburn chastising a theatergoer who disrupted her play. I use the story to teach audience members about the power of completions, taking action now as opposed to letting issues build up or fester. I could simply tell people of the importance of this issue, but my advice wouldn't resonate within them and be as memorable as the vivid portrayal of Hepburn.

- *To entertain.* Public speakers, whether they're primarily storytellers or from business, political, educational, or other arenas, don't necessarily need a cause or mission behind each story they tell. Sometimes stories can be used by speakers to warm up the audience at the outset of a presentation.
- *To acquaint the audience members with themselves.* In addition to telling them more about yourself, stories can help audience members learn more about their own ideas and feelings, as well as those of the people around them.
- *To convey unity.* Stories can impart the message, "I am with you" or "We have much in common." I once saw a speaker talk about one of his relatives who used to live in the area in which a meeting took place. The speaker was seeking to form a bond with the audience, and he did so in an entertaining manner.

Once you understand your own reason(s) for telling a particular story, you can lay the groundwork for improving it. With such self-awareness, you can actively work to emphasize and dramatize those elements of a story that are most poignant.

PERFECTING YOUR STORY

Story-teller Louise Omoto Kessel of North Carolina suggests the following sequence for developing and perfecting a story.

1. The first step in her approach is to determine what she calls the "most important thing," or the MIT. In my Katharine Hepburn story, the most important thing is the moment Hepburn responds to an audience member's disruption by stopping the play. When I tell the story, I build up to this point so that the audience is prepared for something out of the ordinary.

2. The next step is what Kessel calls "word painting." Word painting involves focusing on an object and expanding on it. In the case of my story, it would be a vivid description of Katharine Hepburn's face as she was about to chastise this theatergoer. What was she feeling? What was she thinking? How did her expression change? Did her body stiffen? Everything that I can describe about Hepburn will enhance the audience's experience and "take them there" more vividly.

If you are portraying a character, slip into that character's mode. Turn a different way, contort your face to resemble the character, change your voice, and/or accent particular words or phrases in a way that the character does. Let the character take over. Think about what brought the character to this point in time. What was his or her upbringing? Where might he or she live? What kind of friends or associates did the character have? Where did he travel? What obstacles did he overcome? What impediments is he still facing? The more you know about the character, Kessel says, "the freer you can be about telling the story."

3. While you want to use the appropriate combination of words, phrases, and accents, it is actually the progression of the story and the scenes that are vital. When you think of the scenes first, the words tend to come naturally. So, the next step is to engage in what Kessel calls "mapping." In mapping your story, simply consider what happens first, what comes next, and so on. Draw a scene for each of these "camera shots." Never mind if you are good at sketching or not. When you draw the scene, your mind's eye begins to notice additional details that may not have been part of your story. When I began to draw the scene of Katharine Hepburn, I recognized elements of the stage, the seating, the aisles, the materials used in the construction of the theatre, colors, and so on that had been absent.

RECONSTRUCTING THE SETTING

If the story actually occurred, and you can get back to its location, do so. In my case, it was quite possible to revisit the Kennedy Center, where

Hepburn performed the night I witnessed this situation. I went back up to the balcony and sat in the same seat. I was surprised to find out how the seat, the balcony, the railing, the distance to the stage, and other elements of the actual theatre differed from my recollection. By actually visiting the scene of the story, I was able to more accurately depict the story.

If your story is not based on an actual occurrence, or, if it is impractical or impossible to revisit the scene, do your best to recreate the scene by the means at your disposal. Can you find photos or sketches on the Internet? If so, it will be to your great benefit in retelling the story, and your audiences will derive greater pleasure from hearing you.

CHOOSING YOUR WORDS AND EXPRESSIONS CAREFULLY

The language you use can be vital to the message you try to convey through a story. Professional speaker and author Patricia Fripp suggests telling your story to a number of audiences and transcribing it each time. Then, she advises, closely examine your transcription. Where are the redundancies? What words can be eliminated? What words need to be substituted for clearer, more illustrative terminology?

Are there places where you may lose the audience? Is the sequence the best it can be? Are there words you stumble over? Is the language appropriate for the audiences? Fripp reports that most speakers are amazed when they view the transcripts by how much refinement is necessary.

Practice telling your newly refined story, but not yet to an audience. Tell it to yourself, either in the mirror and/or with a tape recorder or video camera. There is something in telling it aloud, even to a tape recorder or camera, that will help to expose any remaining problems. Examine your facial expressions. Kessel suggests flicking your wrist, raising an eyebrow, leading with different body parts, speaking in a whisper, and exhibiting different facial expressions. As you begin to use these tools with greater competence, you enhance the audience's experience in hearing your story. As you tell your story more and more, keep in mind that the best speakers and the best stories essentially "show," not "tell." Professional speaker Lou Heckler says, "Don't tell your stories; relive them."

PAINTING A PICTURE

When you impart your story in an entertaining manner, relating it in some way to audience members; employing objects, sights, sounds, and/or places; focusing on key words; accenting the most important thing; and closing with a flourish, you all but guarantee that you'll become the type of storyteller that people want to hear. Indeed, the measure of a superb storyteller is that audiences want to hear his or her particular story over and over again.

FITTING IT INTO YOUR SPEECH

Theoretically, an effective signature story can be told to any audience because of the universal elements the story encapsulates. Where to tell it within your presentation is another matter altogether. Depending on what impact you want to have, the story could come first, last, or someplace in the middle.

Wherever you tell your story within your overall presentation, you always want to be able to do so in a manner that does not seem rushed. If you don't leave enough time, and you find yourself racing through your signature story, the audience will sense it and feel uneasy. A great signature story, even slightly rushed, can lose its potency; therefore, you need to know exactly how long it takes, accounting for laughter, applause, silence, or whatever response you anticipate.

Studies say audiences' attention spans last about seven minutes for any one given topic. If a speaker retains the same posture, voice, or focus, he or she has little hope of reaching the audience. To keep a high level of interest, fit your signature story into your speech where it will reinforce a certain point or theme. This technique will keep your speech dynamic and interesting.

THE STORY-TELLING EXPERIENCE

In a 1988 article appearing in *The National Storytelling Journal,* author Fran Stallings discussed the entrancing power of story telling. A well-told story could so completely enthrall audience members that their attention to everything else would recede from conscious awareness. Their experience while listening to a story was likened to that of a light hypnotic trance. Professor Brian Sturm at the School of Information and Library Science at the University of North Carolina has been building on the works of these and other researchers. Sturm has been synthesizing his findings in cognitive science, psychology, literary studies, linguistics, and folklore to explore what he refers to as "the nature of the story listening trance phenomenon." Interviewing listeners at conferences, Sturm transcribes their interviews and then analyzes the results to identify recurrent themes. What was it exactly that put people into an "altered state" during a story such that they listened as if in a light hypnotic trance?

These unique and amazing findings reveal that individuals most definitely "experience a qualitative shift in their state of consciousness when they listen to some stories," says Sturm. He found that six characteristics of the state become apparent, including:

- Story realism.
- Lack of awareness of surroundings.
- Engaged receptive channels (people could see, hear, feel, and experience elements of the story).
- A lack of control or loss of control of the experience.
- A "placeness" to the experience.
- A sense of time distortion.

Sturm's interviewees often referred to words such as "alive," real," "in the story," or "being there," when discussing their story listening experience. Some listeners became so enmeshed in the action that they "took on the personae of the story characters." Some listeners no longer noticed their surroundings while others felt as if the surroundings had simply disappeared.

While all listeners could physically see the storyteller, many reported visualizing the story as it was being told, that is, seeing it in their mind's eye. They were also likely to have a kinesthetic experience, experiencing shivers, gasps, or laughter based on what was being said. "Some listeners identified with the emotions of the storytelling," reports Sturm, "others with the emotions of the story itself, and still others with the emotions of past experiences that were recalled during the story." Listeners also perceived that the story had a locale "they were not 'beside' the story, they were within it, with the story seeming to occur around them."

As a result of his research, Sturm was able to identify 16 positive influences on the storytelling experience (see below) and one negative influence or distraction, which represented any disturbance that inhibited a listener's ability to experience or maintain the story listening trance.

As you review the 16 influences that follow, remember Professor Sturm's observation that understanding of the story listening trance is still in the initial stages and that there is still much to be discovered about this wondrous phenomenon:

1. *Memories.* The more vivid a memory a story can evoke the greater the potential for a story listener to experience the light hypnotic trance state.

2. *Novelty.* A story heard by the listener for the first time has a far greater chance of sparking excitement and inducing the trance state.

3. *Expectations.* Listeners who were ready and willing to be entranced by a story were more likely to achieve the trance state.

4. *Personal preferences.* A listener who likes a particular type of story is more likely to be entranced by that type of story (i.e., those who like adventure stories).

5. *Physical comfort.* Comfort tends to be something that goes unnoticed until it is absent. Given that the listener's seat, prevailing temperature, humidity level, and other meeting place factors were to the listener's liking, the greater the likelihood of the trance state.

6. *Familiarity.* While novelty, addressed above, was a strong influence for some, some people responded favorable to stories that represented "old favorites."

7. *Storyteller's ability.* A storyteller's reputation for and demonstration of excellence can make a huge difference in inducing the trance state.

8. *Rhythm.* A story that is told with a continuing rhythmic pattern can augment the trance state, while breaks in rhythm can disrupt it.

9. *Emotional comfort.* As with physical comfort, emotional calm induces the trance state while any experience of stress or anxiety tends to disrupt it.

10. *A listener's occupation or background.* Individuals in professions requiring vigilance (e.g., police officers or nurses) may experience difficulty experiencing the trance state.
11. *Humor.* Humor may impact physical comfort and/or emotional comfort and in any case is "engaging for many people."
12. *Recency.* The story that is most recent in the listener's memory is often considered the most engaging.
13. *Storyteller's involvement.* Storytellers who become highly involved in their own telling induce a "piggyback" process and thereby their listeners become highly involved themselves.
14. *Storytelling style.* Stories that are appropriate to the situation and are told at a moderate pace with good description help to bring on the trance state.
15. *Rapport with the storyteller.* Listener's who identify with the storyteller in any way have an increased likelihood of achieving the trance state.
16. *Story content.* Listeners find a story more engaging when they can identify with the story theme.

TELLING IT OFTEN

There is no getting around this point—to become a master in delivering your signature story, you have to tell it often. I can think of no substitutes for doing so. I have spoken with many public speakers who report that the telling of their signature story gets better and better each time—not because they are embellishing it, but because details become more clear, their pacing approaches perfection, they learn ways of drawing the audience further in, and they perfect the use of gestures and props at critical junctures.

But, you may ask, won't I become tired of telling the same story over and over again? The answer to the dilemma is that you delve into the story in ways that make it different for you each time. Each time you tell it, something else may come to mind. Perhaps there is someone in the room who inspires you. Perhaps the story reminds you of someone new in your life, or a recent event. By maintaining your own excitement for your signature story, you will continuously capture the attention and emotions of your audiences.

Finding Local Audiences

Now that you have your signature story, it's time to test it out on an audience. You have a ready throng of willing listeners right in your local area. Whether it is the Lion's Club, the PTA, the United Way, the Chamber of Commerce, or any one of a dozen other groups that meet in your town, you will find that many actively seek speakers for their weekly and monthly meetings. Even if you only come on after dinner for 15 to 20 minutes, that is more than enough time to try out a story or two.

With a brand new story, I recommend speaking to at least three groups in this manner before attempting it in a larger venue. Your three early round presentations will enable you to work out some of the rough spots, substituting words here and there, embellishing this element, dropping that one, and refining the story until it is easy for you to tell it to an audience in an attention-grabbing way. The more universal your theme—love, hate, triumph, adversity and so on—the less you will have to do in terms of adapting it to each audience.

Since good stories contain universal elements that could appeal to anyone even if you speak entirely to business or professional groups, highly personal, nonbusiness stories can still work well. Remember, the chances are that most of the adults in your audience are parents. They may also be siblings, they certainly are sons or daughters of their parents, they have friends, they experienced triumphs and failures, they get embarrassed and so on.

Be sure to record yourself even during these early rounds. Doing so, and reviewing the recordings closely, you have the greatest chance for rapid improvement. Still, after all the work you put into perfecting your signature story, the most important factor to remember is to focus on the audience. Keep in mind that most people have never heard of you before and have never heard your story. Even if you are delivering your signature story to a group for the second time, there will be many people in attendance who were not there the first time you told it. Even those in attendance who heard it before will hear it "anew" and will reflect on it in different ways.

As the old proverb says, "You can never stick your foot in the same river." You never tell your signature story in exactly the same way or with exactly the same impact.

DEVELOPING OTHERS

When you feel reasonable adept at telling one story, go back and repeat the process until you have a second one in your arsenal, on your way to at least five. Having the capability to tell at least five vignettes or stories at the drop of a hat means that you have flexibility for all types of engagements. As more stories evolve, you may find ways to improve your original signature story. Continuously use your developing skills to cultivate every story you tell.

Once you have amassed a library of these stories, you can begin to work on the best 20 or so. You'll find that you can recall them easily with only a keyword or two, so that you can carry them all with no more than an index card. Then, when you're preparing for a speech, you can pick two or three that fit easily with your topic and your audience.

15

Pauses and Silences

Thinking occurs four or five times faster than the typical person can speak. This situation leads some speakers to think that audiences need to have fast, peppy, pause-free presentations in order to pay attention. Actually, the opposite is true. The speed at which people think has little relationship to a speaker's ability to hold an audience's attention. Listen to any gifted storyteller, and you'll find that the audience hangs on his or her every word. While some or all of the audience members have the ability to think more quickly than the rate of the speech, few actually do it.

With an effective presentation, whether it involves statistics or an enthralling story, audience members are happy to follow along at the speaker's pace. Moreover, people want to reflect on what they hear. A speaker's pauses and silences give audience members this time to reflect, synthesize, and get ready for what's next. The more emotional a presentation, the more important pauses and silences can be. Audience members are not simply ingesting data or words—they're cultivating feelings, convictions, and images.

BUT I HAVE SO MUCH TO SAY

For some public speakers, the thought of handing back some of their time (through pauses and silences throughout their presentations) seems like an imprudent practice. After all, if you only have 25 or 45 minutes, and you have a lot of information to convey, why would you want to shorten the length of your presentation through self-imposed pauses and silences?

The short answer is that the audience can only hear, absorb, and act on so much, and, in many cases, less is more! Less information presented to them, if it's powerfully offered, can result in a more effective presentation from the standpoint of changing opinions or influencing behavior. As a professional speaker and author of 32 books, I often encounter this dilemma of having too much information to offer. Yet, to try to cram in as much information as possible into my presentation would defeat the purpose of the presentation itself.

PAUSES SEEM LONGER
TO THE SPEAKER

A curious phenomenon occurs when you give a presentation. What you may think is a long and deadly pause of, say, three or four seconds, goes by in almost an instant for members of the audience.

Put down this book for a moment and mentally count to five.

At the typical pace of career professionals, your count to five probably occurs in three seconds. You could pause for three seconds at the end of every paragraph of your presentation, or even the end of every other sentence, and no one would lose interest. The audience would probably be better off in terms of being able to absorb your presentation, and certainly to reflect upon it. You, as the speaker, would be better off since you would be maintaining energy, staying focused, and offering a presentation that is easier to follow. Plan for less time than you're allotted in order to allow ample room for pauses.

PAUSE BEFORE SAYING A WORD

Dave Yoho believes that your level of energy is usually determined before you speak. In his book *How to Have a Good Year Every Year,* Dave says, "Many speakers who wait for exhilaration from audience reaction while dealing with anticipation and butterflies, waste energy through hyper-nervousness. He continues, "If you've prepared your speech, know your audience, and have checked the environment in which your speech will be given, then you can direct your energies internally."

Yoho recommends that you relax, observe your audience, become a part of the milieu, and enjoy the moment. He routinely pauses before launching into his speech and simply "takes in" the whole room. Where else in life do you ever encounter such a magnificent assembly?

PAUSE FOR A POWERFUL CLIMAX

An equally important pause should occur at the end of your presentation. Too many speakers end with a lame, "Thank you," which dissipates the power of their presentations. For maximum impact, offer your final pause after your last few words. This pause signals to the audience that you have maintained control and stopped speaking, and it is time for them to respond with what you hope will be a loud, long round of applause.

If you don't time your presentation, and you rush to finish on time, ending with "thank you," you won't likely receive the strongest audience response. If you end with power and purpose, and offer your final pause, the audience will respond.

PAUSING IN MIDSENTENCE

Some speakers learn the power of the pregnant pause, the pause in mid-sentence, just before delivering the important part of a statement. For example, consider the power of the pause in the following passage:

> At the medal ceremony for a Special Olympics competition, a 26-year-old man had just won the 100 meter dash for his age group. As the judge hung the gold medal around his neck, the young man said, "Thank you." With those words, the volunteer who had worked with him for many years began crying. When asked why she was crying, she said, "It's the first time . . . he's ever spoken."

Former NFL referee and veteran speaker Jim Tunney uses this anecdote in his powerful speech about volunteering and serving. He uses the dramatic pause as depicted here by the ellipses to great effect with his audiences. By waiting a brief moment before delivering the last three words, Tunney invariably captures the hearts of everyone in the room.

Would the story be as compelling if Tunney did not pause prior to saying, "he's ever spoken"? The story would still make a impact, but it wouldn't have the same dramatic effect.

Tunney's pause helps to focus the attention of everyone in the room. As such, it's easy for them to empathize with the volunteer who has given her heart and soul to helping this Special Olympian. People leave Tunney's presentation with a lasting impression. Indeed, I heard the presentation in 1981, and I vividly remember it to this day.

THE PAUSES OF HISTORY

If you listen to some of the great political speeches of the twentieth century with your newfound "ears" for pauses and silences, you may be amazed to discover how often pauses were employed in such speeches. John F. Kennedy's inaugural address, which included the line, "Ask not what your country can do for you, ask what you can do for your country" contains a three-second pause between the two parts of that statement.

The same observation holds true for Franklin Delano Roosevelt's famous line, "We have nothing to fear . . . but fear itself." If you can obtain a recording of it, note the pause between the two portions of that sentence. Delivered too quickly, without a break in the middle of the sentence the line would have been far less effective in calming the anxieties of a nation in peril. Amazingly, if he had said it too fast, people may have dismissed FDR's line as political gibberish. After all, to this day, are you certain of what the sentence means? The way that Roosevelt delivered it, with dramatic pause, undoubtedly gave people a sense of assurance.

NOT FOR EVERY OCCASION

There are, of course, times when some pauses and silences do not favorably contribute to a presentation. You know these instances all too well. The speaker stumbles, unsure of what to say. He loses his place; starts shuffling papers, slides, or other materials; and leaves the audience in the lurch. These kinds of pauses signal ineffectiveness and lack of organization. Perhaps it is fear of appearing unprepared that prompts the more novice speaker to avoid silences altogether. Unfortunately, such a speaker doesn't recognize the power of employing them to his or her best advantage.

What are some of the best times to employ pauses? As you have seen, pauses are effective when you are about to offer the closing item of a powerful or emotional story. Another time to pause is when you offer a startling statistic. For example, if you tell your audience that 61 percent of Americans are now overweight and 27 percent are obese, a simple pause for 5 to 7 seconds will allow the audience to absorb those figures and consider the implications behind this fact.

PAUSES ENHANCE HUMOR

If you add humorous remarks to your presentation, and by now you know that I am a strong advocate of doing so, pause after each one. To give the audience the full measure of your humor, you must be silent—otherwise, your reaction will detract from the desired effect. Masters of the well-pronounced, posthumor pause, such as the legendary Jack Benny, know that sometimes it takes the audience a few moments to gather up its collective faculties and respond. During pauses, Benny would use a facial expression to encourage greater laughter. You can practice your own actions during pauses to discover what works best for you. The look that Jack Benny developed became so well known to his audiences that, in time, all he had to do was pause and give that look, and he would get a laugh even if what he said was only marginally funny.

PAUSES CAN CONVEY SERIOUSNESS

You can take a cue as well from politicians who have effectively mastered pauses and silences. While George W. Bush has long been reputed to be highly effective in one-on-one and small group sessions, his increasing mastery at issuing large-venue, dramatic appeals offers a type of living classroom for all aspiring public speakers, particularly in the area of using pauses and silences.

Bush didn't start out as a great orator, but following the 2001 terrorist attacks on America his series of speeches vaulted him into the rare air of powerful orators. His voice, with its Texas twang, isn't particularly a strong asset, yet he uses it to its best effect. When he makes a factual point or when he says something that touches listeners, he instinctively pauses, seemingly "reading" his audience. He proceeds only after listeners have had time to let his words sink in.

His manner of pausing is so effective that television viewers often feel as if they are in the room with him. During pauses, he looks out at the audience with a facial expression that almost says, "Isn't it true?" Audience members don't say a word, yet it's almost as if he is reading their minds.

PRACTICE YOUR PAUSES

If you have little experience with pausing while presenting to a group, here are a variety of exercises that can increase your capacity in this area:

1. In our media saturated society, you can't aspire to high office unless you have reasonably well-developed communication skills. The next time you watch a speech by the president, secretary of state, or other high official, be on the lookout for their pauses and silences. If the address is not punctuated by audience applause—a relatively straightforward response—then time the length of the pauses and silences. You may be amazed to find that they often exceed five or six seconds.

2. The next time you speak to a group of any size, if only an in-house team meeting, pick a spot in advance in which you will pause for at least three seconds. During this time, look directly at members of your team—don't flinch or look away. After your words have had time to sink in, begin again. You'll find that no one will accuse you of being ill-prepared; on the contrary, your pause likely helped to drive home your point.

3. Practice pausing in front of the mirror. During your true, three-second pauses, note your facial expression. Do you want it to be one of encouragement, concern, alarm, joy, or empathy? You have those options and dozens of others. When you pause, you have the opportunity to "speak" to your audience in a way that you cannot while your mouth is in motion.

4. Practice pausing in one-on-one conversations with friends or relatives. This is tricky, because, in such conversations, a three-second pause can be an invitation for the other party to jump in and start talking. You could preface such encounters by saying something like, "I need to bounce something off you for a few minutes. Please hear me out before responding."

Such a conversation could prove to be a rare and pleasant experience for your listener. After all, the typical conversation, particularly those in which one person is trying to influence another, are punctuated by anything but silences. The person pitching an idea often presents one observation, fact, recommendation, or nugget after another as if swamping the listener with evidence and exhortation will more quickly generate the desired effect and agreement.

Three- to five-second pauses in one-on-one conversations will give the single listener, similar to members of a large audience, the opportunity to synthesize more of what you're saying without feeling overwhelmed and besieged.

5. Go to your computer and find anything on your hard drive that you've written in the last few weeks or months that may also have been communicated verbally. As you review the text, save it under another file name and begin to add instructions on how you might present it effectively. For example, after a powerful statement, you might then type in "pause for three seconds" and then continue on. You only have to mark up two or three paragraphs to put this exercise into practice. Print out your new file complete with inserted directions. Then, practice delivering the information on the page while heeding the instructions (i.e. when to pause, perhaps when to raise your voice, when to lower it, and so on). Notice how much more effective you sound to yourself. When you sound more effective to yourself, chances are high that you will sound more effective to others.

Now that you've learned the techniques for selecting and developing your topic, mapping your presentation, creating a signature story, and mastered the nuances of your presentation, it's time to think about marketing yourself.

PART III

MARKETING YOUR
SPEECH AND
SPEAKING CAPABILITIES

I f no one knows who you are, your topics, how good you are, or how to find you, how will you ever make public presentations? Whether or not you command a fee for your presentations, you need to "get the word out" about your speaking capabilities.

The early chapters in Part III focus on topics such as positioning yourself, developing strategic marketing tools, and broadening and maintaining your appeal. I've saved development of specific materials, such as the one-sheet and videos, for later chapters.

We will not address generic marketing topics such as using direct mail or telemarketing campaigns, as they are topics well covered in books devoted exclusively to entrepreneurial or Web marketing.

Although this part of the book, along with Part IV, on contracting and landing the deal, is geared primarily for those aspiring to professional speaking, the material will be useful for any public speaker. Once you've implemented the advice in Part III, you'll be more enthusiastic about gaining exposure, and you'll be well equipped to generate new opportunities.

The Client's Mind-Set

You'll see the names of 3,500 speakers when you open the National Speakers Association's directory, *Who's Who in Professional Speaking,* and many thousands of speakers and trainers in the American Society of Training and Development's membership directory. What's required, however, to be among the few hundred speakers who are in demand?

THINK LIKE A MEETING PLANNER

Rather than speaking at a meeting, suppose you were planning it. How would you know that you're bringing in somebody who's going to do the job well, deliver the right message, and offer take-home value? While there's no foolproof way to know, here are some telltale markers of the top speakers:

1. *No off-the-shelf programs.* Today, every audience requires at least some form of a tailored presentation. There are no off-the-shelf programs that fit every audience every time, even when the topic is as generic as management, leadership, or stress management. An astute speaker will spend more time asking about the audience than he or she will conveying the essence of the message, at least at the outset. Be wary of any speaker who does not ask a lot of questions but who claims to have just the right message.

2. *Arrives well in advance.* The best speakers arrive in advance and make themselves thoroughly familiar with the meeting venue. No matter how good the speaker is supposed to be, if he or she expects to get off a plane and jump into a taxi and make it to your site with moments to spare, you may get a performance that is not up to your expectations.

3. *Has supporting materials readily available.* Undoubtedly, you'll need a biography, an introduction, and an agreed-on write-up of the presentation. The seasoned speaker has these and other materials readily available.

Many speakers offer such elements on their Web sites. If not on the Web site, the speaker can at least send them via fax or express delivery. In any case, when these materials are not readily available, it may be a sign that something is amiss.

4. *Has a speaker agreement form ready.* If you're hiring a professional speaker, you can save time and energy if the speaker can submit his or her speaker agreement form to you rather than asking for you to prepare a letter or agreement yourself. A detailed discussion about speaker agreements is offered in Part IV.

5. *A toll-free telephone number and fax number.* An experienced speaker recognizes the importance of accessibility and thus offers you a toll-free phone number and fax number. Going further, many speakers also offer their home number, a cell phone or car phone number, if applicable, and a pager number if they happen to carry one. Yes, this may be overkill, but if you need to get in touch with somebody, these are wonderful safeguards.

6. *High-quality presentation materials.* No one should have to endure unattractive black and white overheads or slides when color is available. Today's foreword-thinking speaker uses presentation software to craft audiovisual materials that will be easy to read and understand, pleasing to the eye, and right on target for his or her message. Ask to see the speaker's presentation materials in advance. They can be transmitted via an e-mail attachment. Thus, you get to discuss and agree on what your audience will see in advance of the actual meeting.

7. *Shows respect for your audience members.* Is your speaker willing to meet with audience members prior to the actual presentation? The functionally competent, oratorically stirring speaker who is aloof to your audience before and after presenting does not win over participants the way that the fully engaging, personable, and accessible speaker does. This is something important to ask about when you're in the negotiation stage. You may be surprised by the answers you receive.

8. *Has a pre-speech questionnaire.* Does the speaker have a pre-speech questionnaire (see Part V)? This is a one- or two-page document that he or she submits far in advance of the presentation. The speaker concerned about the audience has taken the time to craft a document that includes questions that will help him or her better know your audience, your organization, what you're trying to achieve, and what message you want delivered. Most importantly, it helps the speaker understand what participants should know, and how you'd like them to feel at the conclusion.

The speaker can send this form to you via e-mail or fax, or may have it available at his or her Web site. The speaker should also be prepared to cover this form with you over the phone. Often, this will be the most convenient way for you to handle this task, and the speaker needs to be accommodating in this area.

9. *The speaker's responsiveness.* Has the speaker been responsive from the first time you made contact until he or she delivers the presentation? You can gauge a speaker's level of responsiveness best prior to the presentation. Are the materials that you request promptly submitted and readily available? Does the speaker return phone calls in a timely manner? If you see any sign that the speaker's level of responsiveness is less than you desire, be wary. This may be a clue to how the presentation and overall interaction with the audience may come off.

Now that you've tapped into how meeting planners initially assess the speakers they're seeking, let's consider the concept of positioning and how to use it effectively with meeting planners.

Positioning Is the
Best Marketing

You don't have as many dates booked on your calendar as you would like and, at the same time, you're leery of employing traditional, over-used marketing vehicles such as mass mailing and cold calling. Is there another way to consistently maintain a healthy speaking calendar without the onerous burden of mass mailing and extensive long-distance calling? Yes, there is; it's through personal positioning. To understand personal positioning, let's first define it:

Positioning is an organized system for finding a window in the mind.

The concept of positioning was popularized by Al Ries and Jack Trout. They observed that "in our over-communicated society, very little communication actually takes place." Rather, you must create a position in the target's mind. Communication occurs when optimally placed and timed. Positioning is as vital today for speakers as it is for Fortune 500 companies.

AN APPROACH, NOT A SET OF RULES

Positioning, and its latter-day relation, branding, is a way of thinking and presenting yourself rather than a fixed set of guidelines or principles. Positioning is not an overnight strategy; it requires considerable effort. Once you establish your "share of mind," positioning translates into more bookings.

Positioning involves risks. It requires a broad, long-range view of yourself and your programs. The position that you develop likely will be right only for you and no other speaker. You may become the leader in an emerging field, or a highly successful how-to presenter in traditional skill areas. Personal positioning can be enhanced through what you say, whom you meet, what you attend, what you read, and even how you listen.

Being the "first" remains one of the quickest and easiest ways to gain a position in someone's mind. Who was the first woman in space? Did you answer: "Sally Ride"? You are correct. Now, name the second woman in space. You may not be sure. (The answer is Judy Resnik, who was a member of the unfortunate Challenger Shuttle crew.)

What if you have no position? Watch out, because you'll be working long and hard to try to fill that speaking calendar. You'll end up undertaking exhaustive direct mail and cold-calling campaigns. Positioning for the successful speaker of today is not optional. As Ries and Trout said years ago, you can either endure the position you end up having by default, or work to establish the position you choose.

The position you occupy in the minds of those you wish to serve contributes to the success or failure of your speaking business. The nice part about positioning is that once you get the campaign in motion, inertia alone often will carry the day: You position yourself as an expert in X, and as you build up your position, more and more people will seek you out when they need a speaker on X. Every time you speak on X, or write an article on it, and so on, you add an extra layer to your position.

Change with care. A major drawback to positioning is that once you've established your position, changing to something else can have its difficulties. For example, Bob Burg made significant progress in his early years as a speaker in the arena of memory and memory enhancement. Years later, Burg switched his speaking focus to networking, and while he generated a good roster of speaking dates, it took some effort.

For Burg to dislodge his previous reputation held in the minds of meeting planners, he:

1. Changed his marketing literature.
2. Began writing books and articles on various aspects of networking.
3. Turned down requests to give presentations on memory.
4. Sought to convince callers to book him for a networking presentation.

Decide and align. After deciding to be known for some topic area, every element of your speaking operation would of necessity be aligned with your position: your stationery, envelopes, business cards, mailing labels, and even packaging materials; also your photos, promotional pieces, and all products such as audiocassette tapes and albums, videocassette tapes and albums, books, CDs, and software. On site with audiences, your participant's packet, wardrobe, grooming, AV materials, briefcase, and professional artifacts need to enhance your positioning.

SPEAK AND CONSULT

Many consultants and service providers use public speaking as a way to generate new clients. I have often watched these experts miss the mark because their presentation style and speech are designed to say, "look at me." What the audience needs, however, is someone who can demonstrate his or her ability to rapidly understand their needs, how they would like to proceed, and what outcome they would like to achieve.

Conveying this capability and then proving it in the field consistently wins over new clients, retains existing ones, builds a strong client base, and lets you increase your speaking fees.

SPEAKING FUELS THE FURNACE

Tricia Santos is the president of her own computer consulting firm. She has achieved considerable success as a speaker because she is intensely dedicated to listening to her clients, and she conveys this empathy in her speeches, while other technical advisors may operate at their own pace and manner. Tricia has the patience and understanding to adjust her presentation. As a result, she is a very popular speaker. For many years, she has been actively involved with NSA-Carolina Speakers Association, attending the quarterly meetings even though they are nearly three hours away in Charlotte, North Carolina. In addition, Santos looks for every opportunity to speak at both peer group meetings and other professional meetings around the state, whether or not she is a member of the group.

Santos knows that every time she speaks to a professional group, there are opportunities both to improve her speaking capability and to generate new clients. She consistently reaps multiple benefits as a result of her presentations because she is giving great value at every presentation and influencing those who are in a position to retain her as a computer consultant.

TARGET A SINGLE INDUSTRY

For a variation on Santos' positioning activities, some speakers target a specific industry and then provide all the services they can for serving that industry. Francis Friedman, for example, is president of his own company, Strategic Initiatives Inc. Whereas Santos provides a variety of computer consulting and speaking services to many different audiences, Friedman exclusively serves the meeting industry itself—groups like the Professional Management Association, Meeting Planners International, and The American Society of Training and Development.

Usually Friedman is either at the headquarters of a meeting planning association, or at a convention or trade show where he is handling multiple clients at once. At such venues, he might be providing prearranged consulting, coaching, training, or speaking. In this manner, Friedman is continually able to generate new clients, further broaden and deepen his understanding of the meeting and trade show industry, and ensure that he continues to offer leading edge services to the industry.

BECOMING A HOUSEHOLD NAME

Bill Lee has been a full-time, industry-specific speaker in construction supply since 1987. One of Lee's primary positioning strategies is his exclusive industry newsletter called *People & Profit$*.

Lee contends that the task of producing an industry newsletter requires knowing the full ramifications of what's involved. Publishing a newsletter is a large undertaking—an eight-page monthly newsletter, over the course of a year, is equal to writing a 240-page book. However, Lee believes that if you choose to position yourself in a particular industry and carve out a niche, then the information contained in even a two- to four-page quarterly newsletter must be highly targeted, timely, and clearly indicative of your status as a key resource within the industry.

"If you intend to stay in such a position, that means you have to maintain your level of excellence in issue after issue," Lee says. The critical factors in creating demand for his newsletter include the following:

- Increasing the number of quotes from key players in the industry.
- Publishing timely and interesting facts, figures, and industry statistics that otherwise are not easily encountered by the readers.

The underlying premise of producing a newsletter such as Lee's is that you and your organization can consistently be counted on as a leading source of industry information. You can enhance your reputation in a similar manner by writing articles and even books. Sometimes a book also turns into an audio book or a video presentation. All of these ventures add to your positioning as an expert.

SPECIAL SEMINARS

One of Lee's other key positioning techniques is to offer associations in his industry the opportunity to book him at their annual convention for only the cost of travel. In return they agree to promote his newsletter and speaking services. Many associations have taken him up on his offer, and once members of the association were exposed to Lee's presentations, the demand for his speaking services began to grow. Lee says, "This marketing technique exposed my message and my speaking style to 75 percent of the owners and managers in my industry."

By his fifteenth year of producing *People and Profit$,* Lee had 2,400 paid newsletter subscribers—a healthy number for a highly targeted niche. Over that time, he has conducted more than 800 seminars and consulting assignments for owners and managers of construction supply firms.

Every time Lee speaks, he creates solid bonds with his target market, gains exposure to more people in the industry, stays on top of the field, creates opportunities to increase his newsletter subscriber base, and gains leading edge information to include in his newsletter. He has created a victorious cycle in which one positioning technique enhances another.

INDUSTRY STATISTICS

Whether or not you produce a newsletter, you have the ever-present opportunity to collect industry statistics and other data that could be filtered into your presentations, articles, Web site, and other marketing vehicles and intellectual properties. Lee says, "When I began speaking and consulting in my industry, no one was doing a thorough job of collecting industry statistics, so I chose these 'stats' to position myself in the marketplace."

18

Making
Measured Progress

Now that I've covered other ways to position yourself as an expert, such as writing an article or a book, I turn to the topic of setting goals for yourself and your positioning. Whatever your goals, it pays to make them challenging. As in many industries, competition among public speakers is so keen that there is simply no standing still.

A goal, as I discuss at length in my book, *The Complete Idiot's Guide to Reaching Your Goals,* is a desired outcome, something that you're seeking, you want, you're willing to strive for, and to which you devote energy. "Outcome" means a result, a situation you can describe, an achievement to which you can point, a feeling that is real and unmistakable.

1. A goal needs to be challenging, but reachable.
2. A goal needs to be quantifiable.
3. A goal needs to be associated with some time line.

In establishing your strategic position, think about how well-known and how in demand you are for your particular type of presentation or topic. You could measure your progress in many ways, including:

- Tabulating the number of unsolicited calls you receive from target industries inquiring about your presentations.
- Preparing a grid that rates your presentations and custom information versus that offered by would-be competitors.

- Tabulating the number of publications or external sources that refer to you as an "expert," "authority," or foremost presenter in the field.

Many other speaking goals that you can set for yourself can support your positioning objectives. Constantly improve the quality of your presentations. Keeping the criteria for effective goal setting in mind, this would mean devising evaluation standards by which you could judge your performance over time. For example, you could gauge your performances by:

- The number of letters you receive following a presentation.
- The evaluation scores you receive from one group arithmetically adjusted to compare to scores you received from another group.
- The frequency of your being invited back.

Enhance the novelty and uniqueness of your presentations. Indicators might include:

- The number of audience participants and meeting planners who report that your presentation is unique.
- The number of hours you spend refining that content.
- The number of hours you spend practicing your presentations with new content.

Increase the demand for your services. There are many potential indicators here, including:

- The number of calls you get in a week, month, or quarter from interested parties.
- The number of groups that ask you back.
- The raw number of bookings in a week, month, quarter, or other period of time.
- Sales of associated tape programs, books, and other learning tools.

If you're a novice in the world of public speaking but have made a commitment to become increasingly more effective as a speaker, there are a variety of other simple goals you can establish including:

- The frequency of your speeches.
- The size of the audience.

- The length of your presentations.
- The types of groups to which you speak.
- The types of people in your audiences—administrative, line, staff, supervisory, management, executive, top management, or CEO.
- Where you are in programs—opening, luncheon, closing, general session, keynote, or breakout speaker.
- The creation of products from your presentations—audiotapes, books, videos, CD ROMs, or transcripts.
- The sales of existing products at your presentations.

Whatever your position and trajectory in the world of public speaking, you'll never run out of challenging, reachable goals. By setting them, you can ensure that your presentations remain vibrant.

REVENUE OPPORTUNITIES

One way to achieve at least some of your goals is to capitalize on the different opportunities to sell your services. One of the first questions I ask myself after having booked an engagement is, "Are there other revenue opportunities with this particular client?" For example, would the meeting planner be interested in ordering books or other learning tools for all the participants? Are they having a board of directors meeting the night before where I could lead a 45-minute roundtable discussion?

EDITORIAL COORDINATION

Whether it's an association, government agency, or corporation, nearly all such entities today have their own monthly publications, either full-fledged magazines or simple newsletters. At the least, you could offer public relations information to the editor to alert more members or staff about your presentation. You could also offer one or more articles at fee or at no cost to further increase your visibility within the organization. It will serve their editorial needs as well.

Are there other association or industry journals, not published by the host organization, to which it might make sense for you to submit public relations materials or publishable articles? If you're working within any one of your chosen niches, then undoubtedly you're aware of most of the major magazines that serve the niche. If you're not aware of them, the reference librarian at any city or university library can readily supply you with the names and addresses of the key publications.

VERTICAL OPPORTUNITIES

If you're speaking in Chicago to a medical supplier on September 19, find out who is meeting in Chicago on September 18 and September 20, especially if your calendar is free. I spoke to a banking association in Texas on July 30, and I was fortunate enough to discover months in advance that the Chamber of Commerce was meeting an hour away on July 29.

The Chamber of Commerce hired me to speak as well; hence, I was able to create a tight circular route. This greatly benefits the meeting planner as well, because I could apportion my plane expense between two clients, thus lowering everyone's overall travel costs.

Another vertical opportunity is making contact with groups similar to the group to which you'll be speaking. For example, if you're speaking to the Kentucky Trial Lawyers Association, it would be beneficial to share that information before and after your presentation with the Tennessee Trial Lawyers Association, Illinois Trial Lawyers Association, and others.

You don't necessarily have to wait until you've made the presentation. The fact that you've been retained by one group is often of interest to a similar group. After the presentation, and particularly if you were well received, by all means alert the other vertical groups. The same process works if you're speaking to a branch, a plant, or a division of a company. Many times no one within the company thinks to alert the other branches. Therefore, it behooves you to ask for a list or roster, referral names, and supporting letters so that you can book dates with the other divisions.

HORIZONTAL OPPORTUNITIES

Whenever you're speaking at a national convention, regional meeting, or state meeting, visit the exhibit hall. Invite those at the trade booths to attend your session. I was speaking to a medical association and was fortunate enough to have an insurance agent who was exhibiting at the convention attend my session. He corralled me in the hall afterward, asked for my card and fee, and told me that he was the planning coordinator for his state insurance association. I hadn't thought of inviting people from the exhibit hall into the session. Once I realized, however, that everyone in the exhibit hall and everyone at the convention in general belonged to other organizations and associations, I knew that I should get as many of them into my session as I could.

Invitations in Advance

Many speakers already are aware of the value in inviting others who reside in the city to their presentations. In three years of seeking to invite guests to sessions, no meeting planner has ever turned me down.

Dr. Judith Briles routinely summons the local media to her presentations. She lets radio, TV, and newspaper producers and editors know where and when she'll be speaking. She is often interviewed before or after her speech in addition to having the reporter or journalist attend her presentation.

Sponsored by . . .

If you're attempting to land a corporate sponsor, that is, an organization that wants to pay your fee as you speak to several groups in their target market, invite potential sponsors to your speeches. Sometimes a complete roster of attendees, including exhibitors, is provided for you, with names, addresses, and phone and fax numbers. In that case, you could call five or six prospects in advance and invite them to your speech.

In all cases, the number of people who actually take you up on your invitation versus the number of invitations you offer is going to be small. That's all part of marketing. People are busy, and it's hard to get anybody to go anywhere. You only have to get one or two key people to attend your session to make your leveraging efforts pay off.

BUILDING YOUR MAILING LIST

Each time you speak to a group, you have the potential to build your mailing list. Such a list is valuable if you have products and learning tools, and to stay in touch. You can add to your mailing list in several ways (to be cleared with the meeting planner):

1. Include an order form in your handouts, or get permission to leave an order form on everyone's seat before the presentation.
2. Mention during your presentation that you have a newsletter, order form, or other materials available, and that anyone who wants to be put on your list can do so by either leaving you a business card or signing up on a sheet that you provide.
3. Find out if there will be a participant roster or list circulated to everyone, as mentioned above. Once again, it's probably best to proceed with the permission of the meeting planner.

AUDIO AND VIDEO OPPORTUNITIES

Every time you speak to a group, regardless of who did the booking, you have the opportunity to create an audiocassette simply by bringing your own equipment. There are at least five good reasons why it's worth taping yourself as often as possible:

1. *Taping affords personal review of the presentation.* There is no better way to review your performance than to hear exactly what you said and how you said it, on tape.

2. *Each tape is potentially salable.* Tape cassette producers, manufacturers, and distributors can professionally edit your tape, supplying voiceovers and transition passages that can result in a salable cassette.

3. *The tape transcript is salable.* Don't overlook the value of marketing the tape transcript to members of the group you addressed. Professional societies frequently offer tape transcripts from symposia and seminars that they have sponsored to those members who were not able to attend or who wish to have a written record of what was said in the speech.

4. *The transcript can be converted into articles.* Frequently, a transcript of as few as three or four pages lends itself to being turned into an excellent article. With longer transcripts, it may be possible to extract

several excellent articles, which in turn can be used to promote your speaking career and earn additional income.

5. *Use tapes to get other speaking engagements.* After your speech has been taped, you can extract a 5- to 10-minute passage that can be used to develop demonstration tapes for distribution to other meeting planners. What better way for them to assess your speaking skills?

VIDEO IN THE MAKING

Both you and the organization can benefit when you produce a product like a video that both you and they can use again. The specifics of what kind of permission to offer, how to charge, who owns the copyright, and so forth is the topic of another chapter. The point here is that each speaking engagement must be assessed for its potential as an audio or video product.

When you are creating such products, you have further opportunities to collect on-site testimonials. Many times after a speech, people will come up to you with praise. If it is captured on audio, and particularly, video, you have valuable footage, indeed.

OTHER OPPORTUNITIES

- Each time I speak, I try to get at least one letter, be it from the meeting planner, room monitor, key attendees, key officers, or key staff, that I can use in my speaker's portfolio (see Chapter 21 on Kudo letters).
- If you're at a convention, you can meet other speakers with diverse topics and compare notes as to what they've learned and what opportunities are available.
- If you're at a private company, schmoozing with the attendees during break or at lunch often leads to other engagements.
- Every time you make a presentation, a world of opportunities awaits, far more than if you simply presented information and ideas for the good of the people in attendance. Your time is precious, and by planning your strategy in advance, you can get your speaking career into overdrive.

Getting Paid and
Selling Your Services

F inding and hiring a professional speaker can be a complicated process for a meeting planner. A planner needs to first narrow the search by deciding on the objectives of the presentation and then choosing a pool of speakers capable of meeting those objectives. The fee is perhaps one of the most important considerations in choosing a speaker.

Selecting a professional speaker doesn't mean randomly picking an affordable speaker, nor does it mean paying a large sum of money on the assumption that more equals better. Rather, it is a matter of finding a speaker who meets the planner's criteria and represents the best value for the fee that he or she charges.

To help in the selection process, many meeting planners have fee ranges. The following is an "unofficial" breakdown of the pay scale, citing the "characteristics" of speakers at each level:

Less than $1,000:
Few meeting planners today expect to retain a speaker for less than $1,000; nevertheless, many organizations have a limited budget. Depending on the situation, some highly experienced professional speakers have accepted payments of $1,000 or less. The speaker who regularly falls into this pay range, however, is local, someone

who gives infrequent presentations, or someone who does not speak professionally.

$1,000 to $2,000:

This is the customary fee for an entry-level speaker or an up-and-coming professional. Speakers charging at this level are generally good at what they do but may not necessarily speak full-time or even frequently. Furthermore, this is an appropriate fee for salaried speakers or corporate employees. Ranges can overlap—$2,000 might be seen as being in the next category.

$2,000 to $3,500:

Speakers in this range are frequently comparable to one another. Often, there is very little difference among the quality of presentations at this level. Speakers who charge $3,500 are often no better than the ones who charge $2,000.

$3,500 to $5,000:

The majority of professional speakers in business today charge between $3,500 and $5,000. Along with greater compensation comes greater expectations. Meeting planners willing to pay over $3,500 are counting on a solid presentation from someone who knows the ropes and has a 99 percent or better chance of delivering a winning performance.

$5,000 to $7,500:

Speakers able to command between $5,000 and $7,500 must meet specific and important goals. In this pay category, a speaker might expect to address an organization's national convention (as opposed to the state convention), a corporate quarterly or annual meeting, or an executive retreat of 15 to 20 people. The speech itself could be either a keynote address or a half day in length. At this level, planners are counting on a professional, seasoned veteran capable of accomplishing the objectives with absolute competency. Competition is stiff in this fee range.

$7,500 and Above:

Understandably, there are few speakers in this range. Many speakers talk about these numbers, but consistently earning figures this great is another matter. Above the $15,000 mark, expect to find few noncelebrities. It is not unusual, however, for a celebrity or high-ranking expert in a particular field to command anywhere between $15,000 and $80,000.

WHEN PRICE BECOMES LESS OF AN ISSUE

At the lower end of the pay spectrum, even relatively small discrepancies between the prices of two speakers can make a big difference in the selection of one over the other. However, this becomes less of an issue as the amount of compensation increases.

For instance, if a planner is willing to pay between $7,500 and $10,000, it's because he or she is looking for a speaker who can achieve specific results. When choosing between a speaker who charges $8,000 and one who charges $9,000, the planner will often opt for the more qualified, not the cheaper, of the two.

However, you can't neglect to recognize the implications of your fee. My colleague Jim Cathcart once said, "Despite all the work that we've done, all the study, all the technique, all the refinement, all the practice in speaking, all the literature we've developed, everything we've done as speakers, the number one thing the market judges us by at first is our fee!" If you are charging $7,500 a presentation, you are automatically regarded as a better speaker than someone charging $5,000. Your background, credentials, and personality are all important factors in setting your fee.

ESTABLISHING YOUR FEE

Deciding how much to charge clients is daunting. You want adequate and fair compensation for your skills and services, but you don't want to sell yourself short or demand more than your experience allows. While $2,000 is a good starting point, your baseline fee should not fall below $1,000 if you want to be taken seriously. Fortunately, a speaker can draw on many resources for help in establishing payment guidelines.

COMPARE YOURSELF
WITH YOUR PEERS

Trade Materials

Write to a bevy of other speakers and establish an information and materials exchange with them. Ask to see brochures, one-sheets, reference letters, and other materials they have produced, and be sure to send them copies of your own published or important documents. Solicit information from speakers whose incomes approximate or slightly exceed your own. Use what they send you to set a few future goals for yourself; you will want to produce similar or higher quality material at some point in your career.

Exchange Videos

Over the years, I've exchanged videos with successful friends and colleagues in the business. I have been able to refine my own techniques by comparing my presentations with others.

A speaker isn't concerned that a peer will steal his or her lines from a demo tape; one person's presentation material is usually inapplicable to another's anyway. Most people will be flattered by your interest and inclined to grant your request. In addition, sharing my videos with my colleagues lets them know what I'm doing so they can have me in mind when approached for a job that isn't right for them.

Elasticity Calculations

Another way to decide how much to charge is to do an elasticity calculation. Suppose you earn $2,000 50 times a year; that's $100,000 in gross revenue. From an elasticity standpoint, 50 speeches at $2,000 generates the same revenue as 33 speeches at $3,033. My personal strategy is to go out a handful of times a month (35 times a year) at $X, rather than 70 times a year at one-half $X. Besides, I want to be opening general sessions, closing general sessions, or otherwise be the prominent speaker on the guest list.

What are you willing to deliver? Will you deliver half-day or keynote presentations? Are you willing to travel outside of your state or to another country? Most speakers are willing to do a variety of session lengths and have a different fee for each. Speakers who charge $3,000 for a keynote might charge $4,000 for a half-day presentation, and $5,000 for a full day.

You may find it helpful to draw a 3 × 3 grid with nine fees to help you establish base rates for offers of any type, length, and location you receive:

Price Schedule

	LOCAL, STATE ($)	LONG DISTANCE ($)	INTERNATIONAL ($)
Keynote	3,000	4,500	6,000
Half day	4,000	5,500	7,000
Full day	5,000	6,500	8,000

Your first box, for example, sets up a guideline for local and keynote address, the lowest fee; the last box is for a full day at an international event, which commands your highest fee.

A trend is to include all expenses in a higher fee. Scott McKain polled several meeting planners and all of them indicated they would rather book a speaker for a $2,000 flat fee than deal with the hassle of paying $1,500 plus expenses. There are two reasons why this is preferable: There are no receipts to deal with, and no complicated paperwork is involved. Planners appreciate the ease and simplicity of flat rates.

If you choose to go this route, prominently indicate your "all expenses included" policy in your literature; otherwise, you're going to lose money and dates because it will appear as though you're charging the same as everyone else.

DISCOUNTS AND FAVORS

Personally, I give a 10 percent discount on the second day if I'm booked with one organization back to back. I give the same discount for multiple bookings. Other speakers charge slightly less if the organization that hired them videotapes the presentation. Better yet, convince the organization of the value of doing a video shoot of you and become a cocopyright holder. (See terminology from the sample speaker in Part IV.)

Other speakers offer a discount if the client will write letters of recommendation on the speaker's behalf or in exchange for other intangibles. I would avoid doing these things, however. The trade-off is not sufficient. If you need video footage or if you are booked for multiple dates, offer a discount. Otherwise, don't discount or do favors.

WHEN TO ASK FOR MORE

Raise your price when you're getting more business than you want at your current rate, or you've done something so compelling in your career that you should no longer charge your current fee.

Don't let the fear of losing clients hold you back from giving yourself a deserved pay increase. When you raise your fee, there are certain groups that will drop out of your clientele, but for every company that can't afford you, one that can will appear.

UPGRADE YOUR MATERIALS WHEN YOU UPGRADE YOUR FEES

Make your materials equal to what you are charging. If you've moved into the $2,000 price range, spend some money and print a brochure. As you keep increasing your fee, upgrade the quality of your materials. You want your printed materials to correspond with your value.

Only after you spend years in the business establishing your reputation can you operate on a "pull-policy," letting the contents of your materials speak for themselves instead of relying on a snazzy production. Until then, continue to upgrade your materials each time you raise your rates.

In addition to keeping your materials updated, also make sure they're formatted for the latest means of communication. The need for on-site speakers at conferences and conventions is not likely to dissipate. Still, online presentations will grab an increasing share of the speaking, training, and consulting market. If you haven't gotten your feet wet in this technology thus far, now is the time to get started. As of this writing, the Internet is the major vehicle shaping the changes in the meeting industry. By staying focused on broad-based emerging issues, even solo speakers with no staff can maintain a firm handle on where to focus their time and attention. The key issues and areas to keep in mind are discussed next.

All Functions to the Web

All meeting planning functions that have not already been will eventually be transferred to the Web. Given this reality, it becomes fundamental to have all the materials in your business Web-ready. This means converting all of your marketing materials as well as pre-speech materials (see Parts IV and V), such as contracts, agreement forms, presentation question-naires, survey forms, product ordering information, and room diagrams, into PDF format so that any form can be sent to a meeting planner quickly and easily. Conversion to PDF format is a painless process once the proper software is installed. Log on to *www.adobe.com* to obtain the Adobe Acrobat softwear necessary for this.

Prepare Dual Formats

Prepare all speech-related materials in dual format—whatever you prepare for an onsite audience needs to be recast for delivery over the Internet and for a net audience. Corel Presentations, PowerPoint, or other slide show software readily lend themselves to use over the Internet.

Ensure that your professional photos, handouts, or participant materials, including charts, graphs, exhibits, and article reprints used in front of a live group can be easily conveyed over the net.

Master Long-Distance Techniques

Speakers today need to become aware of and proficient in making online presentations. Use a headset so that you can maintain hands-free movement while directing a professional slideshow, entertaining questions from your audience, conducting on-the-spot surveys, and tabulating results, all without the slightest hitch.

Securing Strategic URLs

Many speakers, trainers, and consultants recognize the value of securing strategic URLs for purposes of effective marketing and for protecting intellectual property. I own BreathingSpace.com, for example, as well as

JeffDavidson.com and a variety of other URLs that help meeting planners find me. It makes sense for any speaker aspiring to charge a speaking fee to secure those URLs that represent various versions of their name, and company name, products, and services.

For all the talk about URLs being snapped up immediately, even within the .com domain there are many effective combinations that speakers, trainers, and consultants potentially may secure. Visit register.com or simply type "domain registrations" in search engines, and a list of vendors who can help you will appear.

How You Use It

The Internet offers many other benefits to public speakers. If you offer products for sale, for example, how you use the Internet will become one of the principle determinants of your sales success. Those who initially may not have seen the need to purchase products, or felt the urge to, may eventually become repeat buyers, in part because of the relationship you establish and maintain via the Internet. In addition, opportunities to stay in touch with groups to whom you have spoken and to key audience members has never been greater.

Developing a Dynamite One-Sheet

Now let's turn to developing some of the critical marketing pieces referred to earlier. The *one-sheet* is a major tool speakers develop to work in smooth coordination with their video demos. True to its name, the one-sheet is a single sheet of paper that includes the speaker's topic roster, biography, credentials, and product list, among other information.

PROPER ONE-SHEET INFORMATION

The typical speaker one-sheet is a carefully produced, visually pleasing, highly informative document. The one-sheet needs to meet specific criteria:

1. *Name and contact information.* These essential items need to be printed clearly, toward the bottom of the front page and, preferably, reprinted on the back as well. The font and point size should be sufficiently large so that contact information and other descriptive information can easily be read.

Professional speakers who are represented by bureaus often split their print runs in half. Half of the run contains fully printed sheets with their own contact information. The other half of the print run leaves such information blank so that the respective bureaus can fill in their contact information, or even print individual bureau contact information for bureaus to distribute.

2. *Your Web site.* When sending your one-sheet directly to meeting planners, list your Web site along with your contact information. You could make reference to additional information on your Web site, which could include fee information (since it's never appropriate on a speaker one-sheet), longer biographical material, an extended list of clients, praise from clients, possibly an extended description of your presentation, subtopics, and anticipated benefits or results. Detailed information such as your preferences for room setup, travel arrangements, accommodations, and other logistics can be posted on your Web site as well, particularly in locations only for meeting planners.

3. *Photographs.* Professional one-sheets contain at least one color photograph of the speaker. Most of these photos are head and shoulder shots, although some speakers opt to use photos of themselves with a microphone in hand or otherwise gesturing to an audience. Some speakers include two or more photos. In such cases, one of the photos is invariably a head and shoulder shot. It's important to have a current photo, not one from five or more years ago. Running unrepresentative photos invariably surprises the meeting planner and prompts him or her to contemplate the other ways you may have misrepresented yourself.

4. *Grabber headlines.* Unless you're so well-known that your name alone is sufficient to attract recipients' attention, employ a descriptive phrase or grabber line at the top of your one-sheet. Many speakers use an excerpt from the description of their favorite presentation or a truncated version of its title. It is also helpful to have humor or some type of twist in the title as long as the readers are sure to understand it.

Here are some clever headlines that succinctly convey a clear message and invite their readers to continue:

- Sales Techniques for the Twenty-First Century
- A Guided Tour of the Future
- Inspiration for Your Audience
- Winning Strategies for Winning Companies

5. *Topics and brief descriptions.* The one-sheet would be useless without at least one topic, although most speakers list several. The topics need to be succinctly stated in about two to seven words. The topic title is followed by a brief description of what is included. This could be one long sentence, two moderately long sentences, or three short ones. (See the sample one-sheets.)

6. *Previous clients.* Somewhere on the one-sheet you need to present readers with a compendium of your previous audiences. Some speakers merely list the names of the organizations. Some attribute quotes. If you've presented to large organizations you have an advantage over the speaker who only lists rather obscure organizations. If you have only spoken to a handful of "name" organizations, sprinkle them among the listings you offer. After you begin to accumulate enough clients and kudos, you can begin to focus on such issues as balancing your list for male-female split, industries or professions, or corporations versus associations.

7. *Biographical information.* You don't have to reprint your resume here. In succinct paragraphs, present compelling information about yourself. This includes anything remarkable in your upbringing or education, obstacles you've overcome, awards you have received, appointments, promotions, publications, and other citations.

Some people offer a few paragraphs of biographical information followed by a bulleted list of credentials such as degrees, books published, and the aforementioned awards and citations. Any way you choose to present such information will generally be effective as long as it is succinctly stated, relevant to the topics you offer, and answers the questions that meeting planners and other interested parties would most likely have about your background. The most common error with biographies is to go overboard.

8. *Philosophy, benefits statement.* This feature, no more than a few phrases or sentences, encapsulates your philosophy on issues relevant to your presentation or to speaking in general.

9. *Logos.* If you have a company or personal logo, use it on your one-sheet. If you are a member of a widely recognized group, such as Toastmasters International, the National Association of Speakers, or the International Platform Association, you may want to include the group's logo as well because it can lend credibility.

10. *Products.* If you are the author of a mainstream or self-published book, audiocassettes, videocassettes, CD-ROMs, or other professionally produced products, include them on your one-sheet. Some speakers highlight their products by including photos or artwork. Even with all the predictions about the forthcoming high-tech world, books are still the main

---

"Managing in a Sped-Up World"

Jeff Davidson *Informs* ✦ *Entertains* ✦ *Inspires*

"You hit a home run for us."
Independent Bankers of Texas

"What a delight..."
Re/Max

"Not only were you a *breathtaking* speaker for us but you also demonstrated your warmth and generosity as a person."
Employee Relocation Council

"By far the most effective speaker we've every had."
Society of Government Meeting Professionals

"I was thoroughly enlightened and entertained by your presentation."
United Defense, FMC

"You were a real life saver..."
Unocal Corporation

"...you made a strong connection with the audience."
NationsBank

"You come across as fully knowledgeable on your chosen topic, with a great sense of humor and a relaxed confidence..."
U.S. Automobile Association

"Your presentation was marvelous and so appropriate..."
Missouri Heart Institute

"...you're really quite entertaining and inspiring."
America Online

"Thanks for the inspiration!"
United States Air Force

"Your presentation was very entertaining, humorous, and full of valuable information. I would recommend your presentation to everyone."
American Express

"Your message was very timely and very effective."
Farmers Insurance Group

"Your involvement of the audience with your presentation was most enjoyable..."
KPMG Peat Marwick

"Everyone here is raving about your presentation last month. I heartily recommend you as a speaker for any group or organization. Whether they're looking for increased productivity, efficiency, or peace of mind, they'll find it in your talk."
Hugh Broadcast Partners

Hailed as a "dynamo" by *The Washington Post,* Jeff Davidson is a leading authority on innovative career and lifestyle strategies ...a world class expert, helping people more effectively live and work at a comfortable pace while confronting constant change.

Jeff Davidson can move an audience like few others. Jeff offers memorable presentations, combining outstanding content with inspiration, humor, and flair. Jeff supercharges his audiences to take action. He is often featured or quoted in *USA Today, The Washington Post,* and *The Los Angeles Times,* and on 100's of talk shows. More than 725,000 people find Jeff's award-winning books (cumulatively selected by book clubs 21 times), audio-books, videos, keynote presentations, and management seminars to be enlightening, entertaining, and transformational. Jeff's ground-breaking book, *Breathing Space,* reveals how to avoid racing the clock and gain more control over each day. His latest book, *The Joy of Simple Living,* with a foreword by Mark Victor Hansen co-author of *Chicken Soup for the Soul,* is the definitive work on simpler living offering nearly 2000 tips, arranged by every aspect of one's personal and professional life!

Jeff Davidson, MBA, CMC has delivered 550 presentations on three continents to corporations and associations, both large and small. *Vital Speeches of the Day* has reprinted seven of his speeches alongside those of Dr. Henry Kissinger, George Bush and Lee Iacocca. Jeff's tailored approach and entertaining style consistently earns him rave reviews and return engagements.

Topic Summaries

Relaxing at High Speed™
Jeff's most compelling topic, he offers breakthrough perspectives on space, time and stress management techniques that anyone can master. A great opening, luncheon or closing keynote speech, audiences have called this presentation "life-changing."

Managing Multiple Priorities
Jeff presents innovative ways to manage priorities including using hand tools, power tools, and cerebral tools; and implementing multiple-priority grids; conditioning your environment; and using multiple stations for high productivity and notable results.

Managing Information and Communication Overload
Too much paper, too much reading, too many web sites—do these diminish your effectiveness? Jeff reveals the nuts and bolts of using information for maximum gain and offers essential "how-to" type tools for continual improvements.

Prospering in a World of Rapid Change
Even Tom Peters says it's normal to be confused these days! In this riveting presentation, Jeff presents high probability scenarios of the near term future and then outlines specific steps you can take to achieve, maintain, or enhance a leadership position.

Jeff Davidson ▪ Http:// www.BreathingSpace.com ▪ Speaking@BreathingSpace.com
2417 Honeysuckle Road ▪ Chapel Hill, NC 27514 ▪ 919-932-1996 ▪ FAX 919-932-9982

Sample One-Sheet (Front)

source of product credibility for establishing speaker credentials. If your books or other products are produced by widely recognizable publishers or producers, all the better. If the book has gone into multiple editions, say so.

If you have no products at this time, fear not—you can still craft a highly professional one-sheet. Chances are that many recipients will not even notice the absence of product listings.

11. *Professional history.* If your employment history or your service to an industry as a consultant is considerable, feature such information on your one-sheet. If you worked for a prestigious organization, chaired

---

"You were the hit of our sales meeting in Orlando."
Gilbarco

"Your session was the highlight of the convention as far as I'm concerned."
Coldwell Banker

"You have changed my life forever."
Houston Chamber of Commerce

"Your presentation was very effective."
Countrymark

"...extremely informative and applicable to our day-to-day needs."
Subsurface Technology, Inc.

"Thought provoking."
Mayo Clinic

"...a superb talk which has already made a positive difference!"
Naval School of Health Sciences

"Your approach to *Breathing Space* was refreshing..."
Dollar Rent-a-Car

"Thanks for the insight and ideas."
Union Carbide

"You are a rich resource and your insights are invaluable. You will always be on my recommended list of speakers."
IBM

"Thank you for a thorough and thoroughly entertaining presentation."
Volvo

"Your approach was very well suited to our young participants."
Proserv

"Your presentation was outstanding."
Paine Webber

"You had tremendous interaction with the audience."
Intel

"Thanks for a great talk."
Philips Petroleum

"I would definitely like to hear your presentation (and/or a longer version) again."
Burroughs Wellcome

"... enjoyable and enlightening."
U.S. West

"Our audience got exactly what they were looking for and a little bit more--the hallmark of a true professional!"
Westcott Communications

Outstanding Content, Consistent Results

"My passion is helping people to manage information and communication overload, technology and change-related anxiety, and having to do more with less."

Jeff Davidson

The best presentations happen when the audience, meeting professional, speaker, and sponsoring organization all get to win! From the first minute, Jeff Davidson delivers electrifying, interactive keynote presentations geared to meet the needs of each audience. Find out why meeting professionals say...

"You were a pleasure to work with."
"We'll have you back."

Outstanding Achievements/Recognition
- Certified Management Consultant (CMC) awarded by the Institute of Management Consultants.
- Project Manager for restructuring the Innovation Center at M.I.T. in Cambridge, MA.

- Shared billing with Dr. Tony Alessandra, Dr. Wayne Dyer, Knight Kiplinger, and Tony Robbins.
- Books translated into both complex and simplified Chinese, Czech, Dutch, Finnish, French, German, Hebrew, Indonesian (Malay), Italian, Japanese, Polish, Portuguese, and Spanish.

- Featured in 68 of the 75 top circulation American newspapers, also *American Way, Boardroom Reports, Computer News, Entrepreneur, Family Circle, Leaders, McCall's, Men's Health, Meeting News, Nation's Business, Sales & Marketing Management, Success, Successful Meetings, Toastmaster,* and *USAirways.*

Outstanding Learning Resources
BOOKS
- ❑ *The Joy of Simple Living* (Rodale)
- ❑ *Breathing Space* (MasterMedia)
- ❑ *Getting New Clients* (John Wiley)
- ❑ *Marketing Yourself and Your Career* (Adams)
- ❑ *The Complete Idiot's Guide to Managing Your Time* (Macmillan)
- ❑ *The Complete Idiot's Guide to Managing Stress* (Macmillan)
- ❑ *Marketing Your Consulting and Professional Services* (John Wiley)
- ❑ *The Complete Idiot's Guide to Reaching Your Goals* (Macmillan)

AUDIOS
- ❑ *Relaxing at High Speed*
- ❑ *Managing Information Overload*
- ❑ *Getting New Clients*
- ❑ *Creating More Time and Space*
- ❑ *Blow Your Own Horn*
- ❑ *Simplicity*
- ❑ *Get a Life!*

Sample One-Sheet (Back)

Every time Don Hutson speaks, people notice something different... about the person in the mirror.

Don Hutson, CPAE, CSP, is in the business of making people believe they can do better– and he gives them the skills to do it. For over 30 years, he has energized his audiences into action. Throughout the business world, he is known as one who delivers real solutions for business professionals.

Don successfully worked his way through the University of Memphis, graduating with a degree in Sales. After becoming the #1 salesperson in a national training organization, he established his own training firm and shortly thereafter was in demand as a professional speaker.

Don Hutson, Chairman /CEO of U. S. Learning, Inc.

Credentials

Don's dynamic and engaging programs have garnered him many honors and awards over the course of his career. He was elected by his peers to the presidency of the National Speakers Association, and he has received its prestigious "Cavett Award," as a member of the year. He was also honored as the annual recipient of SME-I's International Speakers Hall of Fame Award.

Don has addressed over two-thirds of the Fortune 500 companies, and has been selected by a number of them to help develop their own corporate university. Today he is the Chairman & CEO of U. S. Learning, Inc. and has made over 5,000 speaking appearances. Don is also regularly featured on national television and currently serves on five corporate boards.

Don is the author of *The Sale* and co-author of five other books.

His clients include FedEx, International Paper, Sara Lee, IBM, Sherwin-Williams, Bell South, Target Stores, Hewlett-Packard, Oracle, Bank of America, Prudential, GTE, Blue Cross /Blue Shield, Sony, Cellular One and hundreds of trade associations.

Sample One-Sheet (Front)

important meetings (or simply spoke at them), or otherwise participated in industry activities, accent them.

12. *Special features.* If you guarantee the results of your speech, say so on your one-sheet. Guarantees, however, are not to be issued lightly. This is an effective strategy used by veteran speakers who have proven track

Don Hutson, a pilot since the age of 16, uses entertaining aviation anecdotes to illustrate key points.

Video Brochure Available

Don Hutson creatively designs each of his presentations for individual clients. In fact, every appearance is based on an in-depth needs analysis to tailor content.

"Don Hutson's speech at our President's Meeting was excellent! He gave us valuable ideas in every critical area discussed during our needs-analysis call."

- Bill Rice, President
Airgas, Inc.

"Don did more for the skills and attitudes of our sales force in one hour than I could have imagined!"

- John Kluge, Chairman of the Board
Metromedia

"Our members are raving about your 90-minute keynote address at our Las Vegas conference. Your energizing delivery, coupled with the on-target content, was perfect!"

- David Trust, CEO
Professional Photographers of America

Program Topics:

High Performance Selling

Salespeople will learn cutting-edge skills to effectively develop customer alliances while protecting margins.

How To Make And Keep Customers Happy

Don reveals an arsenal of skills, strategies and pertinent statistics for all team members to utilize for customer loyalty.

The Change Initiative

Learn how to embrace, respond to and capitalize on changes that are coming at us in an ever increasing rate through this captivating program.

21st Century Leadership

Don employs powerful skills on leadership style and management designed to create a loyal, high-performance team.

Cavett Award
Past President, National Speakers Association
Member, Speakers Roundtable
International Speakers Hall of Fame Award
Author of 5 books
CPAE, CSP
Consummate Speaker of the Year Award

For your convenience, Don Hutson's fee is inclusive of travel expenses. Please call for date availability and specific quote.

U.S.Learning inc.
The University Company

P. O. Box 172181 • Memphis, TN 38187
(901) 767-0000 • (800) 647-9166 • FAX (901) 767-5959 • www.uslearning.com

Sample One-Sheet (Back)

records of results. The wording of your guarantee is vital. For example, I have employed the following: "Jeff guarantees that his presentation will meet or exceed your expectations or his speaking fee is waived." In such cases, I'm giving the meeting planner full discretion as to whether or not I have performed as guaranteed. Other speakers have offered guarantees that involve achieving some minimal evaluation score or some minimum ranking among all presenters at a given conference.

Speakers bureaus tend to notice those speakers who offer a guarantee. It is a bold, decisive move and one that public speakers need to delay offering until they are certain of their capabilities. For a given speaker, the repercussions of having to pay off on a guarantee could be personally devastating, so think hard about your capabilities before making the offer.

13. *Claims or assertions.* Making claims on your one-sheet is less professionally aggressive than offering a guarantee. The claims, however, have to be based on documented evidence. If you claim that you receive "consistently high evaluations," have ample evidence at your fingertips.

Assertions are akin to claims. Speakers often include phrases such as, "guaranteed to be an audience pleaser." With this particular assertion, the guarantee is not the same as the type of guarantee stated earlier. Nevertheless, such assertions should not be issued lightly.

Exaggerations are red flags for recipients of your one-sheet. As marketing consultant Marcia Yudkin explains, for each claim or assertion that you make on any marketing document, readers are subconsciously saying to themselves, "Says who?" Professional speakers organizations urge members not to make claims or assertions that they cannot legitimately prove. "The world's best" is a phrase that can get you in trouble, unless, of course, you are the world's best.

14. *Projected outcomes.* While you don't want to make excessive claims of any nature, it is appropriate to list specific outcomes that your presentations tend to produce. Many speakers will offer a benefit statement directly followed by their topic descriptions.

If you speak on leadership, for example, you could follow with two or three sentences on what your presentation is all about. You might then add,

> Participants will leave this session knowing how to let go of some of the reins of power when it makes sense and to prepare staff members to aspire to leadership.

Such projected outcomes or benefit statements help meeting planners decide whether or not your presentation will be right for their forthcoming meetings. If you're not the right speaker or if your presentation is not quite right for the particular event, you want to be among the first to know about it.

THE ONE-SHEET AS DOOR OPENER AND CLOSER

Aspiring public speakers and infrequently booked professional speakers have a tendency to attempt to take on all possible bookings. If you intend to be in the speaking arena for the long haul, you want to ensure that you expertly meet the needs of organizations and audience participants in each of your sessions. Your topic descriptions and any benefit statements or anticipated results as listed on your one-sheet helps the meeting planner determine whether it makes sense to pursue discussing an assignment with you. Hence, you want to accurately and succinctly list the most important benefits of your presentation.

A LOW-COST ALTERNATIVE

One-sheets are expensive. As an alternative, you can refer inquirers to your online one-sheet which you can easily offer on a Web site. You may be able to use a low-cost, desk-top one-sheet as a substitute. While they can't hold a candle to a four-color, professionally printed one-sheet, as faxable place holders they'll do fine.

EMULATING OTHERS

The one-sheets presented on the following pages have been generously supplied by veteran professional speakers. The stark reality for the aspiring public speaker is that it's simply too difficult and time consuming to create a one-sheet without modeling it after others.

Modeling as used here means generating ideas—it does not mean copying or otherwise violating the rights of others. One-sheets are copyrighted documents *whether or not* they contain the copyright symbol. The choice of fonts and various point sizes, coloring, shading, and arrangement of features is up to the discretion of each speaker.

Be especially careful not to lift descriptive phrases or passages directly from another speaker's one-sheet. In particular, be cautious when it comes to the titles of other speaker's presentations, grabber statements, and custom-created designs. My friend Glenna Salsbury spent years listing herself, with great justification, as a speaker of "enduring influence." It would be highly inappropriate for anyone else to claim he or she was a speaker of "enduring influence." These two words are distinctive enough that many other speakers, meeting planners, and bureaus within the industry know that they refer to Glenna. Another speaker caught using the phrase would be looked on unfavorably.

Could a novice speaker who never encountered Glenna's literature decide to use the phrase? It could happen. If the speaker discovered that he or she was predated by Glenna, however, the true professional would cease using the phrase.

YOUR PROFESSIONAL PHOTO

Your one-sheet needs at least one photograph and meeting planners will often ask for a photograph prior to your speech. In the evaluation stage, meeting planners may use your photo to ensure that you maintain a professional appearance. They may want to post it on their Web sites or include it in conference or meeting brochures, booklets, pamphlets, or postcards. They may also use it to create an on-site cardboard poster or placard in the hallway outside of your meeting room.

There are several other uses for professional photos including:

- Newspaper reporters may request photographs for interviews, as will publications that accept your press releases.
- Professional photos come in handy if you write articles or books or produce audio or video products. The cover of a demo video all but demands your photo.
- You also need a photograph for any advertisements you place in professional magazines, listings in association directories, and any other print or online speaker compendiums in which you are asked to participate.

Preparing for Your Photo Shoot

The time of day when you have your photo shoot is important. Most people look better early in the day after having recently showered, gotten dressed, and had a good breakfast. Photographers, too, are freshest at the beginning of the day. So, schedule your photo shoot accordingly.

Like that of many other service professionals, some photographers may have designations, such as CPP (Certified Professional Photographer), CRPhotog (Craftsman Photographer), and MPhotog (Master Photographer) after their names. That means they've studied in their chosen fields and been cited by the Professional Photographers of America. While it isn't necessary that you have your photograph taken by a photographer with such credentials or even one familiar with the speaking industry, it can certainly help. Here are some common denominators of effective "shoots" of which you need to be aware:

- Do not retain a photographer before you see his or her work or get a referral. If practical, visit the photographer's studio prior to the day of your shoot. Ask about line screens and halftones. Such effects may make a particular photo more useful for your purposes. You don't have to be an expert; simply ask the photographer to show you examples of possible effects before your shoot.
- Let the photographer know what you are trying to achieve with your photos. Use a variety of poses and try photographs in color and black and white. It is far easier to pay for an extended sitting than it is to come back several times.
- Speakers sometimes opt to use a sequence of photos on their Web sites, marketing literature, and promotional items to convey a sense of dynamism. If you use dramatic gestures during presentations, a series of still photos can work particularly well. Keep the same wardrobe, although it's okay to take off your jacket for some shots.
- Show the photographer the types of end products on which you intend to use your photographs. If you don't already have such materials of your own, use examples of other successful speakers. For example, "live" candid shots let the meeting planner see how you look in front of an audience. Photos of seminar attendees listening intensely, laughing, and participating can convey a strong image about your ability to dazzle an audience.

- Suggest different angles and approaches. Also ask the photographer to change the filters, lighting, lenses, and even background screens. The subtlest of changes during the photo shoot can result in dramatic differences and ultimately provide you with photos that make all the difference in conveying the best of you.
- Examine the photographer's background screens. The background you choose makes a big difference with how your photos turn out. For most speakers, a soft blue or gray tone works well. Avoid employing a background color that clashes with your hair, complexion, or wardrobe. By changing the amount and color of light, the photographer can complement the colors you're wearing with the background.
- A basic, one-color paper background generally is preferred for speakers over mottled-colored backgrounds. At all costs, avoid "busy" backgrounds. Pose at least six feet from the background so that shadows don't ruin your photos. Ask the photographer to separate you from the chosen background with what's called a "hotspot" positioned behind your back and head.
- Tell the photographer if you have a favorite expression or preferred side and any other subtle preferences. Don't fall prey to the erroneous notion that a good photographer knows all—a hit-and-miss approach to generating the type of photos you seek can be costly in terms of time, energy, and money.
- Get considerable rest the night before your photo shoot. Since photo sessions are not everyday occurrences, treat the day as you would a speaking engagement. You need to arrive in high spirits, with high energy, and a great attitude. Give the photographer the best possible chance of capturing you on film.
- If you wear any type of special garment for your presentations and wish to do so for your photo shoot, make sure that it is cleaned and pressed. Avoid garments with plaids, broad stripes, or patterns since they may divert attention from your face.

Be careful when using props since they can distract viewers. If you are an author and a speaker, holding a book with dark colors presents an educated, forward-thinking image. Remember, however, you need to sell yourself, not the prop in your hand.

For Men Only

Shave within a few hours of your shoot. If you are in need of a haircut, get it done a week before; otherwise, you run the risk of having that just-clipped look. To ensure that camera lighting doesn't give you a shiny face, use powder to achieve a matte affect. If you are balding or bald, lightly powder your head as well.

Chose a tie that is somewhat darker than your shirt. It is likely that your jacket is dark, and, hence, will contrast nicely with a light blue or gray background. Ensure that your shirt collar appropriately accents your face and goes with your style of jacket. A spread collar works well if your face is oblong. A button-down collar works well if your face is more round.

Wear long sleeves to convey an image of professionalism. Even if your sleeves and cuffs will not be visible in the final product, avoid wearing a short-sleeved shirt to your photo session.

For Women Only

Come to your session with a fresh hairstyle that is comfortable for you and looks appealing from different angles. Use powder as necessary to eliminate a shiny face.

If you wear a jacket, choose one that's slightly darker than your blouse. As with men, wear long sleeves. If you choose to wear jewelry, recognize that, unless it is larger than normal, it will be indistinguishable in the photographs.

If you have an oblong face, wear a crew collar for best effect. If you have a round face, wear a V-neck collar.

Reviewing Your Proofs

When it is time to take a look at your proofs, be thorough. You want to select the photos that best represent you and the image you wish to convey. Choose the photos in which you are centered and your pose seems natural.

Options abound for enhancing your photos on the way to the final product, but be careful. You can have a photo retouched (airbrushed) to the point where you appear far different in the photo than in person. As cited

previously, this can lead to unwelcome surprises when you show up looking dissimilar to your photo.

If you're unsure as to which photo(s) to select, have a relative or friend,
not the photographer, help you choose. You want someone who has known
you for more than a few days to help in the selection.

Meeting planners may request a print from you as opposed to simply receiving a photo as an e-mail attachment. They may want to make a display
on-site in conjunction with your presentation. In such cases, you need at
least a 5 by 7 photo and more likely an 8 by 10, so order them as part of an
overall package. When submitting a photo to a meeting planner or other
recipient, affix a label with your complete contact information on the back
of the photo away from head and shoulders to avoid possible bleed through.
A meeting planner working with dozens of speakers will appreciate it.

Ordering Options

When ordering photos, your best deal comes with buying the larger packages. If you buy more photos than you can use in a relatively short time,
you will be tempted to keep submitting photos that no longer convey your
current image. If you are going to err in one direction or another, get too
many photos rather than too few. Your cost per photo will be lower.

Every two to three years, schedule another photograph session. Even if
you think that you haven't changed much during that time, you never want
your personal appearances to contrast your photo. Subtle changes in fashion will also conspire to make your photos appear out of date.

If you're happy with the earlier photographer, book another session
with him or her. However, you still need to undertake all of the preplan-
ning and conversation discussed earlier. As harsh as it seems, photos can
sometimes be the make-or-break criterion when it comes to selecting a
speaker for a forthcoming event. You want to stack the odds in your favor
by submitting an authentic representation of yourself.

When it comes to photograph reproduction, don't forget that you need
permission from the photographer who took the originals. Many photographers seek to charge you over and over again for the use of your own
image, and it is their legal right to do so unless you purchase *all* rights to
the photo. It may cost a little more, but it will be worth it in the long run.

Collecting and Using Kudo Letters

Any entrepreneur who receives a letter from a satisfied customer naturally feels pleased. For speakers, kudo letters are of even greater significance. When you receive a letter of praise following one of your presentations, the letter may have long-term marketing value and support the other marketing materials you're developing for your presentation packet, particularly your one-sheet (see previous chapter).

When people inquire about your speaking services, more than all the traditional marketing tools you may have at your disposal, a single kudo letter from a satisfied meeting planner or audience participant (or several letters if you have them) can often spell the difference between your being selected or not.

Why are letters so important? Prospective clients expect that you will have persuasive marketing materials to woo them. Letters that you've received from people who have heard one or more of your presentations can actually carry more weight than slick marketing materials because someone actually took the time out of his or her busy schedule to write to you.

I WANTED TO TELL YOU

Why do people write a kudo letter at all? Your presentation pleased or moved them. They valued the time that they spent with you. They heard something that changed their lives or at least prompted them to devise a plan that will improve or enhance their careers or their lives.

Some speakers request a kudo letter from meeting planners as part of their speaker agreement, given that the meeting planner appreciated the presentation. I don't advocate such requests because they are too contrived.

It's perfectly appropriate to ask audience members who approach you with words of praise following your presentation to capture such thoughts in a letter. Speakers say, "It would mean so much to me if you could put those words into a letter." Whatever personal appeal you make, the days directly following your presentation often hold your best chance of receiving letters. As more time passes after your presentation, the probability of receiving letters declines.

Some speakers appeal to audience participants for kudo letters during their presentation. Depending on how this is handled it can be appropriate. For example, about two-thirds of the way through, if you adroitly raise the issue of how important their feedback is to you and how much you would appreciate hearing from them in the form of a personal letter, I've found that you might receive between one and four letters for every hundred people in your audience.

YOUR CHANCES FOR KUDOS

Over the years, I have observed that the propensity for audience members to send letters is based on several factors, among them:

- *How far they have traveled to attend the meeting.* Local meetings generate more letters because people get home sooner, are less tired, and are more likely to handle the task within a day or two. Meetings where most participants booked round trip plane flights tend to yield fewer letters per hundred participants if only because by the time they return home, days may have passed, they are tired, and their in-baskets are piled high.

- *The number of other presenters.* If you're the only speaker or one of a few at a meeting, your chances of getting kudo letters are greater than if you are one of dozens of speakers. Don't over look the opportunity, however, to obtain letters from participants in either setting.

- *The type of group to which you are speaking.* People at an association convention are more likely to write than audience members comprising some company division. Women are slightly more likely to write than men, and both younger and older audience participants are more likely to write that those between 30 and 55. I've also found that people either at the top or the bottom of a corporation are more likely to write.

- *What type of speaker you are.* If you're a motivational or inspirational speaker, you tend to generate more letters. If you speak on productivity, cost cutting, or if you otherwise tackle any touchy issues confronting an organization, you tend to get fewer letters.

- *The traditions of the organization.* With some groups, it's considered standard fare for audience participants to send follow-up letters to presenters; in other organizations, sending kudo letters is the last thing on anyone's mind. Charitable institutions, schools, hospitals, universities, and some governmental agencies tend to be populated by people inclined to write letters especially if a speaker requests it.

A Few Good Letters

Any letter of praise, regardless of who wrote it, where that person is employed, where the meeting occurred, and what topic you addressed is better than no letter. The fact that there is one person who stated on paper that your presentation was valued is a feather in your cap and may influence the next meeting planner with whom you interact.

If you speak a few times annually and generate two or three letters, managing your kudo letters is simple. You could keep them in a single file and make copies as inquires about your presentations come in from other meeting planners. If you have several letters from previous participants, then you can pick the two or three that are most appropriate per inquirer.

For example, if you have a letter from the same state as your latest inquirer that could be a letter well worth including. Women tend to respond to letters that you have received from female audience participants, and men seem to respond to letters from male audience participants. Finally, if you have a letter from someone in the same industry as your current inquirer, you have a significant marketing tool. A letter from a meeting planner carries more weight than a letter from a single audience participant, all other things being equal. If a meeting planner or a top officer of the organization writes you a letter of glowing praise, it can be worth its weight in gold.

The great opportunity in collecting kudo letters is that beyond simply running them off on your copier for submission to prospective meeting planners, you can also use the letters in a variety of promotional formats. [Note: With all such promotional uses, ask permission of those who sent you letters. Virtually everyone whom you ask will respond affirmatively. Occasionally, someone from a government agency or other institution may prefer not to be included. That's okay; honor the request.]

- *Collages.* Some speakers arrange an attractive collage of kudo letters for use as a graphic on their Web sites or in hard copy speaker literature. The point size of the letters in collages is tiny, but readable. You want to make the arrangement so that the letterhead and some key phrasing from each letter appears in the collage. Some speakers remove the dates from the letters so that the collage does not "age."
- *Blurbs.* Another technique for employing the letters to great advantage is to extract key blurbs. However, don't use single-word declarations from the letters you receive—offer longer phrases, whole sentences, and possibly brief paragraphs followed by the name of the person, their organizational affiliation, and their state and town. Otherwise, it might appear that you're intentionally trying to mislead the reader.
- *Extended blurb groupings.* On my Web site and on hard copy pages (which I can print as needed) I have blurbs from 18 different categories of audiences such as accountants, attorneys, sales professionals, women's groups, and chambers of commerce. If a meeting planner from any one of these groups inquires about my presentations, I submit a page or more of extended blurbs specifically related to that meeting planner's industry or profession.
- *Letter packets.* The more kudo letters you receive, the easier time you have marketing your presentations. Once you've assembled

more than 100 letters, you could select a subset of them, perhaps four to eight letters, that could pique the interest of almost any meeting planner who may inquire.

- *Online PDFs.* If you maintain a speaker Web site, you also have the opportunity to scan your letters in full color and save them in an Adobe PDF file format. This means that when site visitors click on hyperlinks to your kudo letters they will be treated to a full view of the letter.

- *Compendiums.* I know of two speakers who send out three-ring notebooks or perfect-bound compendiums of hundreds of letters to inquirers. Perhaps this is dramatic overkill (and expensive overkill at that!), yet speakers report that kudo letter compendiums represent an effective marketing strategy. One speaker said that when a meeting planner receives his huge compendium, there is simply no denying his general effectiveness as a speaker and his potential for offering great value with the group in question.

THE SELF-GENERATED KUDO

In lieu of, or in addition to, collecting kudo letters, some speakers have devised and successfully deployed a combination evaluation and marketing form that works wonders. (See the form on page 160.) Veteran speaker Dr. David Meinz gave me this brilliant idea, which I adapted. You might be surprised as to the number of audience participants who not only complete the form and turn it back in to you, but who have generously circled several of your topics that they would like to hear.

MAKING IT EASY ON THE RECEIVER

When submitting letters or admirable evaluation forms, speakers often use a felt-tipped pen or highlighter to emphasize key passages. Meeting planners are busy, and many recipients appreciate it if key passages are highlighted because it saves them time.

Other than when using collages, if you submit letters to inquirers, send the entire letter. Truncations or cutaways raise doubts! If I get kudo

Self-Generated Evaluation and Marketing Form

Feedback and Follow-Up

1. Name: _____ Organization: _____
   Address: _____ e-mail: _____
   City: _____ State: _____ ZIP: _____

2. Your evaluation of Jeff Davidson's presentation (detailed comments help!):
   _____
   _____
   _____
   _____

   What did the speaker do that was impactful? _____
   What one thing could have been done better? _____
   What was your satisfaction level? _____

3. Would you like to have Jeff back? [ ] Yes   [ ] No   [ ] Possibly

4. Which of Jeff's topics would you most like to see addressed further?

   [ ] Managing the Pace with Grace   [ ] Mastering Change
   [ ] Managing Multiple Priorities   [ ] Handling Information Overload
   [ ] Creating More Space and Time   [ ] Relaxing at High Speed

5. Which of Jeff's services might be worth exploring?

   [ ] Executive/staff retreats   [ ] Roundtable sessions
   [ ] Video conference   [ ] On-site consulting
   [ ] Video training   [ ] Day-in-the-field consulting
   [ ] Online conference   [ ] One-to-one coaching
   [ ] Online training   [ ] Video or Cd-rom of the month
   [ ] Custom CD-rom   [ ] Cassette of the month
   [ ] Custom book   [ ] Custom online newsletter
   [ ] Discounts on Jeff's books/tapes   [ ] Cassette of the month
   [ ] Presentations for your clients   [ ] MC or panel moderator

6. Do you belong to another organization that books speakers?
   [ ] Yes   [ ] No

   Name of Group: _____

   Approx. Size of Group: _____ Month/Year Speaker Needed:_____

   Person in Charge: _____ Phone: _____

   May the speaker call you for info on this group? [ ] Yes   [ ] No
   Phone: _____

letters from you, I want to see the entire letter including the name and title of the sender and full contact data. Few meeting planners who receive kudo letter copies call the letter writer. It is usually enough that they have the full contact information including phone, fax, and e-mail.

WHAT ABOUT "IFFY" LETTERS?

What about the situations in which you receive a letter that contains some glowing praise and, elsewhere in the letter, some recommendations or criticisms? Should you use the letter as part of your kudo file? It depends on what the recommendations or criticisms are.

I receive many letters that say, for example, "I wish your presentation wasn't first thing in the morning—I had a rough night," or, "If only there had been more time." I include these letters in my marketing materials if there are other beneficial observations.

Occasionally, I'll receive a letter that says, "I wish you covered XYZ more thoroughly," or "I was already well versed on DEF and didn't need that much detail." With these types of comments, I usually decide to use them or not based on other elements of the letter such as whether it is from a recognizable company or organization, the title or responsibilities of the letter writer, and how strong the praise was elsewhere in the letter. When you use such letters and choose to highlight those passages that you want recipients to see, I suspect that recipients indeed only read your highlighted sections. The comments that were not entirely favorable often are never even looked at by recipients.

MAINTAINING LONG-TERM CONTACT

When people take the time and trouble to write you a letter following your presentations, it is fitting that you reciprocate in some way. I mail or immediately fax back a note to letter writers acknowledging them for the time they took and the effort they made. As with meeting planners, you want to establish some type of bond with your kudo letter writers. Most people who attend a presentation in one capacity are members of other organizations. They often have the opportunity to sing your praises to other people in other groups.

Whether or not you maintain a comprehensive database of contacts you make in the world of speaking, when you receive and keep someone's letter, you have the contact information that allows for staying in touch with him or her if you so choose. I send my kudo letter writers updated versions of my demo video as they become available once every two or three years. I have received many inquiries as a result of such mailings and in several cases was booked for a speech. Keeping in touch with people who have already seen and praised one of your presentations is relatively inexpensive compared with landing another speaking engagement with strangers.

KUDO LETTERS IN PERSPECTIVE

If you've been speaking for a while and previously have not recognized the value of collecting, managing, and employing kudo letters for optimal impact, get started now on this highly productive path. In the course of your next speaking engagement, make sure that everyone in the audience knows how greatly you would value their feedback in the form of a letter. Some will honor your request.

I'm Ready for My Video, Mr. DeMille

Along with setting your fee, developing a dynamite one-sheet, and creatively employing kudo letters, your video demonstration tape (hereafter called a video demo) is a fundamental tool in your marketing and positioning tool bag.

NOT A MONUMENT TO ONESELF

Some speakers are caught up in the planning and production of a video but lose focus and eventually create a product that represents a monument to themselves. Unfortunately, such ventures tend to miss the mark. The purpose of your video is to:

- Heighten your credibility.
- Enhance your position.
- Deliver a brief but specific message to targeted viewers.

You want a video that helps meeting planners and selection committees choose you for a particular speaking engagement. Of necessity, the video has to please your targets and not your ego.

Nearly all video producers will tell you that the product must be 15 minutes or shorter, make an immediate impact, convey audience reaction, and tell the viewer who you are. You want to convey your ability to sparkle in front of an audience, deliver brilliant material, and motivate the viewer to call you. If you are a humorist, the video has to make them laugh. If you are a subject expert, the video must contain segments of you conveying high content information. If you are an inspirational speaker, the video needs to convey your ability to motivate and inspire audiences.

HOW THEY HANDLE IT

Your video will wind up in the hands of two distinct groups: meeting planners and speaker's bureaus. Meeting planners are not likely to shelve, store, or otherwise retain your video beyond the near term because they are focused on a particular conference.

When your video is sent to meeting planners so that they can consider you for a specific meeting, the chances are that they have a pile of other speakers' videos to review as well. Proceed with the mind-set that you have only half a minute or less to capture their attention. If what they see in the first half minute is captivating and convincing, they will continue to view more of the video.

Regardless of your credentials, assume the viewers know next to nothing about you prior to playing the video. People may have glanced over your one-sheet, briefly stopped at your Web site, and perhaps made a few notes about you. What they see on your video slipcover, video face label, and video spine label represents the information that they have about you before popping in the video. As far-fetched as it seems, your video slipcover frequently serves as one of your primary positioning tools.

PRODUCTION STRATEGIES

As you approach the video-making process, first collect at least six other videos demos and carefully watch all of them. Note what you like and what you don't like, decide what you want to include, and determine how you can improve on what you have seen. From your notes, you can begin to sketch out the sequence of events that will take place during, say, a 12-minute video. Anything you want to say or do during the video—even if you want it to appear candid—should be scripted far in advance.

Begin to sketch out the accompanying graphics as well. Ultimately, you'll want to create a video slipcover, face label, and spine label that coordinate with your speaker one-sheet. Some speakers opt to coordinate all aspects of their speaker literature and marketing artifacts.

Your video slipcover must be a brilliant, four-color production that captures the best of you. You will need a photo—a head and shoulders or action shot. You will also need a grabber line, presumably taken from your speaker one-sheet, a brief listing of three to five topics, a listing of your credentials, and perhaps a few excerpted blurbs of praise from previous audience members.

Pizzazz but Not Schmaltz

Offer some pizzazz. While you don't want to overdo it, it is appropriate to tap the power of video graphics. You can spin your presentation topics in and then out, creatively display your book titles or other learning resources, roll your client roster, or attractively convey your credentials. The key in each case is to have them be relatively brief, not overly flashy, and presented in coordination with other elements of your video. Such a production mandates that you go to a knowledgeable video producer. Unless you are well versed in this field, work with a top pro who has been down this trail before and knows how to create a captivating product.

Music is a must. Viewers need to hear upbeat but nondescript music at least at the start and end of your production. Music throughout is okay as well as long as it enhances, not detracts, from what the viewer sees. Fortunately, there are many noncopyrighted music clips available for a nominal fee, and most video producers can supply stock music tracks for you as part of their overall services.

Cut to the quick. Video viewers are not interested in prolonged buildups to your video, however clever. Most will grimace, groan, or fast-forward through spinning globes, street scenes, boardroom shots, or anything else that is prolonged leading up to what should be the start of the video.

Go with a Pro

While the speaker selects the best material for inclusion in the demo video, the video producer then uses the footage to best effect. The producer assesses the footage for its visual appeal even more so than its content. Most speakers lack the capability to objectively assess this important marketing and positioning tool.

In the hands of a video production specialist, your demo can look and sound even better than you might have hoped for. A producer can run your entire demo through an audio console and eliminate extraneous noise while fine-tuning the treble/bass mix, refining nasality, and smoothing out any irregularities.

Is it ethical to manipulate elements of your video demo? Adding back audience sound reactions, for example, that are commensurate with what actually happened is acceptable. Manipulating your video to present false scenarios that have never actually happened is bound to get you into trouble. Remember that when hired, you need to live up to the expectations that the host organization has of you as a result of the marketing materials you submitted.

Since most speakers don't change their video demo that often, it makes sense to go for the best possible production each time you produce a video. The cost is minor compared to the potential returns when you have the job done right and you are otherwise positioned appropriately.

To avoid having to start from scratch, record your footage using DLP format master tape that enables you to separately store your speaking footage, special effects, voice overs, and music. Although you will have a higher initial cost outlay, you will save money in the long run, and be more inclined to update and upgrade your video regularly instead of waiting three to five years.

MANY PATHS

The best path to a final product can be subjective, so we'll examine the advice of several industry professionals rather than follow a set formula. Note some of the predictable commonalities and unpredictable striking differences in approach:

1. *West Coast Producer*—Does your video grab your attention in the first 30 seconds? Is it television broadcast quality? If it weren't about you, would you be interested in watching it further? West Coast along with all the other producers believes that you need to make an immediate impact on your viewers or you will lose them. The first half minute of the demo is crucial, and many meeting planners will make a host of decisions within those 30 seconds. You need to convey who you are, what you do, and what benefits you offer to the audience.

The meeting planner wants to see you in action, so offer footage that displays your presentation skills, an inkling of your content, and audience responsiveness. Some speakers show snippets that are too short; it is preferable to convey a complete vignette. Have audience members come up to you and said wonderful things? Are there top officers of recognized companies or notable personalities whom you have captured, or can capture, on video? If so, they can prove to be highly influential. Strategically place video testimonials throughout your demo.

When you toot your own horn, it can have a detrimental effect in a video. It is crucial to use someone else's voice when it comes to discussing your background and credentials. Using a professional announcer adds to the overall production value of your product.

The sequence of elements contained can vary, but here is one that has proven effective: opening, opening graphics, music, professional announcer, demonstration of platform skills, presentation vignettes, audience responsiveness, candid message to viewer, discussion of credentials, "for more information," and closing.

2. *East Coast Producer*—Too many speakers' demos lack appropriate production quality and filming basics to be considered compelling. They have the wrong lighting, background, sound, and mix of elements. Speakers don't understand the importance of using spot lighting that creates a dramatic effect and increases a viewer's propensity to keep watching. The lighting on speaker videos is often white or very pale creating an eerie effect.

Many videos contain overly distracting background scenery whereas plain or nondescript is preferable. Speakers astute enough to include audience reactions often fail to show a full episode—the audience moving from one point to another with the speaker's presentation. Audiences are rarely miked and since audience reaction is a key to demonstrating a speaker's effectiveness, this critical element is lacking. Audience sounds can be added back.

Use a story board for each element of a video production. Within the 12 minutes, you need at least six but no more than eight minutes of your best material. Testimonials are also high on East Coast's list. As you draw to a close, let the viewer know it is coming through use of music. Show a powerful closing statement, lock onto the frame, and overlay a closing motto or catch phrase that will leave the viewer with a great impression.

3. *South Atlantic Communications*—Make adjustments to your normal presentation style and delivery so that your video matches what you offer in person. For example, even if you use a highly talented production team to shoot your video, you want to use heavier makeup to ensure that your image doesn't come across as washed out. Get a variety of camera angles, settings, and segments that include you standing and face the camera directly, being filmed from the side, and being filmed while seated. The more material you have to work with, the wider your selection of segments that merit inclusion.

Avoid static head shots, as audiences today are accustomed to constant action. You are competing against broadcast footage that viewers see on television. The average sound byte on the evening news is 20 seconds and dropping. As a result, people become bored easily and have frighteningly tiny attention spans when watching a video.

Pump up your energy to an almost uncomfortable level. You need to triple your typical pizzazz on video to match your true energy level when presenting in person. Without "pumping up," you will come across as too mild and mellow. Mild and mellow is okay live, but when your video is one of eight viewed in succession by a meeting planner, the high-energy speakers are likely to make the first cut.

On the big stage, you can make wide sweeping gestures, but for video, keep them close to your body and well within camera range. Employ the most meaningful gestures that most accurately help to convey what you are saying with your words. Keep your sentences short and eliminate any terms that are hard to pronounce. The viewer is only getting a smidgeon of you, and any verbiage they don't understand is to your disadvantage. Speak in complete sentences and show complete vignettes so that there is no danger of your words being taken out of context.

Get plenty of sleep the night before your video shoot and eat a normal but not heavy breakfast. Arrive early so that you have plenty of time to scope out the territory and get into that zone that enables you to project your best.

4. *Southwest Sage*—Work specifically with a video production crew that is experienced in doing speaker video demos and has been fully prepped as to what you are trying to achieve. In advance, give the crew a copy of your previous video and insist that they watch it several times so that they are thoroughly familiar with how you come across, your important points, and what to watch out for.

Speakers fail to recognize that viewers will typecast them based on what the video shows. If a speaker is addressing a group in short sleeves at a resort, then the typical viewer will assume that the speaker addresses short-sleeved groups at resorts. If the speaker addresses an all female audience, the viewer will assume that the speaker does not address male audiences!

As inane as this seems, it gets worse. Viewers will make assumptions about what is not included in the video—if you include no humorous segments, they will assume that you are not humorous at all. If you have no audience footage they will assume that you didn't get good responses. If you speak exclusively from behind the lectern they will assume you have no capability to handle interactive sessions close to the audience. Anything that you choose to convey about your presentations has to be explicitly shown on your video or in the minds of some viewers it is nonexistent.

Stand at least 15 feet from the back wall or you will appear to be standing along the wall. Unlike East Coast Producer, Southwest recommends that you use a spotlight aimed at the ceiling and not at the speaker. This reduces glare and softens the overall effect for the audience.

Any attempt to directly shoot slides or overheads will detract from the overall quality of your video as they may be entirely unreadable. If you use audiovisuals during your presentation, in advance ensure that the production crew does not film them. Instead have them entered in the post-production phases so that they can be smoothly integrated. The end result will be far clearer and sharper.

Once your video demo is complete and you are ready to make copies, do so with a production house that offers one-to-one video dubbing that results in higher quality than if taping is done via slave units with high speed dubbing.

5. *Mid-West Wonder*—In the first few seconds viewers need to see the audience giving you a warm and glowing response as you masterfully deliver some high-level message. So, extract some midportion of your presentation which represents a high point in the overall speech and use that as your opening video segment. As the applause dies down, have a professional announcer briefly introduce you and discuss what the demo is designed to do. Then fade back in with audience background noise. Offer another view of you making a second sterling point from your presentation, followed by another applause fade out, and another the announcer fade in with a word about your credentials and an invitation for the viewer to keep watching. While this approach may seem overly staged, actually, it follows the same pattern as employed by major broadcast media. It generates immediate viewer interest while inviting the viewer to continue watching.

SPEAKERS DISCUSS VIDEO DEMOS

Several veteran speakers, some of whom have created five or more video demos in their speaking careers, have distinct and worthwhile strategies worth reviewing:

1. *Southern Comfort*—Southern Comfort wants to personally appeal to the meeting planner watching the video demo in the same way that he appeals to live audiences. Before video taping, he seeks to have a 10-minute warm-up session with audiences prior to the actual presentation. Thus, audience reactions, particularly laughter and applause, are captured on the tape. This makes having a one-camera shoot yield the same value as having a two-camera shoot. The production manager can simply overlay the audience footage after the presentation has been filmed.

Southern Comfort informs the audience members of the strategy—if they are part of the experience they prove to be more responsive during the filming. Southern Comfort also choreographs elements of the video to steer meeting planners toward other presentations that he has to offer.

2. *Great Lakes*—This speaker believes that the viewer needs to be comfortable and relaxed and speakers should be snappy but not too fast.

The footage with audiences is most important. It needs to be crisp and entertaining but not too formal. Humor is essential, and scenes of audiences having a good time are critical. A few network-quality effects are okay but it is more important to have a credible, solid, potent portrayal of what the presenter is able to achieve with audiences.

Meeting planners don't want to watch interviews, so her video only contains speaking segments. Unlike other speakers, Great Lakes shows "extras" such as handling questions, arriving early and staying late, coming over to touch an audience member, and bringing someone up on stage.

3. *The Bureau Darling*—Bureau Darling is frequently booked by bureaus. He believes that you need to have as many segments of yourself on video as possible so that you can draw from the best of the best to create a super product. When he books an engagement, he includes a clause in his speaker agreement form requesting that the client videotape his presentation. Then he chooses high-energy segments with tremendous audience involvement.

Because he speaks to groups of 1,000 to 3,000 or more, he is able to show dramatic footage on video. As such, he routinely influences viewers that he is the right speaker to open or close their large convention.

4. *Nice and Easy*—This person approaches video demos as a personal conversation with meeting planners. She does no grand standing and uses no special effects. She speaks in everyday tones, using simple language and a direct approach to the viewer, as if the viewer were right there in the room with her.

After a few minutes her demo cuts away to a live segment of her addressing an audience of more than 2,000 people. She explains that she was their first female speaker. The audience response is magnificent and anyone who views her video is immediately impressed. After this segment, she cuts back to another one-to-one conversation with the viewer, talking about her various programs, and her flexibility. She emphasizes how she will work with the meeting planner to ensure that her presentation makes a difference and is one of the most memorable components of the entire meeting. She also says that if she is not the right speaker she will let the meeting planner know immediately and help find the right speaker.

She closes her video by saying "I've kept this message short because I respect your time." She suggests that the meeting planner call so that together they can discuss how to best accomplish the conference goals.

After viewing Nice and Easy's video, whether someone hires her or not, they are certainly going to like her. This approach has proven effective over the years as she has proven to be a popular speaker. Indeed, a great video can be an invaluable asset and marketing tool. Now that you have the marketing tools in place, it's time to think about negotiating and winning engagements, plus having a speaker's agreement ready to go.

PART IV

PREPARING FOR AND NEGOTIATING SPEAKER CONTRACTS

If the opportunity arises to speak for a fee, you'll need to furnish the meeting planner with a speaker contract. Exactly what goes into a speaker contract? The chapters in Part IV answer that question and provide you with a clause-by-clause explanation of what to include.

Since virtually all paid professionals are subject to price comparisons and fee objections, you'll need to learn how to successfully overcome such objections, win over speaker selection committees, and attain the kind of concessions that can make your engagements worthwhile.

The chapters in Part IV will save you time and energy and will incorporate valuable insights from speakers who've already gone down this path. Many missed opportunities and even costly mistakes can happen when you negotiate a speaker contract, but fortunately, you can avoid them.

What Meeting Planners Seek

Unbeknownst to many speakers, when it comes to booking the right speaker for an event, meeting planners often find themselves forced to stretch their resourcefulness and creativity in ways they shouldn't have to. To better understand how to close more deals with meeting planners, it's helpful to learn about their obstacles and frustrations. Here are various concerns voiced by meeting planners, who shall remain anonymous. *Warning:* It is humbling to read this list, especially if you believe you are a meeting planner's "cure-all."

- *Cost.* "Why do speakers charge so much? It seems as if you can't find a good speaker for under $X these days, and our budget simply doesn't allow paying any more than that."
- *Coordination.* "We need a speaker who is willing to make a presentation that not only addresses the theme of our conference, but meshes with what our staff people will have heard earlier that morning. So, it's vital that the speaker attend the few presentations leading up to his or hers."
- *Industry background.* Our conference requires speakers who have a background within our industry.

- *Customized presentation.* "Most speakers who claim to customize their presentations do not do so. They drop in a few buzzwords and consider that to be sufficient. We need someone who understands our industry, our problems, and our lingo."

- *Finding hands-on speakers.* related to the comment above: "We need speakers who offer practical advice that our people can put to use immediately once they're back at work. Theories and stories are fine, but we also have to have real-world tactical tools."

- *Speaker to audience fit.* "A speaker's style is vital. There are many good speakers, but how many of them actually represent a good fit for our audience? We need to ensure that what we hear and read about a speaker matches what the speaker will deliver on stage at our meeting."

- *Universal appeal.* "There are many levels of staff at our meetings, so we need to find a speaker who can deliver a message that reaches everyone in our organization from intern and administrative assistant to chief operating officer and board member."

- *Topping last year's meeting.* "I suppose it's unfair to compare one speaker to another, but we need someone who will be rated more highly than last year's presenter."

- *Audiovisual rights.* "We videotape the speaker's presentation for internal distribution only; therefore, I need to find a reasonably priced speaker who will include videotaping as part of his or her fee."

- *Flexibility.* "It means a lot to our members when the speaker stays after the presentation to autograph books and mingle with audience members. Too many speakers want to cut and run. If we can find a speaker who is willing to attend the reception the evening before, that would prove to be a tremendous benefit to us."

See Chapter 43 for more ways that speakers fail to hit the mark.

GOOD CLIENTS AND BAD CLIENTS

To be fair, meeting planners occasionally disappoint speakers as well. If the scheduling and booking process went smoothly, you may still be in for a Nantucket Sleigh Ride when it comes to coordinating the details that lead up to the event.

Over the years, I've determined a host of factors that reasonably convey how vigorously I might need to monitor arrangements for a forthcoming engagement:

1. *Assigns one person to serve as liaison.* Sometimes, the members of a speaker selection committee also have responsibility for planning and executing the meeting. This is problematic for a speaker. You want a single person who serves as a liaison.

2. *Completes the pre-speech survey.* Meeting planners who have proven to be my best clients routinely complete my pre-speech survey without my having to ask.

3. *Accurately gauges audience needs.* The more you speak, the more you discover that some meeting planners are clueless as to what their audience wants or needs. Often such meeting planners have been assigned to handle a given conference or are amateurs. Some arrogantly believe that they don't need to assess needs.

I've learned that it is vital to speak directly to three to five future audience participants. I seek a well-rounded view of what the people "in the seats" want and need, and, more importantly, expect. Thankfully, each time I have requested names and phone numbers of forthcoming audience members, meeting planners have capitulated.

4. *Demonstrates basic planning skills.* Some people are simply good at producing a meeting and following through on all details. The good ones are a pleasure to work with. They anticipate your questions. They don't need to be reminded. They are methodical in their approach. They use planning tools to best advantage. The bad ones do far less.

First-time meeting planners tend to be troublesome. Fortunately, many first timers are candid about their lack of experience. The more groups you have addressed, the greater your capacity for "coaching" rookies to ensure a mutual win.

5. *Allows the speaker relative free rein with participation packets.* Some meeting planners want to micromanage—even on a line-by-line basis—your participation packet. It is understandable for a meeting planner to review your packet in advance. He or she may have been burned by a speaker who introduced controversial material contrary to the desires of the host organization.

The micromanaging meeting planner, nevertheless, seeks to have a strong hand in every sheet of paper you disseminate. In my experience, such micromanaging rarely makes a measurable difference in the speaker's effectiveness.

6. *Prepares solid conference literature.* You would be surprised how crucial the host organization's conference literature and, in particular, write-up of your presentation can be in terms of impacting your audience. While there is not much you can do about a poor brochure or flyer, strive to ensure that your presentation's write-up is the best that it can be.

Audiences rate speakers more harshly when the write-up of their speech doesn't match the content, however masterful and insightful it might have been. Audiences don't like content surprises for the sessions they attend, particularly in breakout sessions where they have a choice in what they attend.

7. *Gives the speaker "space" prior to the presentation.* Some meeting planners and their respective organizations misunderstand the dynamics of making a public presentation. With the best of intentions, they load up the speaker's time with energy-draining activities. Aspiring public speakers need to conserve their energy, stay focused on their delivery, and maintain equilibrium.

8. *Arranges the room as requested.* An all too frequent surprise that speakers encounter is arriving on site and finding that the meeting room doesn't resemble what they had requested months ago. The best clients actively work with speakers to ensure that as many of their requests as are practical are met. When requests cannot be met, astute meeting planners pass that information along to the speaker as soon as it is known.

9. *Provides appropriate amenities.* The best clients have prepared an effective agenda encompassing food, restroom, and stretch breaks. The worst clients don't recognize the value of such planning.

10. *Hands me a check.* My speaker agreement as discussed later in the chapter states that I am to receive the second half of my speaker fee

directly following my presentation. Some meeting planners and host organizations ignore this aspect of the speaker agreement.

JUST WHEN YOU HAD
YOUR SYSTEM WORKING

The meeting and travel industries changed on September 11, 2001, and
meeting planners need to pay homage to some new realities. When it
comes to working with speakers, here are new concerns among some
meeting planners:

- *Within Drive Time.* Some meeting planner now prefer to seek speakers within a four-hour radius of the meeting place. Why four hours?
  If push comes to shove, a four-hour or less drive may actually save
  time over flying considering the current waits at airports. Further,
  booking speakers within a four-hour driving radius of the meeting
  site provides an added measure of insurance.
- *Appropriateness of Terminology.* Depending on the audience, it may
  be inadvisable to book a speaker whose presentation language is
  peppered with war and attack metaphors including "pounding,"
  "beat them into submission," "taking a beating," "all out attack,"
  "in the trenches," or "bombs away." Such terms may concern audience members and detract from the overall presentation.

WORK WITH ME AND YOU'LL SEE

In anticipation of meeting planner's general concerns and questions when
booking me for the first time, I prepared a document called "What Is It
Like to Work with Jeff Davidson?" which I patterned after a more sophis-
ticated, professionally printed flyer developed by Jim Cathcart. Here are
some excerpts on pages 180–181.

This single document answers many, if not all, of the questions most
meeting planners would like to know and undoubtedly has tipped the
scales in my favor when it comes to landing the job.

Working with Jeff

"What Is It Like to Work with Jeff Davidson?"

Pre-speech, I will:

- Learn as much about your organization as I can, including your mission, your values, and your objectives.
- Make myself accessible in order to plan a presentation that addresses the needs of your audience participants.
- Understand the needs of your participants before I arrive. I will also attempt, however, to arrive a day early to learn firsthand the needs and wants of audience members.
- Integrate my presentation into the overall theme of your meeting so that the union is seamless to audience participants.
- Send my travel itinerary to you as soon as it is established.
- Have a least one suitable back-up speaker in mind who could fill-in on short notice.

On site, I will:

- Notify you the moment I arrive.
- Be open and accessible to you during my entire time on site.
- Get sufficient sleep so that I am alert, energetic, and tactful during my presentation.
- Visit the meeting room at least 30 minutes before my presentation to do a complete walk-through.
- As time allows, sit in on other presentations and incorporate relevant points into my presentation.
- Meet with AV and set-up staff and other presenters to ensure we're coordinated.
- Offer a succinct, easy-to-read introduction and, if necessary, spend time with my introducer so that he or she is comfortable delivering the introduction.
- Come dressed appropriately for the occasion based on your specifications.
- Be ready to make my presentation whether called on time, late, or even early.

Working with Jeff (Continued)

During my presentation, I will:

- Start with high energy and engage the audience from the first minute.
- Encourage audience involvement throughout the entire presentation.
- Deliver high-content, on-target information that participants want and need to hear.
- Employ personal anecdotes, case histories, and lots of humor to reinforce important points.
- Avoid questionable language at all times.
- Let all audience members know that I am there for them; they are not there for me.
- Use your participants' terminology and their buzzwords.
- Not use the platform for sales, politics, or therapy.
- Remain within my allotted time frame, adjust on the fly if necessary, and stop as agreed to keep your meeting on schedule.
- Continually summarize the important points and key issues.
- Handle as a speaking professional problems that arise, be they related to audiovisuals, outside noise, temperature, air circulation, lighting, or medical emergencies.

Post-speech, I will:

- Be accessible to participants following my presentation.
- Answer questions individually, striving to make each audience member feel as if his or her individual needs are served.
- Send no bill for travel expenses—I do not charge for these.
- Quickly and accurately fulfill any information requests, orders for my products (previously cleared by you), or any other requests.
- Call you three to five days following the conclusion of the meeting to obtain your firsthand feedback and recommendations for being even more effective.
- Never share your organization's proprietary information.
- Be available for phone, fax, or e-mail correspondence.
- Secure appropriate transportation for departing the meeting facility without having to request your assistance.
- Support you in reinforcing the themes and messages of my presentation among your participants, if you so desire.

Jeff Davidson

CLEARING THE LOG JAM—
WINNING OVER COMMITTEES

If only you had a single meeting planner to persuade! Too often it seems, you encounter a meeting planner who must report to a speaker selection committee. So, it is not simply winning over the meeting planner, it is winning over the entire committee.

The existence of a speaker selection committee means that several speakers are being considered along with you. To favorably steer the committee, many professional speakers routinely prepare multiple packets so that if and when the meeting planner asks, a packet for each committee member is readily available.

When a committee is selecting a speaker the single most influential element for you is having someone, in a position of influence, on your side, who has heard you, and absolutely insists that you're the best speaker for the job. Short of that, an excellent video demo or Webcast is the next best alternative. If you're simply one of 10 speakers being considered, you have a 10 percent chance, at best, of being selected—not great odds.

If you don't have a bird dog on the inside, as is most often the case, you may have to send the packets. Here's how to win that way:

- Everyone wants to see letters from people in your previous audiences. The letters are more powerful if they are from people in the same profession or industry as the group to which you are currently appealing. The more recent the letter the better, but don't worry if you have letters that are several years old as long as they speak to your proficiency and mastery, and what you were able to achieve with the audience.
- The traditional presentation kit with all the great things about you included is fine, but all the other speakers will have them, too, so be innovative!
- If you published a book or articles, copies of the book jacket or reprints of the article can be influential among committee members. Some speaker/authors are willing to submit a copy of their book to every committee member. The value-added impact of a book is significant. Once a committee member has your fine book in hand, you've helped establish your position as a subject matter expert. People might toss an article or flyer, but few will toss a book.

- Some speakers send their audience participant packet—actual examples of what audience members will receive. Depending on how attractively you can package your packet, and what's included within it, committee members may be quite impressed. A compelling packet prompts them to want to know more about you and your program.

Audience participant packets work best with a how-to type of presentation. If you are a storyteller, a political pundit, or a motivational or inspirational speaker, you may not have a packet, but that's okay. As I'll discuss in the next chapter, there are yet other strategies for closing the deal.

Preempt the Pack and Close the Deal

Suppose you have correctly determined that you have strong capabilities to serve a particular group and the meeting planner would like to arrange a conference call. When I am faced with having to favorably influence a selection committee, and a conference call is suggested, I'm all for it. I am confident that in as little as 10 minutes I can convince everyone on the line that I am the speaker person for the engagement.

The phone is no substitute for being there in person. However, your speaking style and vocal power can be very persuasive. It is to your advantage to present to the committee "over the phone" precisely because they *can't* see you—you can have notes all over your desk to ensure that you make the right points.

PREEMPT AND WIN

When I have a choice, I go first. Studies indicate that the first candidate in a selection process has a statistical advantage, all other things being equal. Also, you have the opportunity to preempt the field. You might be so impressive by phone that the quest to interview other speakers diminishes markedly. Busy committee members may have been dreading the entire selection process all along—preempt and win!

Rather than proceed as most speakers do—relating how wonderful one's own presentations are—take a different route initially. Tell the group that you need to know more about them, because realistically you *do* need to know more about them. Speaker David Alan Yoho sums it up nicely: "Suppose you went to see a doctor to talk about your chest pains and the doctor spent the next 20 minutes talking about his degrees, report cards, referral letters, and other awards."

- How many hours or days is the overall meeting?
- What will attendees experience before the speaker comes on?
- Will the big bosses be in the room, or will it simply be the district managers who are free to voice their concerns?

Ask about expectations:

- How should audience members feel when the session ends?
- What should they be able to do, as a result of hearing the presentation?

As the conversation continues, you ask the meeting planner questions that reflect on the bigger picture:

- What is your organization's mission or philosophy?
- What are the two biggest challenges facing your organization?
- What are the two biggest challenges facing your attendees?
- What are you particularly proud of as an organization or industry?

As you learn more, ask more directed questions about what should transpire:

- What types of subtopics do you want the speaker to cover?
- How much emphasis should be put on the subtopics?
- Is a workbook or packet desirable?

Finally, having gotten as much information as you comfortably can during this phase of this crucial call, feel free to start talking about yourself, focusing on the impact and results you can help create!

What if the group likes you but is uncertain of your ability to be successful presenting within their industry? Every speaker had to start somewhere. When you get asked "What background do you have in our industry?" and you have precious little, don't be afraid to say, "Not nearly as much as I'll have on (the date of the meeting). That also means that I'm not rooted to age-old points of view as others within the industry might be. I'll bring new insights and fresh perspectives that will energize the meeting."

SELL THEM ON THE TRUE IMPACT OF A PRESENTATION

Aspiring public speakers are grateful for any feedback that indicates that their presentation was well received.

When we delve more deeply into the true impact a presentation has, four distinct levels emerge: reaction, learning, behavior, and results. When you discuss these distinctions with a meeting planner or a selection committee, and discuss your track record in this context, you can't help but be the one selected:

- *Reaction.* There are several ways that an audience can indicate approval of a presentation. These include applause, laughter at the appropriate times, a standing ovation, high evaluations on the speaker rating sheet, crowding the speaker after the presentation, having many questions, and requesting to have the speaker back.
- *Learning.* In assessing the learning impact of a presentation, explain to committee members how you handle fundamental issues such as, "What do I want audience members to know when they depart? What behaviors, skills, or changes did I observe before they left?" Many speakers establish presentation objectives before they speak to a group. Moreover, to win the booking, some organizations require that a speaker orally or verbally convey presentation objectives. In such cases, through audience participation, planned exercises, or audience response, how can you demonstrate that your "learning objectives" for the presentation were met? Committee members will want to know the answer.

- *Behavior.* A strong positive reaction from audience members and the visible exhibition of learning are desirable outcomes for any speaker. A larger question, however, is "What impact did the presentation have on job performance?"

  It behooves you to make follow-up efforts to determine what changes in behavior, if any, on the parts of audience members resulted from your presentations. Have audience members done anything differently since the presentation? Has their performance improved? Do groups handle their responsibilities with greater ease?

  Occasionally, a host organization will survey their members or staff to determine the impact of a presentation or training session. If you can get a hold of such reports, do so, because little else in this world will tell you how you can be even more effective as a presenter. Moreover, this data is invaluable in influencing your next client.

- *Results.* Of all the impacts that your presentation can have, achieving results is indisputably what hiring organizations care about most. Anytime you can gain feedback that indicates your presentation benefited productivity, it is to your extreme benefit.

SELL THEM ON YOUR
OVERALL SERVICES

When you're being considered for a presentation, particularly in those instances when the meeting planner or committee does not have significant experience in managing the full gamut of responsibilities involved, you can serve as a highly valuable resource to the organization. This benefits you, the meeting planner, the selection committee, and the host organization in major ways: (1) You help close the deal by positioning yourself as more than a speaker, but as a key resource and a friend; (2) the meeting planner saves valuable time in planning and increases the probability of having a successful meeting; and (3) the host organization potentially saves cost, labor, and other resources as well as having a higher probability of achieving its meeting objectives.

Here are some of the ways that you can assist meeting planners.

- *Consult on meeting room setups.* An astute public speaker automatically suggests the best room setup for her or his presentation. Based on the time of day, for example, it might make sense to have participants facing different directions so that the sun does not distract them.
- *Discuss audiovisual considerations.* If you have knowledge of overhead projectors and screens, slide projectors, closed circuit monitoring equipment, and so on, you can be a valuable resource for the meeting planner who has little experience in these areas.
- *Help develop the theme.* Perk up if and when a group asks for advice on its conference theme. If you have experience in this area, you can help develop a theme from which answers come as to what kinds of topics are necessary, what the sequence ought to be, and what the overall meeting objectives are.
- *Assist in house presenters.* When you're a veteran speaker compared to who else is on the program, your assistance to the other presenters can be invaluable, so as a bargaining chip, suggest the possibilities. Even if you were to spend as little as 5 to 10 minutes on the phone with two or three other presenters, your assistance could be enormously helpful.
- *Review program materials.* Related to the previous suggestions, early in the game, when speaker selection is yet not complete, ask if the program materials, be they flyers, announcements, or brochures, are still in formation. Why not volunteer to lend a hand and review such program materials? Your willingness to do so could seal the deal for you. In 5 or 10 minutes, you could perform an invaluable service in terms of how effective the program materials prove to be.
- *Volunteer to serve in an additional capacity.* When a meeting planner or selection committee has you on the phone and is seeking to know if you would be the right presenter for a particular presentation, probe further to find if the group could also benefit from your services as a panel moderator or panel participant, an MC at an awards dinner, or an introducer or announcer for other presentations or other conference activities. You might also offer to assist in administering a post speech evaluation.

BUT WE CAN'T AFFORD YOU

Many speakers who would otherwise have served admirably at a conference, are stopped in their tracks when told, "We like you, but we can't afford you." There is an axiom in the meeting industry that is worth considering: "The speaker with the highest fee costs the least." This is true either because such speakers generate more revenue for the host organization, more interest, or more of something valuable. The speakers who charge little routinely cost the group the most.

"So, what are you selling? You're selling outcomes and return on investment," says veteran trainer Ron Karr. "If the outcome is perceived as invaluable, clients will do what it takes to acquire the solution." Prudent meeting planners will not risk an inexpensive speaker on an expensive meeting.

Costs Can Be Deceiving

After you've discussed the results or outcomes you've been able to help other groups achieve, proudly state your fee. Charge high rates with confidence. They expect it if you're good.

If you're asked, "Do you negotiate your fees?" respond by saying, "Occasionally I negotiate my fees, but you're not asking if I simply reduce my fee for no reason are you?" Most likely that's precisely what they intended. Questioning them about it often deflates their gambit.

> The ability to see the situation as the other side sees it is one of the most important skills a negotiator can possess.
> Roger Fisher and William Ury, *Getting to Yes*

Groups willing to pay more for the right program often seek to bargain for extras. Are there instances when you can legitimately fit an organization's budget without altering your fee? "Absolutely," says speaker and negotiating specialist Jim Hennig, PhD. He says, "You can charge different fees in different situations." For example, the following may require special fee consideration:

1. *Multiple engagements.* Two or more bookings deserve quantity discounts. When somebody hesitates at your fee, ask what other meetings and conferences they're having in the next 12 months. Suggest that the more they hire you, the less it will cost per event.

2. *Dual purpose engagement.* Maximize your potential to any group by exploring all of their needs and seeking to meet more than the one initially requested. (See Chapter 26.)

3. *A shared speaker.* Many times when an organization cannot afford a speaker, they include another organization to share the costs. Chamber of Commerce groups often do this, as do local chapters of national organizations. Two local chapters in close proximity may join forces to retain a speaker who simultaneously would address both chapters.

4. *Tape, book, and product sales.* Many speakers quote different speaking fees when they are able to sell tapes, books, or different products. Some speakers provide a percentage of the product sales back to the organization. Jeffrey Isomer says, "When there's ABSOLUTELY no way to get your entire fee because of their budget, ask them to share half the cost of your products with participants. If your presentation is compelling, 75 to 90 percent of the audience will buy your products at half price. The host organization pays the other half. This will make up the lost revenue for you."

"Products and books often come from another budget area," observes Isomer. "The decision maker loves the fact the audience members are investing in more training, and the audience appreciates that the organization is willing to share the product cost. You get full retail for your product—everyone feels like they got a great deal—especially you."

5. *Trades.* Many speakers will trade a portion, or all, of their speaking fee for a needed product or service from the organization hiring them. Some examples include cellular phones and phone time, future hotel accommodations, advertising, automobile leases, and insurance. You might ask for a spouse airline ticket or extended stay at the vacation site of the meeting, knowing the meeting planner often has special airline rates or complimentary rooms. If a group offers to pay only 75 percent of your fee, suggest they publish four articles monthly, before and after your presentation, and that they offer you a full-page advertisement for your products in their monthly publication.

6. *Different fees for special groups.* Speakers often establish discounts for nonprofit organizations, government agencies, health care, or educational institutions. Some speakers grant lower rates to local or in-state groups.

DON'T QUIT UNTIL YOU'RE BOOKED

If you perceive that a group wants you, tell them, "If we can hammer out the details, I'm highly committed to having this work and to offering a superlative presentation to your members (or staff). Are you determined to make this work as well?"

Once you arrive at this point, you increase the chances of closing the deal instead of merely ping-ponging between issues without coming to agreement. Adopt the attitude that when a group calls you, you're going to work with them to find a way to satisfy their needs and yours.

Your best deal may yet be in formation. Keep the conversation alive long after most others would have quit.

WHAT IF YOU LOSE THE BOOKING?

If you fail to close a deal, remain objective! Probe for the underlying issues, and ask yourself the following tough questions:

- Did I do my homework on the group (given time to do so) or did I try to wing it?
- Did I emphasize the results that I could help them achieve or did I simply tout my credentials?
- Did I listen patiently and then answer questions or concerns convincingly or did I jump in with preconceived answers?
- Did I offer my full and undivided attention to this group's needs and concerns or was I preoccupied with something else?
- Did I go the extra mile in addressing the prospect's issues or could I have been seen as uncooperative?
- Did I seek to superimpose my ideas over those of the prospect?
- Did I employ language appropriate to the caller and the group, or did I come off sounding high and mighty?

Rather than feel defeated or deflated when the group selects another speaker, remain professional. Regard the interlude as another step in your overall development, learn what you can, and leave the meeting planner feeling as if it makes sense to re-contact you for future meetings.

Sales trainer Jim Pancero advises not to be shy. Ask: "What would have been required for me to have been equal competition for the speaker you chose?" Don't ask what it would have taken to exceed their selection because that would put pressure on them.

"Once finding out what it would have taken to make it a harder decision, you have valuable information on what to do next time," says Pancero. "This also lets the meeting planner know that you're still in the ball game and interested in getting the job next time."

What Goes into a Speaker Agreement?

When a meeting planner asks you to send your speaker agreement, you're as good as hired. I advocate keeping speaker contracts, also known as speaker agreements, as simple as possible. Most meeting planners, whether acting alone or with a committee, accept most speaker agreements carte blanche. Any concerns usually are handled over the phone prior to submission of the agreement.

The more complex the agreement—the more clauses it has and the more involved it is—the longer it takes for your client to get approval and the greater the risk that the date won't be booked. Also, if you are booked, there will be a greater probability of you having to make major concessions.

Note that the language throughout is simple and straightforward and, hence, can be read and understood by anyone—no use of "heretofore," "whereby," or "wherein"! I'll expand on a few points.

I. CONTACT

For your own peace of mind as well as for all future communication, you want to have the client's name, address, phone, fax, zip, and e-mail prominently listed.

Speaker Agreement

Program Agreement

Speaker: Jeff Davidson, MBA, CMC   **Client:**

Client Contact:

E-mail: _____

Phone: _____   **Fax:**_____

Topic Areas: *Streamlining Your Career and Your Life*

Presentation Date: Feb 28   **Time Jeff presents:** 2:00 to 4:00 P.M.

No. of Attendees: 250, plus or minus 25   **Location:** Washington, D.C.

Speaking Fee: $X000, no travel expense, no hotel, no ground transport, and no other costs.

Deposit Due: $½X000—This nonrefundable portion of Jeff's speaking fee is required as confirmation, to be returned with this signed agreement. The balance is due directly following the presentation.

Cancellation: In the *highly unlikely* event that this agreement is canceled by the client *and* the unlikely event that the date is not resold by Jeff Davidson, MBA, CMC, the following scheduled percentage of the fee will be in effect from the time Jeff Davidson receives written notification:

   0–40 working days prior to scheduled engagement = 100 percent
   41–80 working days prior to scheduled engagement = 75 percent

Meeting Room Arrangement: Jeff is 6'3" and prefers to interact closely with the audience. Hence, a wraparound or chevron seating plan is preferable. (Okay if seating pattern is fixed, as in an auditorium or conference room.) Jeff will visit the room well beforehand and at least 30 minutes before the scheduled starting time.

Audiovisual Needs: A lavaliere (clip-on microphone, wireless preferred); an overhead projector and screen; one display table 3' by 6' or larger.

Educational Materials: Jeff will send a master copy of the participant packet. Is there an additional budget for educational materials for this program? If so, would you like to make my section of the conference extra special by having an educational workbook and cassettes or books provided for each attendee?

[ ] Yes, we would like to order _____ copies of XYZ product

Speaker Agreement (Continued)

(Optional) Filming: The Breathing Space Institute grants to the Client a nonexclusive, nontransferable, nonsublicensable license and right to make a videotape recording for internal purposes, of Jeff Davidson's presentation and to produce and retain a copy of the recorded Presentation in $1/2''$ VHS video tape format only. Every video in the opening billboard of each Tape shall read:

> © 2003 Breathing Space Institute. All Rights Reserved. No portion of this tape may be reproduced without written permission from the Breathing Space Institute, 2417 Honeysuckle Road, #2A, Chapel Hill, North Carolina 27514.

[ ] The Client wishes to film on video.

(Optional) Taping: The same guidelines above apply for cassette taping. The client further agrees to provide to Jeff Davidson at the client's cost and expense the original Master Recording, within seven (7) days following the Presentation.

[ ] The Client wishes to tape on cassette.

Please Complete, Sign, and Return One Copy of this Agreement along with a 50 percent deposit to Jeff Davidson by December 11 to Confirm the Engagement

Authorized Signature: _____ **Client:** _____

---

2. NUMBER OF ATTENDEES AND LOCATION

The number of attendees helps guide you in your planning as the presentation date approaches. The location, which can be vastly different than the client's location, can give you an idea of how far people are traveling to attend, as well as define your own travel time frames.

3. SPEAKING FEE AND TRAVEL EXPENSES

This needs to be spelled out succinctly: List your total fee; then, if there are any reductions in fee, put them in parentheses. Some speakers offer a predetermined discount to nonprofit organizations.

Travel arrangements may vary widely from one organization to another and from one speaker to another. State how travel expenses and accommodations are to be handled. It inconveniences everyone involved when reimbursement policy and procedures are not spelled out in advance. The following gives an example of the style of language many speakers employ in their speaker agreements: "We will make all necessary travel arrangements, pro-rating airfare when the itinerary involves additional clients. You will make all necessary hotel arrangements. Please be sure to guarantee reservations for a late arrival and notify our office of the confirmation number. Please arrange for room tax and authorized food expense to be direct-billed to your master account."

Another popular travel clause used by speakers when they prefer to handle airfare arrangements themselves is as follows: "Due to the speaker's hectic schedule it is best to coordinate speaker's travel plans through his or her local travel agency. The speaker always seeks Super Saver airfares by scheduling as far in advance as is practical."

If you're driving to an engagement, it's standard practice to charge the host organization 36 cents per mile. This figure is based on the latest established figures from the IRS.

4. DEPOSIT DUE

All professional speakers I know ask for 50 percent deposit up front, to be received usually within 10 to 14 working days following the signed return of the speaker agreement. As discussed in the next chapter, collecting this deposit is fundamental to your business and to maintaining the integrity of your speaking calendar. Once you have half of your speaking fee in hand, you are both obligated and protected.

5. CANCELLATION

As discussed previously, in the event of a cancellation you want to alter the range of days and percentages of the fee that you retain prior to the scheduled presentation. For speakers who have had some canceled events or when potential disruption looms on the horizon, insert added clarification regarding their refund policy. For example, "If the event is canceled, the speaker will gladly refund the entire deposit if he is able to rebook the date." Or, "If the client cancels the presentation, the speaker agrees to apply the deposit to a rescheduled appearance within six months from the originally scheduled presentation. If such rescheduling does not occur, the speaker will refund the deposit if he or she is able to rebook the original date with another client."

6. AUDIOVISUAL NEEDS

State your preference in microphones, and details of other audiovisual needs will follow. I don't want to provide too much detail here because the mission of the speaker agreement is to garner a booking with a 50 percent deposit. In the same package I do include a checklist specifically on audiovisual needs and room setup preference.

7. EDUCATIONAL MATERIALS

If you're offering a participant packet, commonly referred to as a "handout," say so and when you intend to supply master copies to the meeting planner. Don't fall into the trap of bringing all copies yourself.

Some speakers feel compelled to spell out that they will be supplying master copies only, and will not be responsible for copying or assembling copies for each attendee. For example, "Per our agreement, we will provide you with complete originals of the speaker's participant packet at no additional fee for you to duplicate and assemble. You will be responsible for copying and assembling enough copies for all attendees, having them shipped and ready at the meeting site, and distributing them based on the speaker's instructions."

Elaborating on this clause makes sense when you routinely speak to large groups and/or you are flying from city to city and it would be simply untenable for you to be schlepping large packages of participant packets. If you have a book, tape, or other products, give the meeting planner the opportunity to purchase the product at a significant discount. Some meeting planners frown on any mention of product sales during a presentation but, surprisingly, are not averse to ordering such items in advance.

During the preliminary conversation leading to a booking, many speakers ask if the host organization has an additional budget for educational materials, and specifically, for this program. If the answer is affirmative the speaker then asks, "Would you like to make my section of the conference extra special by having an educational workbook and cassettes provided for each attendee?"

8. CLOSING INSTRUCTIONS

The closing instructions ask the meeting planner to complete, sign, and return one copy of this agreement. Include two agreement copies, both of which you have signed and dated. I routinely include a self-addressed, stamped envelope and a Post-it pad on one of the copies with the handwritten note "Please sign both, retain one, and send one to Jeff."

Variations on Product Sales

Speakers with products offer different types of clauses in their speaker agreement. For example, "The speaker extends to the client the option to buy his book at the special quantity price of $X each, plus shipping, when purchasing quantities of 10 or more."

Speakers then offer the meeting planner the opportunity to check one of two boxes, followed by the words "Yes, we wish to exercise this option! Please ship X number of copies prior to the program date." The other option is, "We regret that we cannot exercise the option at this time. You may make your educational materials available for individual purchase at the time of the program."

Note, that there is no option for not making educational materials available! Some speakers do this intentionally. It is bold but not so aggressive as to turn off meeting planners. If the meeting planner doesn't wish to have any educational materials at the session, he or she will probably write a small note right on the agreement, but certainly will mention it over the phone should the topic come up.

Some speakers include a paragraph that refers to educational materials on an attached page. For example,

The speaker has other educational materials available and many of his speaking clients request that he makes them available at the presentation site so that the audience participants can purchase them for educational reinforcement. If you'd like the speaker to provide these materials for your audience members, please initial here.

Some speakers then add a page titled "Program Reinforcement Materials" or "Educational Materials," which essentially represents their product order form reworked slightly and tailored to the individual circumstances.

TALK ABOUT PRODUCTS

Professional speaker Elizabeth Jeffries forgoes including extra verbiage on her speaker contract and instead has a conversation about educational products. Once she has secured the engagement, Jeffries says:

> As you may know, I am a published author of a popular book on leadership. Many of my clients include this inspirational business book as part of the learning materials for the program I am presenting. It reinforces my message and helps insure that the ideas are put into action when audience members return to their workplaces. Besides, it seems as if people listen more to someone when they know that he or she is an author! We can offer discounted prices for group purchases. What would it take for you to include the book for your managers?

The last sentence is key, and Jeffries has long labored over it. "What would it take" is a far softer and more effective approach than other harder types of sell. Some meeting planners who might be resistant to a harder sell find themselves wanting to cooperate with Jeffries because of her gentle but focused approach.

SAY IT IN A LETTER

Some speakers make mention of product sales in a cover letter to the meeting planner and do not include product sales in their speaker agreement form. For example, if any mention of product sales has been made over the phone, the following paragraph might be inserted in a cover letter to the meeting planner.

> As we discussed, we recommend that you include a copy of my book as part of the program materials. Beyond lending credibility to the presentation it provides an excellent resource on and reinforcement of the strategies and ideas I will be presenting. An $18.95 value, I am providing it to you at the special quantity price of $12 each for this presentation. I have enclosed a copy of it for your review—enjoy! We can work out the final count nearer to the presentation date.

This, too, is a softer sell that can prove effective with meeting planners who have been besieged by speakers offering products of all manner, using ploys of all kinds.

AUDIO AND VIDEO TAPING

How do you handle requests from the client for audio or video taping your session? If you're relatively new at public speaking, you may consider it an honor to be audio or video taped, and you may want a professional product; hence, your terms are not stringent. On the far end of the spectrum, if you're a highly paid professional speaker, with lots of products, and are fearful of diluting your own market by allowing the client too much leniency, then your terms will be more restrictive.

On pages 202–203 is a sample video taping agreement that I adapted from Dan Burrus, a savvy professional speaker who has developed many high-end products specifically for clients as well as for general retail sales.

For audiotaping, Burrus issues an agreement for association clients that essentially charges a per tape royalty. For each tape sold he receives a percentage of the sale or a predetermined fixed dollar amount. When corporate clients wish to audio tape him, Burrus charges a flat fee, usually several thousand dollars, plus a royalty percentage per tape. He does so to protect himself in his chosen marketplace.

Burrus' taping agreements enable him to depart following his presentation with the audio or video master in hand. Thereafter he sends a copy of the tape with his company label on it back to the host organization. The

04–04 Audio Taping Agreement

Jeff Davidson, MBA, CMC
2417 Honeysuckle Road #2A
Chapel Hill NC 27514-6819
919–932–1996 ▪ Fax: 919–932–9982

AUDIO TAPING AGREEMENT
Client Name
Address
Phone, Fax, E-mail

1. Jeff Davidson, MBA, CMC (hereinafter referred to as "Jeff Davidson"), hereby grants to the Client a nonexclusive, nontransferable, nonsublicensable license and right to make an audio recording (hereinafter referred to as "Master Recording") of Jeff Davidson's presentation at the above-identified program (hereinafter referred to as "Presentation") and to produce as well as sell copies of the recorded Presentation in audio cassette format only (hereinafter referred to as "Cassettes") solely in the United States and Canada (hereinafter referred to as "Licensed Territory") for a period of ___ days following the Presentation date. At the expiration of this license period, all rights herein granted to Client shall expire and thereafter Client shall not produce, give away, exchange, or sell the Cassettes or retain any copies of the Master Recording.

2. Client hereby acknowledges and agrees that Jeff Davidson shall be and is the owner of all right, title, and interest in and to the Presentation, Presentation Material, and the Master Recording, including the copyright. Client further agrees to provide to Jeff Davidson at Client's sole cost and expense:

   a. The original Master Recording, no later than seven (7) days after the end of the license period.

   b. One (1) Cassette copy of Master Recording no later than one (1) week following the Presentation;

   Client shall mail the Cassette and deliver or mail the Master Recording by insured carrier at Client's expense to Jeff Davidson as addressed above.

04–04 Audio Taping Agreement (Continued)

3. Client shall affix to each Cassette labels provided by Jeff Davidson. (Client may affix a special convention label to Side "A," and if this is done, then Client will affix Jeff Davidson's label to Side "B.")

4. Client shall not produce or sell more than ___ Cassettes, which is the estimated total number of people attending the Presentation.

5. The Cassettes shall be of first-class merchantable quality, consistent with prevailing industry standards for such products. Jeff Davidson reserves the right to review and approve the Master Recording quality prior to Cassette distribution to confirm that Jeff Davidson's quality standards are met. If said standards are not met, Jeff Davidson shall notify Client and as a condition of and prior to Client's right to distribute the Cassettes. Client shall take all necessary corrective action to meet Jeff Davidson's standards. Client shall not distribute any Cassettes that do meet such standards.

6. All Cassettes, labeling, packaging, and promotional material shall be produced, distributed, and sold by Client in accordance with all applicable federal, state, and local laws and regulations. Client shall not issue any material that will reflect adversely on the name of Jeff Davidson.

7. Client shall pay an audio taping fee of $_____ within _____ days after the Presentation as a condition of Client's right to produce and sell Cassettes.

8. In the event it is necessary for Jeff Davidson to enforce the terms and conditions of this Agreement, the prevailing party shall be awarded its reasonable attorney fees, costs, and expenses for such action.

JEFF DAVIDSON, MBA, CMC   **CLIENT**

_____   _____
(Authorized Signature)   **(Authorized Signature)**

Date: _____   Date: _____

client may use and sell that tape based on whatever other negotiations have occurred between Burrus and the client.

Unlike other speakers, Burrus also maintains a corporate highlight video contract whereby the client is allowed to use no more than, say, five minutes of his presentation, at no fee. Burrus retains the master and edited master and any other copies made on site that day.

PHILOSOPHY BEFORE PRODUCT SALES

Burrus' philosophy is that any taping is an additional service and therefore merits an additional fee.

Burrus carefully explains to clients that he sells information in many forms. Speaking is simply one of them. A speaking fee is based on selling a single speech to a single audience. If they want additional forms of his information, which could represent a book, tapes, newsletters, CDs, and so on, there will be an additional fee. Burrus says, "It is important to limit the client's right to the stated intended uses, otherwise your information will be reproduced, transcribed, electronically published, and before you know it, you are competing with yourself at no profit."

Because Burrus is at the top of the speaking business as an in-demand futurist, and he continually provides leading edge observations and research findings to clients, his argument is well conceived and highly appropriate. Most other speakers do not so stringently guard their materials. Many regard the distribution of audio- and videotapes of their presentations as promotional tools that may result in additional bookings.

ALTERNATIVE PATHS

One professional speaker routinely allows taping but with a varying fee structure that ranges all the way from free to as much as double the speaking fee, all depending on the situation. This speaker always requires the original master, and wants to have in writing from the client exactly how the recording will be used. The ultimate goal, however, in each case is to best serve the client's needs.

Another speaker, veteran Rosita Perez, asks that the audience be miked so that listeners can hear the laughter generated from her presentations. Hence, whenever she is audio taping, it is highly likely that the tapes she is creating represent both potential products and/or demo tapes that can be submitted to new meeting planner prospects inquiring about her services.

Dan Burrus' agreements include a time limit that, in essence, makes them licenses. At a predetermined time, the client may no longer sell or distribute his audio or video products. This clause further protects Burrus, and conveys to the client that in selling the tape to generate revenue, time is of the essence

It's not a bad idea to strive to convert every presentation that you give into a product. Many meeting planners seek to videotape speakers either for a fee or as an added value to the client. Joe Calloway from Tennessee says, "I've had great response from clients with the following idea: If they are going to video my speech, I ask if they would like me to customize it for them by taking a few minutes either before or after my speech to let their video crew do an interview segment with me."

Calloway explains that it's not an interview as much as "it's me talking into the camera—I'm usually sitting in a chair—and making some comments about their company and how my ideas from the speech can be of use to them." Calloway reports that the tactic gets a great reaction from the client and that the meeting planners love it.

OTHER ARRANGEMENTS

What about the speaker who has little or no concern as to the client's taping? Some speakers allow audio taping all the time without a fee. They often ask for one free copy and suggest that both the client and the speaker become co-copywrite holders. The client may sell the tape and the speaker may sell the tape. In a big world and a big marketplace the theory is that it's unlikely that the two vendors will collide.

I prefer to limit the client to selling within his or her own organization or industry. That way, all other industries remain open to me.

27

Show Me the Money

The aspiring public speaker is often delighted and amazed to find out how much he or she can charge for a professional presentation. Regardless of your fee, if you don't receive payment, you haven't earned a dime. It behooves the professional speaker to ensure that he or she does receive payment and in a timely manner. Most professional speakers insert clauses in their speaking agreements that state how they wish to be paid.

We're going to focus on the importance of collecting a deposit up front, long in advance of ever giving the presentation. This element alone gives you more protection and assurance than nearly anything else you could request. Later, we'll focus on what it takes to earn big fees.

Let's start with a hypothetical fee, $3,000. Suppose the XYZ Company calls you in January and wants to book you for a date in June. As a result of your telephone discussions, the client understands how much you charge and has agreed to your fee. Invariably, he or she will ask you to send your speaker agreement form or contract. If you can send your own agreement, you can largely dictate your own terms.

In the case of a January booking for a June event, I would suggest the following terms. First, state that you ask for one-half of the fee upon completion of the agreement. If the event is canceled for any reason, you are in a superior negotiating position. Remember to state in your agreement the terms for payment should the client cancel.

In general, you want to inform the client as follows:

In the *highly unlikely* event that this agreement is canceled by the client *and* the unlikely event that the date is not resold by Jeff Davidson, MBA,

CMC, the following scheduled percentage of the fee will be in effect from the time Jeff Davidson receives written notification:

01–60 working days prior to scheduled engagement = no refund

61–90 working days prior to scheduled engagement = 50 percent refund

91–120 working days prior to scheduled engagement = 75 percent refund

121–150 working days prior to scheduled engagement = full refund

PROTECTION VIA EFFECTIVE LANGUAGE

Proper terms and language give protection to both you and the client. "And if the speaker is not likely to re-book this date . . ." also benefits both parties. If you are able to re-book the date, you return *all* of the client's money. If you are not able to re-book the date, you can still benefit the client by offering to use the deposit toward some other date in the future, preferably within six months from the canceled date. When a large, high-tech firm canceled my speaking engagement with them last year (my first such instance in 19 years), I offered the company a nine-month period in which to re-book me. I held the deposit applied and maintained that price for them, regardless of whether my fee increased in general.

Note the sliding scale for refunded amounts, depending on how late the client cancels.

Your Precious Inventory—Dates on the calendar are the speaker's only inventory. If somebody ties up your time, then ends up not hiring you, they have essentially tied up your inventory and perhaps even spoiled it so that it can't be resold. Hence, you are entitled to keep some of the money.

Here is the beauty of this sliding scale, based on how far in advance you are booked by clients. Suppose that the client booked you nine months in advance. How might your scale change? Here is an example of terms I have actually used with a client:

01–60 working days prior to scheduled engagement = No refund

61–90 working days prior to scheduled engagement = 50 percent refund

91–180 working days prior to scheduled engagement = 75 percent refund

181–270 working days prior to scheduled engagement = Full refund

Suppose the client books you only three months out. How might the terms change?

01–45 working days prior to scheduled engagement = No refund

46–90 working days prior to scheduled engagement = 50 percent refund

As you can see, in each case, you want to both secure a 50 percent deposit and offer terms that protect you to best advantage.

SOME CONCERNS, NO DISPUTES

In all my years of professional speaking, I have had no client dispute, refute, or even discuss the sliding scale aspect of my speaker agreement. On a handful of occasions, over all those years, a few meeting planners have discussed the 50 percent deposit requirement.

Some asked if they could pay by credit card. Some said their organization's policy is to not make such payments so far in advance, but they could, by special request, perhaps pay 30 or 60 days prior to the presentation date. In those few cases, in consideration of the size, prestige, and reputation of the organizations, I agreed.

The more prominent your client, the greater protection you have. Your meager speaker fee—and it is meager compared to the overall cost of the meeting—is not going to bankrupt major firms. Moreover, if they were to unfairly withhold your payment, the trouble you could cause would be far more costly than the size of your fee. Consequently, as cited earlier at the close in my speaker agreement, for added protection, I state specifically:

Please Complete, Sign, and Return One Copy of this Agreement along with a 50 percent deposit to Jeff Davidson by December 11 to Confirm the Engagement

I do this so that the meeting planner has no confusion whatsoever as to the fact that I expect the deposit to be included with this returned signed agreement. Generally, I offer a completion date 15 to 18 working days past the time in which I send the speaker agreement to the meeting planner.

On occasion, meeting planners will call, fax, or e-mail stating that they are processing the agreement, but it is not likely that they will be able to make payment by the date I have listed at the bottom of the speaker agreement. In such cases, I automatically tell them, "Okay, cross out that date and insert the date that is convenient for you." Their newly inserted date has always been within a week or two of what I had originally requested. Given that the presentation date is still many months off, you can afford to give meeting planners some slack as to when they will submit the deposit.

OBTAINING THE SECOND PAYMENT

My speaker agreement requests that I receive the second payment directly following my presentation:

The balance [of Jeff's fee] *is due directly following the presentation.*

Even with such wording, about one in four meeting planners fails to hand me the check directly following my presentation. I never raise the issue on site—it would seem far too mercenary. In such cases the check usually arrives by mail between one and four weeks after the presentation. I have experienced five cases in which groups took longer than one month to make the payment. When this occurred, I wrote a quick note thanking the meeting planners for everything and reminding them that I was awaiting the second half of the speaker fee as per our agreement.

KEYS TO EARNING BIG CHECKS

Invariably, public speakers on the track to becoming professional speakers want to know what it takes to command big checks. In a word, it is celebrity. If you are a politician, actor, best selling author, sports hero, or otherwise a household name, then your speaking fees from the get-go can be over $10,000. However, being a celebrity is not an option for 99.9 percent of public speakers who aspire to professional speaking.

What can you do to raise your speaking fee to its highest possible level? The primary vehicle in achieving high fees is to have people hear fantastic things about you through word of mouth. When clients are calling bureaus or are calling you directly and are requesting your speaker services adamantly, your fee is going to rise.

What if you are new to a group? Dr. Tony Alessandra says, "The best marketing for speakers is to have a strong video-demo with many topics and audiences, bolstered by a strong relationship with a handful of speakers bureaus." In fact, he advocates having fewer marketing items but having all of them be first class.

Your credentials bolster your video. What can you cite within your video, list on your materials, and present on your Web site? Are you the author of any books? How about a highly respected, well-circulated article? Do you hold any positions in noteworthy organizations? Or, do you simply have unique experience? Adding compelling credentials to a strong video demo helps build your ability to charge a high speaking fee (see Part III on *Positioning*).

IN SYNC WORKS BEST

Any materials that you develop, including a one-sheet, brochure, Web site, and any other supportive items need to reflect your fee level. You can't be a $10,000 speaker with a $5,000 brochure. Those investigating your speaking services want and need to see consistency between who you are, what you offer, how much you charge, what materials you supply, and your operating procedures. Anything less than consistency raises red flags.

> Envision that you're receiving several times your actual fee. If you strive to offer a presentation commensurate with that heightened speaker's fee, your actual speaker's fee will rise more quickly than you might otherwise have supposed.

RULE YOUR NICHE

Speakers who become well-known in a small niche, perhaps with industry specialists, for example, can often successfully charge high fees. Similarly, if you conduct original research, your fees are bound to rise.

Sometimes, as a result of luck or circumstances, a speaker can temporarily charge a high fee. This is the case of U.S. journalist Nicholas Daniloff who was on assignment in Russia when he was held captive by the Soviets and eventually exchanged for a Soviet spy. On his return to the United States, he was in high demand as a speaker and could charge a high fee while his "celebrity" lasted. After the currency of the event wears off, such instant celebrities have no basis to continue charging a high fee, and may have trouble being booked at all. As a group, business and social forecasters tend to do relatively well. Many groups are eager to have a knowledgeable forecaster at their conference or convention.

GUIDANCE ON FEE LEVELS

As your speaking fee begins to climb and you want to become more aware of what others are charging, you have a variety of tools at your disposal. Many bureau Web sites list speaker fees or ranges of speaker fees. These listings give you a good indication of where you may fall within the spectrum. If you work with bureaus, they may tell you when to raise your fees. Listen carefully, because they know what they're saying.

If a bureau feels confident in booking you at a higher fee, who are you to resist? Sometimes meeting planners will disclose to a speaker that he or she is undercharging. Usually these meeting planners impart such information after having booked the speaker! If you maintain a network of other speakers, and this is highly recommended, exchanging fee information with them on a one-to-one basis does not violate antitrust laws.

Regardless of what you charge, a fundamental speaking fee applies: At every point along the trail, you want to be regarded as a bargain based on your fee. It is okay to be a $10,000 speaker who charges $5,000. It is not okay to be a $5,000 speaker who charges $10,000.

A CAREFUL MOVE

Make your move to another fee level carefully. When those booking you tell you that your fee is too low, raise it.

Generally, it is advisable to move up in measured increments. If you are charging $5,000, perhaps you should rise to $6,000 or $7,500. You don't, however, leap from $5,000 to $10,000 unless compelling circumstances prevail.

If you set your fee at a certain level but later find that you are not commanding that fee often enough, it can be difficult to scale back. Backpedaling isn't pretty. Many a speaker has backpedaled and accepted lower fees, often in the form of outrageous concessions, discounts, and other ploys for accepting engagements at far less than one's stated speaker fee.

As you learned in Part III, whatever you charge is likely to be one of the strongest indicators of your value in the marketplace, given that you haven't completely overcharged. A $5,000 speaker is categorically deemed to be more effective than a $3,500 speaker. A $10,000 speaker is regarded as altogether being in a different league than a $5,000 speaker. The $10,000 speaker is expected to deliver on a higher level at every engagement.

If you have any reservations about charging more than your current fee, then you already have your answer: Don't raise your fee.

PART V

GROUNDWORK

Once you book an engagement, you need to take care of many issues in advance of your speech so that you have the highest probability of success. Part V covers a diverse array of topics, including a variety of pre-speech considerations and preparations. Your dual mission is to understand the groups to which you'll be speaking and to work with meeting planners to ensure mutual wins.

Specific topics include managing your time, doing homework on your future audiences, deciding how specific to make your presentations, staying in touch until show time, comprehending the dynamics of meeting facilities, and moving toward mastery by "owning the room" whenever you speak.

28

Responsiveness and Balance

Ralph Waldo Emerson once said, "We form habits and then our habits form us." Realistically, regardless of what work you set out to do on a given day, there will always be more things competing for your time and attention than you can possibly respond to. There will be a constant flow of mail and e-mail. People will call. You'll have to send out packages. You'll receive things that require your attention. Do you have the strength to focus on the few things that will propel your speaking career?

Make work easier for yourself. Set up systems within your office so that you're prepared for incoming tasks. As we're about to discuss, if someone calls and wants to get your demo, you need to have the package in a near-ready state. Ideally, you'll have everything ready except for the final cover letter that you will address to the caller.

The key point for any speaker is this: Much of what goes on in your office is predictable. Therefore, things can be prepared for in advance.

RAPIDLY REPLYING TO MEETING PLANNERS

Even if you've been diligent in developing the array of marketing vehicles that will support you in your quest to garner speaking engagements, unless you have the ability to respond quickly when meeting planners call, too often someone else gets the booking.

The most effective speakers can find things when they need them. They are aware of the resources at their disposal, and they create personal systems to draw upon. Top speakers, not coincidentally, are super organized, and they are able to synthesize the diverse elements necessary for high achievement: managing people, resources, tasks, funds, and themselves.

You don't have to have a cell phone and pager by your side at every moment in order to respond quickly to an inquiry, although many professional speakers have these capabilities. Rather, you only have to field calls, gather information about the caller, submit requested materials, create effective follow-up communications and contacts, and dramatically increase your probability of landing the speaking engagement.

PREARRANGED ELEMENTS

Sit down at your computer keyboard and start typing. Would the clicks be audible to someone on the other end of a phone call? If so, replace your current keyboard with a no-click keyboard. These are relatively inexpensive and widely available. The reason you want to make this exchange is so that you can take notes on your computer while conversing with the meeting planner without running the risk of disrupting your conversation.

For the conversation itself, you want to get an answering machine that has two-way recording capabilities. These were more available in the early 1980s than they are today, but, with a little digging, you can find one. Look for the feature "two-way recording" on the packages of the answering machines that you investigate. The models change so quickly that it is hard to recommend one here; however, over the years, Panasonic and Radio Shack have carried high-quality machines.

When meeting planners call, two-way recording will prove to be invaluable. Sometimes people catch us off guard and we can't take notes fast enough. Often, the meeting planners give us the essence of what their group needs then and there on the first phone call.

Armed with that knowledge, you have a high probability of being successful in both landing the engagement and making a successful presentation. In subsequent discussions, you can prove that you understand the needs of the media planner and/or speaker selection committee. You will demonstrate that you are a good listener, you are going to be easy to work with, and you are client-focused.

DOUBLING YOUR PHONE PRODUCTIVITY THROUGH HEADSETS

Whether you and your staff use the phone five times a day or all day long, simple, inexpensive technology is available to immediately double your phoning efficiency. If you need both hands free to take notes or maintain better organization during a phone call, the typical phone receiver is not practical—you have to balance the receiver between the ear and shoulder while taking notes or leafing through files. Sometimes it drops on the desk. Sometimes you have to put it down or switch to the dreadful speaker-phone option. One of the best ways to alleviate such problems and attain greater efficiency and convenience is the telephone headset.

Using headsets also helps you to minimize distractions. While you are wearing earphones, you don't hear a lot of the background noise that is typical with regular phones. You are not likely to hear phones ring in the next office, and your attention isn't diverted.

USING CONTACT MANAGEMENT SOFTWARE

Undoubtedly, you already have telemarketing or contact management software. Popular brands include ACT, Goldmine, and Microsoft Office. Set up a directory or field exclusively for meeting planners. When a meeting planner calls, you want to be able to quickly enter his or her name, full contact information, the names of other important parties within the organization, and other information that is relevant to the situation. Anything that you miss will be captured by the two-way recording machine.

Pocket Dictators

Voice recognition software is not yet viable for your needs. Thus, you might want to have a pocket dictator nearby. Even if you are a fast typist on a silent keyboard and have two-way recording capabilities, the capability of recording key thoughts on a pocket dictator is invaluable.

MEETING INDUSTRY WEB SITES

You can find the information you want or need about a particular meeting on the Internet, often while you're still on the phone with a caller. Industry Web sites tell where meetings will be held, if transportation is available, how the rooms are configured, and even phone numbers of facility staff members. Here is a brief summary of some of the top sites in the meeting and convention industry:

- www.eventplanner.com   This site offers a directory of meeting planners, a facility search, planning tools, and a special vendor section. Event Planner also maintains message boards for new products, services, and meeting venues.
- www.lecruises.com   Profiles of cruise ships, news of the cruising industry, a bookstore on cruise meetings, and other industry publications are presented here. More importantly, information on keynote speakers, entertainers, and specific onboard programs, as well as links to several cruise lines and meeting associations, are also provided.
- www.mpnetwork.com   Use this site to fill out detailed reservation forms. After doing so, you are privy to a wide variety of features such as an events calendar, supplier data banks, a roster of event sites, destination profiles, a trade show search engine, travel tips, and meeting industry news.
- www.starsite.com   This site provides complete data on meeting and hotel properties by location, name, chain, size, and other criteria. It also contains a supplier search of speakers.
- www.asaenet.org   Hosted by the American Society of Association Executives, you need to register to use this site, but you don't have to be a member of ASAE. It offers a supplier listing, including speakers, speakers bureaus, and other venders such as printers, publishers, and technology services.
- www.iaeme.org   Exposition managers and others can use this site of the International Association for Exposition Management to shop

for services, products, and educational materials. It presents industry news as well as a trade shows directory, a list of upcoming events and seminars, and a job board.

- www.mpiweb.org   As you would expect, the Web site of Meeting Professionals International contains voluminous amounts of information about the meeting industry. In addition to the usual fare, mpiweb.org also includes information on destination resources, other association sites, airline sites, and even a meeting industry "Net" glossary.
- www.pcma.org   This site of the Professional Convention Management Association provides all kinds of research and statistical data about convention management, as well as offering a meeting technology section, checklists for convention management, industry links, and an industry calendar, and convention management news.
- www.tcae.org   This site, maintained by the Trade Show Exhibitors Association, has a comprehensive industry links section that includes allied member product links, trade show industry links, and travel links. It also includes a bookstore, job bank, industry news, and a research section. TSEA White Papers are based on various topics related to the trade show industry.

Alternatively, procure one or more national directories that contain full contact information for corporations and associations. Many contain vast amounts of information on media outlets that becomes highly useful for promotional campaigns. Some of the many worthwhile directories you can choose from include:

- *National Trade and Professional Associations of the United States* Published by Columbia Books, this directory lists 7,500 national trade associations, professional societies, and labor unions. Visit www.columbiabooks.com/books.cfm for information on this volume and the two listed directly below.
- *State and Regional Associations of the United States*   This publication lists 7,300 of the largest, most significant state and regional trade and professional organizations in the United States.
- *Washington*   This book is a guide to 5,000 major organizations and institutions in the U.S. capital and the 25,000 key individuals who run them.

- *Federal Directory*   Offered by Carroll Publishing, this directory combines all three branches of government into one volume and provides bimonthly upgrades throughout the subscription year. It includes nearly 46,000 names, titles, telephone numbers, and e-mail addresses. Visit www.carrollpub.com for more information on this publication.

Why would you want such directories in hand? On many occasions, I have been able to look up the name of a meeting planner's organization in a directory (it can be even faster than using the Web) and interject pertinent information into the conversation. I can say things such as, "You are based in Cleveland; aren't you?" These insights often amaze and delight the caller.

The quality of your interaction with the meeting planner, from the first few seconds, must be so high that you make an impression that is virtually indelible. Whether or not you are ever retained for a speaking engagement by this meeting planner, you have set yourself apart over the phone as few speakers ever will.

THAT'S NOT ALL FOLKS

In a case in which a meeting planner has requested a video demo, presentation kit, or book copy, preassembled packets will help you quickly get them into the mail.

The personalized letter you want to add with such mailings is vital. Begin with a phrase like, "I appreciate our discussion earlier this morning" This phrase conveys that you got right to work on putting the requested package together. It adds to your image of being someone who is highly organized, effective, and responsive.

Five days after your mailing, call to make sure that the meeting planner received the package. This is more than a courtesy call; mail can go astray. Some meeting planners will request that you send packages via overnight mail. I eschew such mailings whenever possible. Most people don't need your information overnight; they simply ask for it reflexively. There is a big difference in mailing a $10 to $15 package when a few dollars for "media mail" will do.

After this initial volley of communication, remember that all of the marketing fundamentals applicable to a traditional vendor-customer relationship apply here: professional, timely follow-up is vital, and you have to take responsibility for meeting the prospect all the way, not half way.

SERVE DESPITE THE CIRCUMSTANCES

What happens if you do not become the speaker for a particular occasion, whether it's because of your fee, schedule, or subject matter? In such cases, continue to serve the meeting planner as if you were booked for his or her engagement. Suggest fellow speakers at the desired fee with requisite skills and applicable speaking topics who might be available. You will be amazed by how delighted meeting planners will be when you make a strong suggestion that meets their needs.

29

The Diversity Factor

In 1982, I attended a week-long executive marketing seminar sponsored by a university. In the last days of the conference, one of the professors referred to an ethnic group with a slang term. Notions of political correctness and sensitivity to diversity issues are at the forefront of social and political arenas, certainly in the enlightened sphere of a college campus. The minority members of the audience in this case immediately felt the sting of this professor's injudicious use of terms. Most people, including myself, looked away from him. He continued on, apparently unaware of his transgression. For the rest of his presentation, hardly anyone looked at him directly; those who did seemed to be sizing him up as opposed to paying attention to his presentation.

INSENSITIVE TERMS

Had this speaker developed the capability to read his audience, he might have discovered that, following his remark, he lost much of the audience.

Hopefully you will never make such an utterance in any of your speeches. You will periodically say or do some things, however, that may prompt the audience to fall out of favor with you. If an unawareness of diversity issues is at the root, there are steps you can take in advance to minimize such occurrences.

EVERYONE CAN BENEFIT

If you appreciate your audiences, strive to ensure that they have the best possible environment in which to receive your message, and pay your respects individually and collectively, you should be able to avoid being biased, insensitive, or socially offensive.

However, anyone can inadvertently make a remark or imply something that causes audience members to feel hurt or disrespected. Lenora Billings-Harris is president of Excel Development Systems and an expert on the topic of diversity. With her audiences, she establishes the premise that "the willingness and ability to create an environment where all people, regardless of differences can achieve their highest potential, contributes to the overall success of the organization

"When we value diversity," says Lenora, "we have a greater capacity and willingness to recognize, understand, respect, and use the unique talents and contributions of all individuals, regardless of their packaging."

Lenora says there's "no place like home" to become more aware of diversity issues and better prepared to make presentations that respect individuals' differences. "Start by examining your own attitudes, values and beliefs," she says, "and how you portray them when interacting with others. The effort is easy—the rewards many."

You might be wondering, "How am I supposed to know about the belief systems of everyone in my audience, especially with large groups?" Relax, it's not that difficult. Your preprogram questionnaire (see previous chapter) will contain questions that ask about the unique aspects of audience members. Review the answers to these questions with the meeting planner in advance and you will understand that you simply can't make assumptions about the composition of your audience.

Most meeting planners will readily raise important diversity issues in addressing their audience. Visit www.religioustolerance.org. Such sites, Lenora says, "often include information on 20 somethings, 30 somethings, seniors, people of color, sexuality, and much more," that can help bring you up to speed.

Before a speaking engagement, ask to speak to five people who will be in your audience. Most meeting planners will readily supply contact information. You could ask specifically to speak to individuals who represent different religious or ethnic groups. You'll be pleased and surprised to learn how eager and willing individuals are to share information with you and how much they appreciate the chance to contribute to your understanding of the overall group.

Lenora also suggests demonstrating your sensitivity to various ethnic groups "if appropriate to your topic or story that you share, by referring to an ethnic heritage month being celebrated."

DEFERENCE TO THE HIGHER SPIRIT

When addressing audiences whose members hold differing religious beliefs, diversity expert Carol Copeland Thomas says, "Refer to religious organizations as faith-based organizations, instead of always using church." Suppose you're speaking to a large audience and you learn that Jains, Sikhs, and Shintos are in the audience. They are all members of long established major world religions.

No one expects you to have a scholar's knowledge of world religions. You should merely make qualifying statements and personal disclaimers when you employ religious references within your presentations. For example, you could use such phrasing as:

"Since I grew up Catholic,"

"In my congregation,"

"As a lifelong Methodist . . ." and so on.

Audience members will appreciate this, since nearly everyone in the audience practices some sort of religion.

"As your own knowledge base expands," says Carol, "include other religious references in your message." Audience members will be impressed if you are a Christian speaker and you can make references to Judaism, for example, or if you are an Islamic speaker and you make references to Hinduism. For more information visit www.tellcarole.com.

LANGUAGE THAT INCLUDES
NOT EXCLUDES

Using the right terms to describe a particular group or individual can be trying. The word "race," for example, was once the preferred term when referring to groups of different ethnicity or nationality. The prevailing view now is that there is only one race—the human race.

Lenora Billings-Harris offers a brief list of current terminology on her Web site: www.Lenoraspeaks.com. The first column offers terms now regarded as socially insensitive; the second column offers currently acceptable alternatives. Today's acceptable terminology will shift, so stay current.

SEXUAL REFERENCES

Sexual diversity requires some special sensitivity. The term *gay* is inclusive of all individuals who are homosexual, but as Lenora points out, in the gay, lesbian, bisexual, and transgender (GLBT) community "It is used specifically to refer to gay men."

A *transgender* person is a man or woman whose physical body does not reflect his or her inner identity. Since the legal status of gay and lesbian unions varies from state to state, the term *domestic partner* is the preferred way of recognizing committed unmarried couples.

Lenora observes that it is acceptable for GLBT individuals who are open about their sexual orientation (referred to as "out") to employ self-directed humor about their status. "It is not okay for a straight speaker to make jokes about GLBT people," she says, "nor is it okay for a speaker to 'out' a GLBT person without his or her permission."

"While the guidelines seem simple enough, here is one you may have to reflect on: It is okay to say 'husband' or 'wife' when referring to your personal situation," says Lenora, but when addressing a group, particularly a large gathering, it is "not okay to only refer to husbands and wives. Include domestic or life partners, and significant others if you want to demonstrate heightened sensitivity to diversity issues."

30

Staying in Touch All the While

Once you've gathered the brunt of the information you need to understand the group, don't coast. Staying in touch with the meeting planner leading up to the presentation, and thereafter as well, is a sound approach to maintaining and building a solid working relationship. Moreover, it helps ensure that your presentation will come off as planned.

Depending on the length of the gap, I schedule a series of communications with the meeting planner, each designed to make it apparent that I have him or her in mind. I let the meeting planner know that I am looking forward to the presentation, that I'll be ready, and that I'm the type of person who can be a resource for the long haul.

Here is the typical contact sequence that I follow for an interim period of six months.

INITIAL CONTACT

When about a quarter of the time has elapsed between being scheduled to present and actually making a presentation, find an article or some other information that would be of interest to the meeting planner. This task is not hard if you revisit the organization's Web site to determine its current issues.

You can then look for more information about these issues using any one of the popular search engines, or by visiting the Web site of any of the popular industry magazines, such as *Successful Meetings, Meetings and Conventions, The Meeting Professional, Professional Speaker,* or *Presentations* to determine if the issue has made its way into these publications or onto these Web sites. Then, it is simply a matter of printing the relevant pages and sending them off with a simple note that says something like, "I thought you might be interested in this."

Following such a mailing, the meeting planner is not likely to respond. That's okay—he or she is extremely busy. Your gesture has probably still been noted. Think of all that your meeting professional's job entails during a given season or year. He or she may deal with many different venders: speakers, coffee service venders, banquet hall sales representatives, airlines, and perhaps even local tour guides.

Include your business card in this first mailing. Don't send a flyer or any other promotional material about yourself. You already have the job with this particular client; therefore, submission of additional marketing materials will be skeptically viewed.

THE SECOND ROUND

About half way between the time you're booked and the scheduled date of the presentation, send a message that simply states that you are looking forward to meeting the meeting planner in person if you haven't done so already, and that you are eager to speak. This message can be sent by e-mail, fax, or traditional mail.

Again, the meeting planner virtually never responds. However, he or she will be impressed by the fact that you took the time to make a second contact.

THE THIRD CONTACT

When three-quarters of the interim time has passed, I send the meeting planner a carefully worded letter that says:

We will soon all be together in (the city of your meeting). I am greatly looking forward to being a part of your gathering. Much time has passed since we first arranged for my presentation, and I wanted to assure you that I will fully meet your needs.

With all that is going on in the world and within your industry, if anything has changed since we first made our arrangements, or if you would like me to accent any particular issues or cover anything that we did not originally discuss, I will be happy to do so. Please call me toll-free at _____, or use fax, e-mail, or mail at your convenience. As always, I am ready to serve you.

Yours truly,

Jeff Davidson

This third contact lends itself to a direct phone call. These days, you are likely to get the meeting planner's voicemail. Proceed anyway. Leave a detailed message that essentially repeats what you said in your letter or e-mail. Use your voice to convey sincerity, support, and professionalism. Well-timed messages can do wonders in terms of enhancing your pre-speech positioning with the meeting planner.

He or she may not reply. Yet, your gesture indicates that you are willing to be flexible, and that speaks volumes about your professionalism. Moreover, it gives the meeting planner the opportunity to request changes.

Letting the meeting planner know that you can be flexible can help relieve considerable stress in addition to logistical burdens. If another speaker can't make it, would you be willing to do a second session? What if the slant that you were going to give your topic is not entirely appropriate, and the meeting planner and his or her organization needs you to approach it from a different angle? The longer the time between the booking and the presentation date, the greater the probability that things have changed and that the meeting planner will respond to your third contact.

The busier the speaker, the less inclined he or she is to maintain this simple system of contact. Yet, you can build this activity into your routine quite simply. Directly following the booking, you can use contact management software to list communication dates in advance. If you work with a staff, your staff people can schedule, track, and monitor this sequence of contacts.

REAPING THE BENEFITS

As a result of these preparations, by the time you arrive at the meeting location and greet the meeting planner, you are among the handful of venders that he or she is truly pleased to meet. I know firsthand that this works. These contacts have helped me form strong bonds with meeting planners.

Your campaign serves two major functions. You provide assurance to the meeting planner on a periodic basis, and you increase the probability of getting another booking, provided that you give a sterling presentation.

Planning for Audience Involvement

Alittle planning can make your efforts to get audience participation even more successful. The effectiveness of any audience-involvement technique is dependent on the context—the kind of presentation you make; to whom you make it; and time, date, room layout, and internal atmospheric considerations.

PREPARATION TECHNIQUES

Many speakers like to involve their audiences at the beginning of their presentations. I find it trite to say "Good morning" or "Good afternoon" to the audience as an inducement for them to say it back. I have seen speakers, however, who do this masterfully and receive a strong return greeting from an eager and receptive audience.

- Some speakers arrive armed with an audience participation packet or printed visual that encourages audience participation. Don't discount this time-honored technique for encouraging involvement—giving audience members something to write on, follow along with, and uniquely mark up creates a higher probability that they'll retain your information.

- Some speakers ask audiences to write down goals for their sessions, goals for when they get back to work, the coming year, or their lives.
- Some speakers issue on-the-spot surveys, usually containing only a few brief questions. Here is an example from my own presentations:

Name   **Date**

A Quick Survey on Breathing Space in Your Life

1. In the last year, the feeling of being time-pressured has:

Decreased Greatly	Decreased Somewhat	Stayed about the Same	Increased Somewhat	Increased Greatly
☐	☐	☐	☐	☐

2. In the past five years, the feeling of being time-pressured has:

Decreased Greatly	Decreased Somewhat	Stayed about the Same	Increased Somewhat	Increased Greatly
☐	☐	☐	☐	☐

3. I am facing more to do today than at this time last year.

Disagree Greatly	Disagree Somewhat	About the Same	Agree Somewhat	Agree Greatly
☐	☐	☐	☐	☐

4. In the past 12 months, I've been taking more work home than previously.

Disagree Greatly	Disagree Somewhat	About the Same	Agree Somewhat	Agree Greatly
☐	☐	☐	☐	☐

5. My best tip for having more breathing space on the job or off of it is:

_____

_____

Employing a quiz as an opening gambit can work well to encourage participation. The quiz does not need to be anything more than 4 or 5 quick questions that can be answered with yes or no, true or false, or a score such as 1 to 5. The speaker can then review the quiz with the entire audience and encourage people to voice their individual answers.

Exercise Card

Breathing Space Exercises

1. Give cards to the first five attendees. The card has two questions:

   - Cite an example when you handled a pressing deadline with grace and ease.

   - What is your favorite technique for reducing stress after a hectic work day?

   - Collect the cards before the presentation and incorporate them into your speech.

   - Give recognition to the individuals submitting the ideas.

2. Ask participants about subscriptions:

   [ ] List all of your subscriptions.

   [ ] Circle those which you do keep up with.

   [ ] Put a line through those you don't.

   [ ] Discuss with your partner.

3. Ask participants about household and domestic chores:

   [ ] List all the domestic chores that you don't like to do:

   [ ] Which ones can you temporarily drop?

   [ ] Which ones can you do less frequently without consequences?

   [ ] Which ones can you hire someone to do?

   [ ] Which ones can you drop for good?

   [ ] When will you put these plans into action?

   [ ] Discuss with your partner.

Either as an opening gambit or later in the presentation, some speakers request that audience participants take out a piece of paper and write down a question that they want answered during the presentation. Others ask participants to give their best suggestions to the presenter. The example of exercises I refer to at longer sessions to encourage participation is on page 232.

Other opening audience-participation techniques involve having audience members nod their heads or raise their hands based on a question. You can also ask them to stand, stretch, greet one another, exchange business cards, repeat after you, or even sing along with you.

USING MUSIC IN YOUR PRESENTATION

Depending on the type of presentation you offer and how long you have been making speeches, you may have an inclination to use music before, during, or after your presentation.

Music can heighten audience members' anticipation during an introduction or render a powerful closing. Some presenters use music long before their presentations begin so that any early arrivals or people simply walking the halls will be curious. Presenters and trainers have used music to signal breaks in their session, to maintain an effective atmosphere during breaks, and to call all participants back to the session when the breaks are over.

Jeffrey Gitomer has upbeat music playing prior to his arrivals on stage. As he comes across the stage, he claps in rhythm to the music and his gestures induce his audiences to do so as well. Once the music stops and everyone stops clapping, he begins his presentation by playing off the energy already created in the room. Thereafter, he maintains a high-energy presentation, which invariably keeps audience members on track with him.

PROTECTING YOUR RIGHTS . . .
AND THOSE OF OTHERS

Most speakers don't understand that music is a form of personal property, each creation belonging to the person(s) who created it. Legally, when someone wants to use a piece of music, he or she must seek permission from the owner. You should check with the American Society of Composers, Authors, and Publishers (ASCAP) based in Atlanta, Georgia, about the works of its members. ASCAP represents the performance rights for nearly 100,000 composers, writers, and publishers in the United States, as well as thousands more from across the globe.

Rather than having to pay a per-song or per-performance fee, a user can perform "any or all of the millions of copyrighted music works in ASCAP's repertoire as often as they like" for a modest annual fee. This form of blanket license not only cuts down on paperwork but keeps licensees from even "inadvertently infringing on the copyright of ASCAP's members." For more information, visit ASCAP.com.

Approach the use of copyrighted music the same way you would approach any other copyrighted material. Song composers wish to retain their rights, as well. If you sell or otherwise distribute any type of recording during your presentation that includes the copyrighted music of others, you need to obtain an entirely separate reproduction right for which you would appeal to the copyright owner.

Preparing a
Seamless Presentation

Gathering intelligence about specific audience members prior to your presentation is a popular technique for keeping the entire audience awake, alert, amused, and involved. For example:

Who is the most popular person in the audience?

Who is the least popular?

Who wins the contests or gets all the honors?

Who never gets any of them?

Who has been with the organization the longest?

Who recently came on board?

Who is the biggest kidder?

Who is known for falling asleep in presentations?

If you can learn the answers to any of these types of questions in advance, you have excellent tools at your command. If this knowledge is used skillfully, the people to whom you refer during your presentation will be utterly surprised, as will everyone in the audience.

The fact that you go the extra mile by finding out such information gets people buzzing about you and your presentation and makes you more memorable.

Incorporating Audience Observations

You already know the importance of doing homework on your audience—collecting information about the group, the host organization, and other presenters. You also know about the value of reading any in-house publications, particularly the most recent ones. Beyond what effective speakers traditionally do, with a little extra effort, you can act like a virtual insider. You can appear as someone who has a strong affinity and empathy for the group.

If you start out speaking to three or four attendees, beyond simply furthering your understanding of the challenges the group faces, you could actually use some of the points in your presentation. With their permission, you could either reference the people to whom you speak or, if they prefer, have them remain anonymous. Hence, you would simply say something along the lines of, "I had the opportunity to speak to several of you weeks before this meeting and a recurring observation emerged."

The power of delivering such a line, beyond showing your willingness to make the extra effort to understand the group's issues, is that the observation undoubtedly will ring true in the minds of many people in the audience.

Working Off Other Speakers

If you will be one of many speakers presenting, ask the meeting planner if you could have the names and contact information for other presenters. Many speakers use this information to great effect. For example, if you know that Jan is presenting directly before you, by having knowledge of what she is going to say well in advance of your presentation, you can craft your speech to incorporate and build on what she says (given that you agree with it).

Getting Materials

If coming a day early is not feasible or desirable, there are other techniques you can employ to add to the aura of seamless presentations. For example, can you obtain a cassette presentation of one of the prior speakers? Perhaps the cassette presentation will be fairly similar to what the speaker will present to this group. If not a cassette, can you get an article or printed materials from the speaker? Perhaps you can get the speaker's outline or notes, a "10 tips" list, or other paraphernalia that conveys the essence of the speaker's message.

When you are speaking in a corporate setting, and a top-ranking official of the host organization will precede you, you can ask for a transcript of the presentation. More often than you might think, they are available.

In the representation questionnaire that I employ with meeting planners, one of the questions I ask is if I can get a copy of the descriptive literature for the group's previous meeting. If I am speaking at an annual meeting, I seek brochures and flyers from last year's annual meeting. Any materials you can gather related to the most recent meeting, or any prior meeting, is to your advantage. You then have the opportunity to weave in speakers from a month or even a year ago.

Another strategy is simply to read the conference material for the event at hand. If you know, for example, that, following your presentation, all participants will be going on a tour or having some other memorable experience, work that into your presentation.

Standing Alone

If you can employ even one of the techniques discussed even once in the course of your presentation, you may be the only speaker who does so. Contrast this preparation with the speaker who does not even refer to the name of the group, its products or services, or any of its buzzwords or jargon for the duration of his or her presentation.

Seamless presentations, while seemingly spontaneous, rarely just happen. Time, effort, and forethought in your presentation can add to an audience's overall enjoyment.

ALWAYS BEING AT YOUR BEST

As a presenter, if I'm not out to make my next speech my best, then it's likely to fall short. Public speaking is one of those endeavors in which you cannot stay "even"—there is no coasting. You're either getting better, or you're falling behind. When you consider the variety of presenters on stage, screen, and television, and compare the presentation skills of today with those of the previous generation, it is evident that they have been on an upward trajectory.

The goal of making your next speech your best, and treating it as if it were your last, is entirely worthwhile and imminently attainable.

Your Introduction
Is Crucial

Prior to launching your presentation, someone will introduce you. Since you write your own introduction, its length is usually up to you. Keep your introduction as short as is practical. The longer the introduction, the more work for your introducer, the more likely that he or she will botch some words, and the higher probability that the audience will be put off.

WRITING YOUR INTRODUCTION

I've sat through introductions that were truly boring. They went on and on, offering a laundry list of the presenter's accomplishments. Following pertinent facts, veteran speaker Al Walker recommends that the introduction have three essentials:

1. Something interesting about you, even gossipy.
2. Why you were chosen to speak, including why the topic should be addressed at this event.
3. Some particulars about yourself.

Your succinct introduction must be reviewed again and again before submission. You need to ensure that it flows. You want to eliminate difficult words. Spoon-feed the introducer. Make it so easy for him or her that success is all but inevitable. Here's an introduction I've employed to great effect:

Humorous Introduction

Jeff Davidson is a full-time professional speaker, author, columnist, certified management consultant, entrepreneur, and former paper boy.

On the way to writing 32 books and speaking to nearly 675 groups, he has been:

> . . . the tackle dummy for the Dallas Cowboys,
> . . . a wardrobe advisor for Dennis Rodman,
> . . . and the personal fitness coach for Rush Limbaugh.

Growing up in the Hartford, Connecticut, area, Jeff was recognized as one of the 10 funniest people in his neighborhood. All told, Jeff's books have been selected by book clubs 20 times, and, over the course of the last nine years, on average, someone in America buys one of his books every eight minutes. You can look it up.

He is author of *The Joy of Simple Living* published by Rodale Books and read by stressed-out people everywhere. From the major themes in that book, Jeff offers several presentations including:

- Managing the Pace with Grace,
- Managing Multiple Priorities, *and*
- Handling Information and Communication Overload.

Jeff has spoken on three continents to organizations such as:

- American Express, IBM, Wells Fargo, AOL, and Uncle Joe's Eat & Run.

You're in for an eye-opening experience and a real treat. Here today to help us stay focused and balanced in a world of rapid change and too much information, please welcome *Jeff Davidson* . . .

I prefer that my name in a heightened volume be the last word from the introducer. Prior to a presentation, I ask the introducer to truncate particular lines if I sense that:

- The introducer is inept and can handle only the briefest of introductions. I've been introduced by people who have been so nervous that they were barely able to complete my 30- to 60-second introduction.
- The mood of the event is not as festive as I had hoped.
- The proceedings are running behind schedule or time will otherwise be tight.

I employ the following introduction (submitted weeks or months in advance) when it appears that the meeting will be more somber or serious:

Serious Introduction

Today in business, people increasingly feel pressed for time, regardless of their title, to whom they report, the size of their support staff, the tasks and responsibilities they face, and even the education and training they bring to the job. Studies show that effective use of time is a critical aspect of management effectiveness.

Your success now and in the future depends on your ability to maintain control despite accelerating change and an explosion of information and communication.

The Washington Post called our speaker, Jeff Davidson, a "dynamo of business-book writing." Upon hearing him speak at business and association meetings, many people comment that his presentation makes an immediate impact on their lives. Jeff has worked with many groups, sharing his innovative ideas and fresh perspectives on how to have more breathing space. He's the author of 32 books, including *Breathing Space: Living and Working at a Comfortable Space in a Sped-up Society,* which is now published in 14 countries.

Here today to help us do just that, please give a warm welcome to . . . *Jeff Davidson.*

Consider giving the meeting planner the option of choosing which portions of your introduction would be most appropriate for the group. If your introduction is on the long side, and I recommend against it, allow the meeting planner to cross out the portions that likely will be the least meaningful for the audience.

PREPARING YOUR INTRODUCER

It's important to ensure that your introducer is fully briefed and supported long before the meeting date. The introduction to your presentation sets the tone and can actually impact your overall effectiveness. Aspiring public speakers too often bring their introductions and hand them to someone at the last minute, or worse, they ask their introducers to wing it—a recipe for disaster.

The typical introducer has little or no experience in properly introducing a speaker. Start with the basic assumption that your introducer is not skilled in this area, ill at ease with making introductions, and prefers to do anything else. Then, if you encounter someone who has a flare for introducing speakers, you're ahead of the game.

Making contact with your introducer far in advance of the presentation day is highly recommended. The larger the group, the more important it is to have such contact. While your introducer may only take up 1/50 of your overall presentation time, what the audience hears about you prior to you stepping up to the lectern has its effects on how they perceive you and rate the overall effectiveness of your presentation.

If he or she knows a little about you as a person, not only as a presenter, the introduction takes on a warmer, friendlier tone. The audience senses that you have some type of relationship with the introducer, which enhances the overall effect.

SUBMITTING THE INTRODUCTION

Tips for maximizing your introduction include:

- If you mail or fax your introduction, use a large point size, preferably 14 or more. Twelve-point type can look awfully small.

- If you e-mail your introduction, suggest at the top and the bottom of the e-mail that the introducer print it out in a large font. Again, size 14 or more, on an 8.5 by 11 sheet of paper. For some reason, some people think note cards are best. Not so. Cards are too small to be of practical value for this critical function.
- Peter Urs Bender prudently advises that you send a letter along with your introduction as a form of coaching.
- I include a note at the top of my printed introduction so that the introducer cannot possibly claim that he or she was unaware of my wishes:

    Notes for Introducer: Your job is important! It sets the stage for my whole presentation. Please deliver this introduction word for word *(my opening comments following directly from the introduction)*. Remaining upbeat and enthusiastic, yet conversational, they won't remember all you said, just how you said it. Please lead the applause to bring energy to the group. Thank you.
- Concurrent to submitting your introduction and any instructions to your introducer, place a back-up copy in the file folder that you're retaining for this group. You never want to show up at your presentation without a copy of your introduction, just in case.

Literally review your introduction line by line with that person. Ask him or her to read it to you and for both of you to edit the introduction with a pen or pencil and cross out or substitute words that may prove problematic.

URGE THEM NOT TO STRAY

Both early in the game and when you finally meet the introducer, urge him or her again not to stray from the printed text. Many introducers offer ad-hoc lines, which squelch your planned transition.

THE APPROACH

The question often arises as to whether or not the introducer should read the introduction. In most instances, the answer is yes. Virtually everyone in the audience knows that the presenter had a hand in writing the introduction, if not totally controlling its contents. It's no surprise for an introducer to read the introduction verbatim. If he or she feels comfortable enough to memorize the introduction, and many have this capability, great.

The happy medium is for the introducer to attempt to memorize the presentation, and use the printed sheet as a crutch, while looking up at the audience for those words or passages that he or she is able to utter without looking down at the sheet. In any case, what's on the printed page needs to be treated as gospel.

Here are some further points to remember:

- In preparing your introducer, let him or her know how important it is to not rush the introduction. The nervous introducer wants to get it over with and too frequently flies through words and sentences that he or she is not able to effectively articulate at high speeds.
- If any part of your name is difficult to pronounce, or any words within your introduction are difficult or unfamiliar to the typical person, write them phonetically.

Once the introducer finishes, it's your responsibility to make a smooth transition, which is discussed in Part VI: "Captivating and Inspiring Your Audience."

Have a Great Trip

Current to maintaining correspondence with the meeting planner and your introducer, there are additional steps to ensure success. When you know in advance that you'll have everything you need when you arrive at your destination, you'll be more confident when it's time to make your speech.

One easy way to lessen your prepresentation stress is to mail packages to yourself. By doing so, you reduce your time getting through airport security checks and lighten your load as you travel to long-distance speaking engagements.

Send the packages ahead to the meeting place, care of the convention or conference services. Every hotel has some kind of closet or storage room to retain such packages until arriving guests claim them. Send your packages as close to the arrival date as practical.

If you're concerned as to who is authorized to receive the package, call the hotel or conference facility and get a contact name. Then, use that contact name on your mailing label. Don't take chances with your important presentation materials—employ only delivery services that offer tracking and proof of delivery.

Mark your package "hold for arrival" with your full name, the name of the conference you're attending, and your arrival date all succinctly printed between the recipient's address and your return address.

With all major long-distance delivery services, you can go online and find the exact time and date your package was delivered, and even who signed for it. You can also call the facility or the person to whom it was sent to confirm reception.

Once you arrive, pick up your package immediately. Don't wait until an hour or two before presentation time. You want to make sure that everything arrived intact. You also want to refamiliarize yourself with what you sent. Many speakers prepare a list of materials they packed and bring that list with them.

PROPER PACKING

Some speakers routinely bring much more than they need even on short trips. Here are some tips to enable you to fly the friendly skies or travel the highways a little lighter and a little freer than usual:

Pack the smallest amount of toiletries/cosmetics possible in the smallest containers possible. Many drugstores sell plastic containers roughly the diameter of a silver dollar and ½ to ¾ of an inch deep with watertight twist-off tops.

Don't bring anything that you know your hotel supplies. You can call in advance to get a list.

For lengthy travel with many stops, bring clothes that wash and wear easily. Take advantage of any valet services.

MAKE THE MOST OF YOUR TIME

If you are about to board a short flight, with your palmtop, you can dial up and download your e-mail just before getting on the plane—no papers, no wires, little weight. During the flight, you can answer all e-mail, sending it to the outbox. You can read correspondence, correct it, make notes, add to a database, calculate complex cash flow analysis with spreadsheet software, listen to a lecture, you name it. The moment you step off the plane, you can send all your e-mail, pick up any new e-mail, and answer calls.

There is no need for lugging weighty stacks of paper or incurring long bouts of lost time anymore; it's a traveler's choice. The key, of course, in every travel encounter, is desire and preparation. What do you want to get done, and will you take the time and energy to assemble tools that will ensure your high productivity? For the seasoned traveling speaker, this is old hat. If you're starting to travel for business, a new world of efficiency awaits.

MAINTAIN RECORDS

Do you have a file folder, notebook, or magazine box in which you keep all travel-related materials? This would include booklets on hotel and air fares, frequent-flyer numbers, passports, numbers for taxis and other transportation, and vacation club folders. I keep such phone and membership numbers in one long file on my hard disk; a printout in a small point size tucks into my portable appointment calendar. Wherever I am, day or night, I have the information I need.

SANITY IN AIRLINE RESERVATIONS

Never, *never* buy tickets at the airline counter. Buy them in advance and have them sent via first class mail. Get seat assignments 30 days before your flight.

- If you book your ticket through a travel agency, review the itinerary included with your ticket. This indicates your scheduled arrival and departure times, stops, and meals. If you book your tickets by phone with the airlines directly, the first page of your packet often has the same information.
- Anticipate delays at your meetings, expecially when you are one of many speakers. Now, before departing by plane for a meeting, I print the flight schedule (from the Internet) of those flights heading to and departing from my meeting destination. My travel escapade following the AOL speech is no longer feasible, so I want to know my options when I am late getting back to the airport or if any of my flights are going to be delayed.

- Drink plenty of water. Water plays an important role in maintaining high energy for your forthcoming presentation. Often when you're exhausted, you need water more than you need sleep. Drinking a glass of water can keep you active longer. During your flight, staying hydrated is crucial.

PREVENTATIVE MEASURES WHILE CHECKING IN

There are also engagements that merit staying for a night or more. Once you get to your hotel and are checking in, here are a few tips that will increase the probability that you'll have the full night's sleep that will support your performance the following day:

- Explain to the check-in staff that you are a speaker, you have a speech in the morning, and your sleep is crucial. That alone might prompt them to give you a room that is in a quiet section of the hotel.
- Get a room facing east if you can; that will give you early morning sunshine, and it will be cooler in the evening than will a room facing west. Specifically ask for a room in which you'll have quiet.
- Ask for a room without a door adjoining another room.

You deserve to get a good night's sleep, and it's essential for you to be at your best. Do everything you can to achieve an optimal level of rest to be alert and energetic the day of your presentation. You might also look into the latest in noise-reduction technology goods. Some products I recommend are: Sound Screen® and Sleep Mate® from Marpac Corporation (P.O. Box 3098, Wilmington, NC, 28406–0098) and Noise Filters®, available from Cabot Safety Corporation (5457 W. 79th St. Indianapolis IN, 46268.

35

Meeting Room Layouts

The more often you speak, the more apparent it will become that meeting room setups come in almost endless variations. The meeting planner can often tell you far in advance what type of room you'll be in and how it lays out. Most facilities also offer Web sites containing room-by-room sketches, aerial schematics, pictures, and dimensions. Still, most speakers, myself included, become acquainted with the meeting room only the night before or an hour before their presentation.

Starting on page 250 is a fairly nonjudgmental review of more than a dozen meeting room setups and the types of meetings for which they are most appropriate.

WALK THE MEETING ROOM

Once on site, do a prepresentation walk through of the meeting facility exploring every facet of it. Beyond the usual equipment, sound, and temperature checks notice the potential for glare. Are there large windows with the curtains open? On a sunny day this is the death knell in terms of retaining the attention of your audience.

Glare may arise from TV monitors, mirrors, glass, light fixtures, fire hose boxes, or anything shiny in the room. Walk the room and sit in various seats to detect possible glare that audience members might experience. To minimize glare try hanging drapes, changing lighting, and repositioning chairs.

Theatre-Style Seating—More than half of all the rooms in which you'll speak are simply set up theatre style, with one big aisle down the middle, a stage or podium at the far end, and seats in symmetrical halves that go several rows deep. Some of your energy is lost with theatre-style seating because you directly face large, empty center aisles.

**THEATER STYLE
WITH CENTER AISLE**

Crescent Theatre Seating with Side Aisles—This is an appropriate set-up for keynote or general session presentations to large audiences. Because of the curvature of the rows, all parties can easily face you without craning their necks. No energy is lost in this setup because there is no center aisle. Patrons in the middle seats receive the brunt of your energy while those on the left and right wing are often no less involved.

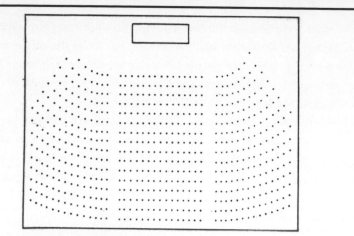

**CRESCENT THEATER STYLE
WITH SIDE AISLES**

Classroom Style—Classroom style is reminiscent of rooms in your high school classes of years past. There may be one center aisle or several aisles between rows of desks or tables. If tables are used, there may be one, two, three, or four audience participants at each table. Classroom style can be effective with groups of up to 100. For audiences of

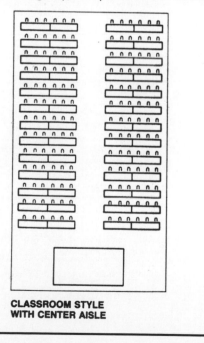

**CLASSROOM STYLE
WITH CENTER AISLE**

(continued)

more than 100 people, effectiveness depends on the skill of the speaker and the factors related to room dynamics. For example, classroom style seating in an amphitheater arrangement, whereby the presenter is at the basin of the amphitheater and the seats fan out in a semi-circle, would allow for far more than 100 attendees.

Herringbone Classroom Style—Similar to the basic classroom style described above, the herringbone arrangement consists of desks or tables that are tilted in a V-shaped fashion, such that all participants are directly facing the presenter and can easily view participants across the aisle. This set-up facilitates greater audience participation and louder laughs because participants can clearly see each other.

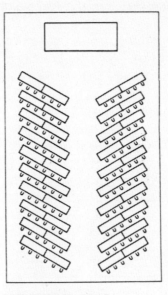

**V-CLASSROOM STYLE
(HERRINGBONE)**

Standard U-shaped Seating—With this configuration, the presenter is situated at the opening part of a U. In a banquet situation, participants might be seated inside the U. After dinner, they would have to turn their chairs in order to face the presenter. In a strict classroom or seminar environment, the inner portion of the U is often left open so that all participants can at least indirectly face the presenter without having to turn their chairs.

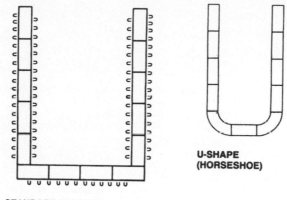

STANDARD U-SHAPE

U-SHAPE
(HORSESHOE)

The underlying premise in using the U-shaped setup is that everyone is important. There is significant work to be done, and participation is widely encouraged. The coveted positions are at the bottom center of the U, although a wise presenter can help all participants feel as if they have a good seat by frequently roaming into the middle of the U. No more than 150 people should be seated in such configurations. For presentations of any length, less then 40 and as few as 20 seats are advisable. A variation on the U-shaped configuration is the use of curved tables on the corners to form a true U- or horseshoe-shaped configuration. The meeting dynamics stay the same.

Hollow Square—This seating configuration is like the standard U-shape with the top filled in to form a square. There may be a presenter, moderator, or group leader at the top center. There is no seating inside the square. This arrangement is often popular for board meetings during which all participants have a vital stake in the outcome of an organization. A variation on this theme is to have rounded tables at the corners to yield oval configurations. The meeting dynamics stay the same.

(continued)

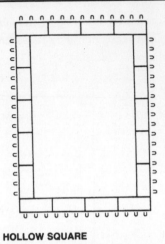

HOLLOW SQUARE

Closed Boardroom Seating—Participants are seated at an oval or oblong table, or at a set of tables arranged in an oval or oblong fashion. The cabinet of U.S. presidential administrations uses such a meeting setup. The presenter, host, or moderator is usually in the center of one of the long sides. Closed boardroom seating gives participants a feeling of intimacy, although those seated on the long sides cannot easily see many of the attendees.

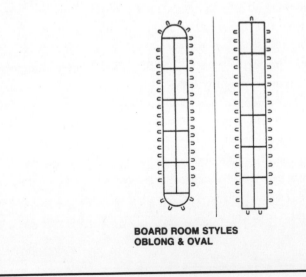

BOARD ROOM STYLES
OBLONG & OVAL

Boardroom-style meetings encourage quick bouts of participation. Often, other meeting participants are seated within the room away from an oval or oblong table setup. A speaker at such gatherings will usually stand so as to be more easily heard and seen by others. Such presentations tend to be relatively brief, on the order of three to five minutes. The set-up is not appropriate for sessions any longer than eight to ten minutes.

O-Type Setup—Similar to the hollow square, an O-type setup is an octagonal arrangement ensuring that each participant can see all other participants. Such arrangements are conducive to meetings including 8, 16, or 24 people for 1-, 2-, and 3-person tables, respectively.

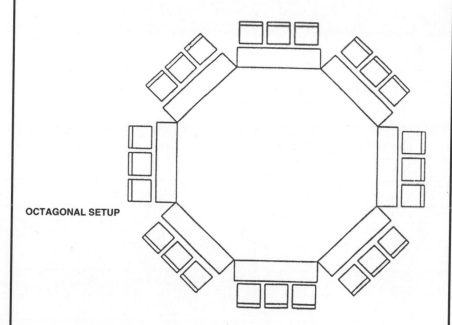

OCTAGONAL SETUP

T-Shaped Setup—The T-shape configuration is also used in banquet settings. Presumably, the guests of honor sit across the top of the T, the cross bar, facing guests seated on the left and right of the stem. As with other such meeting room setups, the person in the dead center seat at the top of the T is the presenter, moderator, or host. As with

(continued)

other "alphabetical" type arrangements, any words spoken here need to be mercifully short.

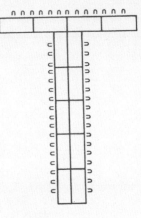

T-SHAPE

Facing Parallel Tables—This configuration is like the letter H without the cross bar. Two rows of tables of equal length are placed in parallel fashion with space in the middle. Such an arrangement has been used for debates, negotiations, and other planned, verbal confrontations. Generally, a public speaker won't have to deal with such an arrangement.

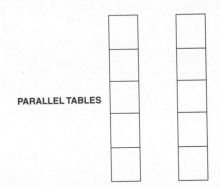

PARALLEL TABLES

In the Rounds—This term refers to people seated at round tables of 6 to 12 participants who will eat preceding or succeeding a speaker. When it's time for the presentation, at least one-third, and up to one-half, of participants will have to turn their chairs to see the speaker. Such presentations tend to be shorter than those offered in theatre or classroom arrangements.

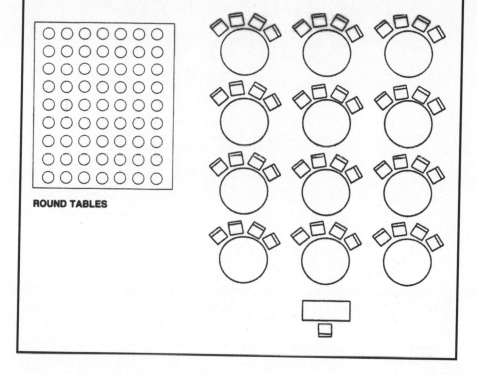

ROUND TABLES

Glare will reduce the concentration level of anyone in the audience who is experiencing it.

Fortunately, the better meeting facilities have been designed by professionals who are aware of the impact of meeting room colors, textures, lighting, and furniture as their impact on audiences. When you perceive potential decor problems that may diminish your audience's experience of your presentation, don't be shy—tell the meeting planner.

Check for uneven lighting and any seats that may lie in a "dark zone." Audience members seated in a dark zone will be at a disadvantage compared to the others in the room. The cure might be as simple as switching on or off certain lights.

36

Handling Speaker Challenges

Audience members who see speakers prior to the presentation have a predisposition to make contact with him or her, particularly if the speaker is well-known or if the presentation has been highly anticipated. Thus, public speakers who want to appear professional need to get the room in order long before people start arriving. By making the necessary preparations before the day of the meeting, and becoming familiar with the room in which you will present, you will have more time before your presentation to meet and greet audience members.

It may be unfair, but the presenter who seems flustered by "disturbances" from audience members prior to the formal start of the presentation is not going to win over those audience members and ultimately may suffer from lower evaluation scores, even if his or her actual presentation was sublime. If you have handled preparations far in advance, then you have even more opportunity to engage freely in your pre-speech rituals or to converse with audience members who approach you.

SHIELDING YOURSELF FROM OTHER SPEAKERS

In addition to all the groundwork activities you've been undertaking, you need to recognize that often you won't be the only speaker for a particular function. While it is important to familiarize yourself with other speakers, and the order in which everyone will speak, if you're relatively new as a public speaker you may not want to be present for the presentations preceding yours.

If the room and venue logistics allow you to be out of earshot of the prior presenter, take advantage of the situation. "Try not to sit down too much while you're waiting to speak," advises veteran speaker and executive speech coach Patricia Fripp. "If you're scheduled to go on an hour into the program, sit in the back of the room so that you can stand up occasionally. It's hard to jump up and be dynamic when you've been relaxing in a chair for an hour."

Most public speakers can eventually arrive at the point at which they don't have to engage in a variety of remote or private personal preparation routines. They are comfortable being in full view, listening to a prior presenter, or greeting members of their audience. Only you can determine when you're ready to make the change. For now, rest assured that it's perfectly natural to want to sequester yourself from outside distractions prior to your presentation.

JITTERS

What if you experience a case of the jitters right before you're about to go on? Patricia Fripp paints a vivid portrait: "You're waiting your turn to make a speech, when suddenly you realize that your stomach is doing strange things and your mind is rapidly going blank. How do you handle this critical time period?"

There is no single answer to this question. "You need to anticipate your speech mentally, physically, and logistically. Mentally, start by understanding that you'll spend a lot more time preparing than you will speaking," Fripp says. "As a general rule, invest three hours of preparation for a half hour speech, a six to one ratio. When you've become a highly experienced speaker, you may be able to cut preparation time considerably in some cases, but until then, don't skimp."

She offers a technique from acting that is helpful for speakers. Find a private spot, and wave your hands in the air. Relax your jaw, and shake your head from side to side. Then shake your legs one at a time. Physically shake the tension out of your body.

Fripp observes that part of your preparation will be to memorize your opening and closing—three or four sentences each. "Even if you cover your key points from notes, knowing your opening and closing by heart lets you start and end fluently, connecting with your audience when you are most nervous."

ANXIETY ABOUNDS

The renowned psychologist Rollo May once said, "It is well to remind ourselves that anxiety signifies a conflict, and so long as a conflict is going on, a constructive solution is possible." It may be illuminating for you to know that for at least the first few years in public speaking, everyone experiences some form of anxiety. Many learn to minimize the effects.

One step to quell feeling anxious is to choose to be where you are and to do what you are doing. Some speakers find it helpful to make specific affirmations prior to presenting. For example:

- I choose to enjoy my time on stage.
- I choose to feel comfortable in front of this group.
- I choose to make all preparations to ensure a smooth delivery.
- I choose to easily maintain eye contact and clarity with my audience.
- I choose to draw strength and energy from my audiences.
- I choose to speak with a clear voice.
- I choose to be an effective and persuasive speaker.

THE CONTROL FACTOR

Much of the fear that people experience prior to making a presentation is due to an *anticipated* loss of control. An individual might unwittingly, unproductively focus on losing one's place, slurring words, saying the wrong things, or embarrassing oneself. Yet, a different focus entirely is desirable and achievable.

Consider the focus of veteran speakers who look forward to addressing groups. They gain energy from being on stage. They appreciate the opportunities.

You can't expect to instantaneously assume the orientation and mindset of a veteran professional speakers. You can, however, take steps to minimize your pre-speech concerns. The primary activity is to practice, practice, and practice.

TAKE A DEEP BREATH

Many speech coaches recommend that in preparation for a presentation you focus on your breath. By drawing in slow deep breaths, you can realign your physiology. In the late 1970s, Dr. Herbert Benson demonstrated that meditation, which facilitates deep breathing, could induce direct physical benefits, such as reduced muscle tension, decreased heart rate, and lower blood pressure.

In *The Relaxation Response,* Dr. Benson discussed his belief that the "core of meditation" was what he called the "Relaxation Response," which represents the body's inbred physiological mechanism. This mehcanism diminishes or prevents one's fight or fight process—the stress response. Taking slow, deep breaths will bring your heart rate down and your respiration back to normal when you are tense.

Drawing deeper breaths helps to disperse adrenaline which would otherwise leave you feeling in a highly charged state, to decrease your blood pressures, to decrease your rate of ventilation, and to fortify your body's ability to respond to stress.

CREATE A FAIL SAFE ENVIRONMENT

If you are concerned about slipping up during your presentation, create backup systems for yourself. There are no "rules" against taping key words to the stage floor or podium for your eyes only. If you work from an outline, enlarge the print size so that you have little trouble keeping your place. Befriend audience members in advance of your presentation, as previously suggested, so that you have some "friends" in the audience to speak to.

Except in rare and other readily discernable situations, audiences are not "out for blood." They would prefer to see you succeed rather than fail. Most people can sympathize with you if you stumble and will forgive various transgressions. So seek to relax and stay as loose as you can to help keep any anxiety at a manageable level. That way, the audience has a better chance of getting the best of you.

PART VI

CAPTIVATING AND INSPIRING YOUR AUDIENCES

Serving and, more importantly, inspiring your audiences are perhaps your greatest responsibilities as a public speaker. You can impact your audiences in many ways so that they gain optimal benefits from your appearances. Surprisingly, some of these ways occur before you launch into your formal presentation.

The seven chapters in this section cover critical elements of effective public speaking such as pre-speech warm-ups, thanking your introducer, and opening with a flourish. I also discuss the idea of "reading" the audience as you go, post-speech considerations that require your attention, and pitfalls that may be looming. Your quest is to have meeting planners regard you as a unique presenter, someone worth knowing for the long haul.

37

Pre-Speech Activities

GREETING THEM AT THE DOOR

To leave an indelible impression on your audience, you can engage in a practice I saw undertaken with aplomb by author and speaker Roger Dawson. Prior to a presentation in Tampa, Florida, Dawson positioned himself at the entrance of the lecture hall. More than 400 people piled into the room, and he virtually shook hands and greeted every one of them.

I hadn't met Roger before, but I was aware of several of his best-selling books on negotiation. At first, I was a bit bemused. I thought, "Why is this guy standing at the door and pressing himself on us? Isn't this a little aggressive?" Yet, as his speech unfolded, I realized that he had taken control of the room. He was making a personal connection with every single audience member. The greeting solidified people's connection to him, enhanced their willingness to follow along with his presentation, and made them more favorably disposed to what he was saying. Undoubtedly, he got high marks for his speech.

Setting Yourself Apart

It takes time and energy to engage in such a gesture, and some speakers are leery that the energy required to greet several hundred people might detract from their presentation. To be a master speaker, however, you have to find the requisite energy. Some professionals feed off this early

265

interaction with audience members and generate even higher energy once they begin their formal presentations. One-on-one encounters don't occur often enough between speakers and audience members.

Marking Your Territory

Being a student of the speaking profession, I took full advantage of the next opportunity to greet members of my audience. Fortunately, it was a group of only about 50. I positioned myself at the entrance to the room so that they had to encounter me as they came in. I wasn't as skilled as Roger Dawson in pre-speech greetings; however, I knew that the gesture was appreciated. The speech went well, and I received high evaluations.

I repeated the practice at more speaking engagements, even with groups of several hundred. Eventually, it became second nature to me. Now I wouldn't think of giving a presentation without greeting as many people as possible.

What's in It for You

By making one-on-one pre-speech greetings, you get to experience audience members as individuals and not part of the mass of people in front of you during your presentation.

Making pre-speech greetings also takes the focus off of you. Of the many reasons that speakers get nervous before speeches, one of the foremost is focusing too much on themselves. When you greet others, you shift the focus from yourself to the participants. If you have the time, you can glean valuable information from audience members that you can then insert into your speech. Beyond that, simply casting your attention on audience members can provide a greater sense of perspective.

A Different Approach

If greeting people at the door is too confrontational for you, here is a variation. As early arrivals take their seats, move around the room offering your greetings. This affords you much more control than simply standing at the door. Because they're seated, you get to monitor how much time you spend with each party.

Often, early arrivals are seated in groups or pairs. It is somewhat easier to greet two people at a time than it is to approach individuals. Think of the last time you were at a reception or party and easily fell into conversation with two or three others as opposed to approaching one person and starting a conversation from scratch.

I vary my pre-speech conversations with early seated arrivals using such phrases as "Glad you made it to this session," "I am always appreciative of people coming in early," or something as bold as, "I am eager to know what you hope to get out of today's sessions." These and similar phrases can help put audience members at ease while gleaning valuable cues for you.

An Added Bonus

Another pre-speech crowd pleaser is to give something of value to the early arrivals. I often bring an extra packet of article reprints that aren't included in the general audience participant packet. This gift to early arrivals helps cement the brief encounter.

I approach seated audience members and say something like, "Thanks for coming early today. Here is a bonus article for you. I only have a few of them left, but I want to reward those who arrive in the room early." You may think such a gesture doesn't have great impact, but I have seen people's faces light up following the reception of such a gift. Many people are pleased to receive *anything* directly from a speaker. Nearly always, the gesture pays off.

APPROACHING SHOWTIME

It's your responsibility, and your introducer's, to make a smooth transition. Ideally, you can reach the introducer within 5 to 10 seconds following his or her summons to you. Audience applause gives you time to move to center stage.

Extend your right hand as you approach your introducer to indicate that you're ready to shake hands. Then, especially if your mike is on, say something seemingly private to the introducer that is audible to at least the people in the first few rows, and perhaps the entire room. I routinely greet my introducers with "That was wonderful, thank you," "Excellent job, I appreciate it," or "Great job, thank you."

By giving your introducer such immediate high praise, you further set the tone for your presentation. You have sincerely and lavishly praised someone who undertook a job that might not have been so comfortable for him or her.

Because your praise was audible, you help win over other audience members who were within earshot. After all, they might have been up there, they might have felt nervous, and they would have appreciated your lavish praise as well. You've endeared yourself to the audience in a way that few presenters consider doing.

The one-to-one personal praise that I advocate has greater impact on many levels. Also, by not stopping, standing, and facing the introducer and thanking him or her, you get to launch right into your presentation with more power, more pizzazz, and more potency. (See Chapter 38, "Open with a Flourish.")

Nuances designed to inspire your audience, such as marking your territory, individually greeting audience members, and thanking your introducer are not small potatoes. Even if the atmosphere isn't all that it could be, there is still a touch of magic in the air.

Open with a Flourish

Talk to 10 veteran speakers and you will get as many as 10 views on what makes for a successful opening to your presentation. The common factor is that your opening has to fit your style and comfort zone. You have to establish rapport with the audience members and convey to them a sense of energy and enthusiasm.

Traditionally, speech coaches taught that first you thank the introducer by name, then you look to the whole audience, then you "catch fire." This is still the preferred approach for large convention hall speeches, which most of your presentations will *not* be. The traditional pattern involves an introductory icebreaker (a verbal transition from thanking the introducer to addressing the audience), a brief preview of what you're going to cover, the order of what you'll cover, and a conclusion.

THAT OH-SO CRITICAL FIRST SENTENCE

With my method, because you are semi-privately thanking the speaker and hence not dissipating the power of your first sentence to the audience, the first sentence is vital. Select it carefully. If you open with some tepid line like "Mr. Speaker," "Madam Chairperson," and so forth, you're merely following what you have seen on television. If you say what an honor it is to speak to such-and-such group, then honestly explain why; otherwise, your words are empty. If you open unconvincingly with something such as

"Good Morning," "How are you all doing today?" "It's great to be here," and other inane greetings, you have already lost several audience members who consider such openings contrived.

With whatever approach you choose, your goal is to immediately and completely capture the attention of the entire audience. Here is the opening of a speech by Garry Trudeau, the "Doonesbury" cartoonist, at Yale University's Class Day. Note how it draws on the traditional large gathering-type of opening, but then goes way beyond that:

> Dean Kagan, distinguished faculty, parents, friends, graduating seniors, Secret Service agents, class agents, people of class, people of color, colorful people, people of height, the vertically constrained, people of hair, the differently coiffed, the optically challenged, the temporarily sighted, the insightful, the out-of-sight, the out-of-towners, the Eurocentrics, the Afrocentrics, the Afrocentrics with Eurail passes, the eccentrically inclined, the sexually disinclined, people of sex, sexy people, sexist pigs, animal companions, friends of the earth, friends of the boss, the temporarily employed, the differently employed, the differently optioned, people with options, people with stock options, the divestiturists, the deconstructionists, the home constructionists, the home boys, the homeless, the temporarily housed at home, and God save us, the permanently housed at home.

A powerful opening requires homework. Undoubtedly Gary Trudeau spent considerable time on his opening and did his homework on the audience. Good openings necessitate that you know your audiences, what they're up against, and what they've heard from previous speakers, whether at the last meeting of this type or from their CEO or president.

Perhaps some article in the monthly publication had great impact. Perhaps something in the industry is currently commanding everyone's attention. Link the hot button item that you uncover with how you open your speech, and you have the ingredients for a powerful opening. Here are examples:

- Will anyone here lend me $10.5 million?
- The *New York Times* reported today that this organization has failed to . . .

- The last time I addressed this institution, most of you were still in college . . .
- When I look out at this fine audience . . .

You have lots of options for openings—don't fear that they won't emerge. You could start with a human interest story, pose a challenging question, refer to an event (the more recent the better), pay a compliment to someone in attendance, or open with a joke. If your opening appropriately grabs the audience's attention, then it works.

Do not make your opening more than 80 percent of your highest energy. You have to build to your highest energy level. Otherwise the rest of your presentation could seem flat.

FALL IN LOVE WITH YOUR AUDIENCE

Many speakers report a deep-seated belief that prior to going on and delivering your opening line, you need to "fall in love with your audience," so that, when you formally begin, the audience feels that sense of love. I concur with this approach for several reasons:

1. The most effective speeches by far are those in which audience members feel as if the speaker is on their side and that he or she is empathetic and prepared to address their current needs. Even if the speaker were to give a stern speech, he or she nonetheless could offer "tough love" to the audience.

A speaker who doesn't convey such affection could be regarded as talking down to the audience, acting superior, or falling prey to the "here-comes-the-expert" syndrome.

2. Conveying a sense of love to the audience is self-serving in some respects, but it's also highly practical. At some point during your speech, you may falter and your energy may drop. There may be some sections that you botch. A joke may not work. If you've already conveyed your depth of feeling for audience members, then they'll be far more supportive during any rough spots in your presentation.

Don't underestimate the value of having an audience err in your favor. You need all the advantages you can muster during a presentation. No one is so good so often that he or she never needs to worry about losing favor with an audience.

3. The feeling of love that you convey does not imply that you're going to sugarcoat important topics, gloss over tough issues, or otherwise diminish your authenticity. Often, the more sternly you wish to speak and the more contentious your material, the more important it is to convey a sense of love to your audience.

Be sure to show your affection to the people who sit in the front rows. Everyone behind them can observe and sense the caring that you convey. In that manner, you can win over the whole room.

> The deepest principle of human nature is the craving to be appreciated.
> —*William James*

BECOME MEMORABLE

To tell people what they already know in a new and intriguing way has its benefits but does not make for a memorable speech. Challenging conventional wisdom makes a speech memorable. What old industry rule or axiom are you now ready to overturn? What have members of this group always counted on that now needs to be regarded in a totally different way?

Freeze the Moment

Recall from Part II, "Developing and Enlivening Your Presentation," how a professor stood up on his desk in the middle of his lecture and poured a pitcher of water over himself, shocking the class and freezing the moment. While it's not likely that you are going to pour a pitcher of water over your head on stage, you do need to consider options for freezing the moment. Standing on a table, making an exaggerated movement, or raising your voice can effectively shock your audience members and cause them to remember your point. Review tapes or transcripts of your speeches to determine where and when you may be able to appropriately add a gesture that will freeze the moment forever in the minds of audience participants.

Have a Flair for the Dramatic

The memorable speakers and speeches within the past half-century share a common component: the flair for the dramatic. Mario Cuomo, Jesse Jackson, John F. Kennedy, Ronald Reagan, Margaret Thatcher, Donald Rumsfeld, and General Norman Schwarzkopf have all instinctively known how and when to raise and lower their voices, draw the audience in with their stories and anecdotes, and appeal to the expectations and emotions of their listeners.

They use the lectern and the stage as their playing field. They use facial expressions, eye movement, hand movements, and other gestures as their tools of the trade. They engage their listeners and make it hard for them to turn away. They get into a rhythm. Whether or not you agree with them, you feel compelled to keep listening.

EMOTION ON THE PLATFORM

What role can conveying emotion on the platform play? Depending on the circumstances of your presentation, you may believe that emotion plays a small role in your overall effectiveness. If you're delivering a technical or how-to presentation with cut-and-dry instructions, what role would emotion play? Read on.

Dan Clark says, "The most memorable speakers are the emotional speakers." Clark believes that emotions are an international language. "Our audiences relate to our imperfections more than our perfections and we reveal them only through emotion," says Clark. Moreover, "in the absence of emotion there is no change."

With regard to technical presentations, Clark says that "emotion is the permission statement inviting each audience member to get involved in our presentation. Too many people in our audiences are hurting inside, living their lives as Thoreau wrote 'in quiet desperation.'" Even in a technical presentation, as Clark explains, ours "might be the only positive affirmation that they receive all week/month/year. The essential catalyst to inspire them to better deal with pressure."

With nontechnical presentations, audience members certainly need to have an emotional experience for the message to sink in. Clark says, "Our special responsibility is to guarantee a significant emotional experience. We are ambassadors of living, laughing, learning, and loving, not news anchors reporting facts.

Manipulation of Poignancy?

In essence, a memorable speech takes the audience on a roller-coaster ride of emotions—not wantonly, not arbitrarily, not haphazardly, but in a choreographed, synchronized fashion. They experience laughter, mirth, and joy. Later, they experience sadness or sorrow. You can overdo it, however, when it comes to emotions.

Ensure that the emotional components of your presentation belong there because they contribute to the flow and essence of what you wish to convey. Do not use them as tools of audience manipulation. Use emotion to emphasize the points you're making. Life is full of highs and lows, of happiness and sorrow. It is perfectly permissible, and indeed highly desirable, for your speech to emulate life.

39

Audience Involvement

Aspeaker can no longer automatically expect to have the complete and undivided attention of an audience. The primary reason is that the concentration levels of audiences everywhere have dropped considerably within a generation. Television and radio producers are well aware of today's shrinking attention spans, so news and features grow shorter and shorter.

Effective public speakers come to grips with the reality that they need to employ a variety of techniques for ensuring that the audience stays focused, involved, and entertained.

In this chapter, we'll look at a number of techniques you can draw on to keep audience members involved in your presentation.

EXERCISES FOR AUDIENCES

For speakers who prefer to have audience members interact with one another to get everyone loose (and perhaps awake), exercise variations are endless, including:

- Some speakers have everyone in the room stand and meet one new person and exchange information such as why they are here today, what they hope to get out of the session, one unusual hobby they have, and so on so that participants have a better chance of remembering one another.

- For long sessions with significant audience participation, speakers have directed audience members to find out even more about each other:
  —Where they were born.
  —Where they went to school.
  —If they have any brothers or sisters.
  —Where they were first employed.
  —Their favorite movie, book, food, and so on.

In all cases, the underlying goal is to have audience participants become more vocal and involved in the day's proceedings. Giving everyone the chance to interact with everyone else, however brief and minor the exercise, can significantly increase the probability of greater audience participation for the balance of the presentation.

AUDIENCE INVOLVEMENT BY BEING YOURSELF

Audience members have an instinctive capacity to immediately determine when someone is putting on an act. You've heard the expression, "Who you are speaks so loudly that I can't hear what you say." In front of a group, if you assume a persona that does not reflect the real you, people will feel uneasy.

If your focus is on you, it can't be on the audience. So, your need for approval limits your ability to connect with your audience and strips you of any authority you may have had. However relevant your message, it comes across as less so.

How do you work yourself out of this dilemma? Rather than pander for audience approval, strive to offer your approval to them. Sincerely acknowledge them for being there, for listening, for the jobs they undertake, for the challenges they face.

Your ability to embody your genuine self might be the single greatest factor in generating high levels of audience participation. Allen Klein, who has written such poignant books as *The Healing Power of Laughter*, says, "My best programs have been when I convey a heart connection with the audience. I am not thinking about my material, my delivery, or even how the audience is reacting, but just being there to meet their needs even when they don't match my own agenda."

WHAT'S IN A NAME

In any type of presentation, use names of audience members when it is practical to do so. If you are giving a keynote speech or a general session presentation, while you may not be able to actually see individuals or their name tags, undoubtedly you know the names of meeting organizers and top officials.

In smaller settings in which you are able to read name tags or place cards, freely use names throughout your presentation. Besides keeping people awake and alert, you also increase the odds of them staying tuned in to your presentation. Think about the times when you were in school and your teacher dropped your name into the middle of a sentence. Thereafter, you approached that lesson on a different plane. It is no different with adults today.

WHAT IT MEANS TO YOU

Because audience members are so distracted these days, have so much on their minds, and may have trouble relating what you say to their own situation, there is a magic phrase that you may need to insert throughout your presentation: "What it means to you." Here's how to employ it to best advantage. Suppose you are laying out a scenario in your presentation, carefully providing the audience with background information on a situation for which you will then offer solutions.

In my "Managing the Pace with Grace" presentation, I first lay out a scenario for the audience. I discuss what I call the five mega-realities of our frenzied existence. If I have an hour presentation, I might devote as much as 20 minutes to describing these five mega-realities, perhaps devoting four minutes to each.

At about the 18th or 20th minute, I noticed that members of this particular audience were a little befuddled. Some were getting frustrated, some were confused, and some had tuned out. Twenty minutes is a long time to spend laying out a scenario, no matter how important it is. I realized that unless I linked what I was saying to the people in the seats, I would lose them. So, as I discussed why the world has "sped up," I inserted the phrase "and what this means to you is . . ."

I then related the overall situation to what they encounter in everyday life. For example, the first mega-reality is the ever-growing human population, to the tune of nearly one million more people on earth every four days. That is a startling statistic, and certainly some people in the audience will be startled to hear it. But if I keep adding statistics about the growth in human population, even my most ardent supporters will soon grow weary.

Now, suppose I say to them, "What this means to you is that each day when you head out on the highway, you're likely to see more cars and more vehicles of all kinds, clogging up all the lanes, slowing traffic, and making your commute more arduous." I might talk about how, even in the country, you will see another house going up on the hill, another boat on the lake, another traffic light installed at a corner that years ago you never would have guessed would acquire one. Now everyone in the room can relate to what I have said. Why? Because we are all facing the onslaught of a growing human population in our own environments on a daily basis.

The more how-to or technical your topic, the more important it is for you to keep relating what you are saying to the everyday experiences of members of your audience.

If you are an astrophysicist, a microchip developer, or a gene-splicing specialist, there is no need to fear losing your audience as long as you can continue to make vital links to which people can relate. The following are alternatives to the phrase "what this means to you":

- The point I'm making is that in your own careers . . .
- So, how does this relate to you . . .
- As a result of all this, you will likely experience . . .
- The upshot is that each day . . .
- This should be of concern to everyone in the room because . . .

I recommend employing a variety of these phrases throughout your presentation, particularly if you are giving a longer presentation. All audiences today need a higher level of spoon-feeding than their counterparts of previous decades. The situation is not likely to change in the foreseeable future.

Better How-to Presentations

1. *Reinforce what you say to an audience with participant packets, formally known as handouts.* They could be distributed before, during, or after your presentation, based on your method of delivery, how you want audience members to interact, and what you want them to retain. Opt for a shorter, rather than a longer, participant packet. Lengthy packets may overwhelm audience members.

2. *Shorten your lists.* Rather than give them a list of 10 things to consider, give only five. People are exceedingly busy these days, and having five, or even three, things to do is much more palatable than ten.

3. *Spoon feed your audience at every opportunity.* The old saying, "tell them what you are going to tell them, tell them, and then tell them what you told them" has never been more important. However, you need to implement this strategy in a creative way.

4. *Mix your brilliant high-content how-to information with some stories and anecdotes.* There is nothing worse than listening to a brilliant speaker who overloads the audience with observations and insights, facts and data, but doesn't break up the material with stories. These stories give listeners a visual picture.

5. *Recognize and acknowledge the listeners' pain throughout your presentation.* Nothing will endear you to your audience faster and help maintain that precious relationship longer than a keen display of your knowledge of their hardships and predicaments.

PLAY ALONG WITH AN AUDIENCE MEMBER

Almost any type of direct audience interaction, especially with a single member of the audience, will increase everyone's level of attention.

- I have seen Tony Alessandra humorously interact with a single audience member, usually someone in the center of the room in the first row, thereby drawing everyone else in. When Alessandra talks about the four basic personality types, he calls upon "Andy," who is seated in the first row, to play along with him. He'll ask Andy how he would approach different people with different personalities. Virtually everyone in the room follows along closely as Alessandra helps Andy work through the lesson.

- As a variation, you could simply have a conversation with one person in the audience for the purpose of raising the attention levels of everyone else.
- Some speakers rely on a single vocal audience member who has perhaps voluntarily offered some witticism. That audience member then becomes the focal point for bringing out the speaker's humor. It must be done in a good-natured way, of course. Near the end of the presentation, the speaker generously thanks the audience member for being such a good sport.
- You can shake hands, give high fives, or offer pats on the back to selected audience members.

40

Audience Responsiveness

I an effort to maintain audience responsiveness, some speakers loudly communicate all the time. That is not an effective presentation technique, and it tends to drain audience energy.

Raising and lowering your voice, as well as being silent, are effective tools for increasing audience responsiveness. People don't need to have a presentation pounded into them to ingest the key points. A combination of loud and soft volumes works far better. Choose what you want to accent via increased volume and do it in a controlled fashion.

Getting softer can work well depending on where you are in your presentation. If you're speaking about something on which you want people to reflect, slowing down and speaking at a low volume can work wonders. Suppose you arrive at a critical part of your presentation and you want to encourage audience agreement. In a low voice, you could say, "Haven't we all experienced that at one time or another?"

For a vivid example of how well reducing your volume can work, tune into a *Barbara Walters Special.* She uses that particular technique to great effect. When she wants to ask interviewees a question that requires them to disclose some personal or highly confidential information, she leans forward and looks directly at them. In a soft voice, she poses her question as if the cameras aren't rolling and the answer won't be broadcast to millions of homes.

The same technique works with audiences of any size. If you're behind a lectern, lean forward a little. If you're in the middle of the stage, come to the front. Look directly at some segment of your audience and, in a low volume, pose your question. Then, give audience members time for mental reflection.

Alternatively, simply make a statement, perhaps a provocative one. Wait for participants' reactions. Don't rush the process—let people have time to absorb the full weight of your statement. Resist the temptation to launch immediately into what you want to say next.

NOW LOOK AT THIS

I discussed telling stories, employing print and audiovisual materials, and using humor to great effect in Part II: "Developing and Enlivening Your Presentation." There are endless variations for using these time-honored tools.

- One way to combine all three techniques is to read an amusing or dramatic tidbit from a book or an article. For some reason, when you deliver your own material, it doesn't seem to be quite as dramatic as when you say, "Allow me to quote from XYZ." Or, if you pick up a recent magazine or newspaper and say, "Let me read you a passage from the ABC edition of XYZ," you tend to have the attention of everyone in the room.
- Referring to other media seems to draw everyone in. I've seen speakers show *themselves* on a video monitor and gain higher audience attention. Apparently, the dominance of television ensures that people will pay attention, for at least a short burst of information. Drawing on this principle in a public presentation essentially means that anytime you can get your audience to look at a screen, you will have a temporary upward fluctuation in attention levels.

AUDIENCE PROPS

It's one thing for a speaker to bring props to a presentation. It's another to have audience members create their own.

- You could ask everyone to grab a coin, throw it in the air, and see if it comes up heads or tails, as a form of answering a question, dividing up the group, or having people advocate one viewpoint or another.

- You could ask people to write down their troubles on a piece of paper, then crumple the paper and throw it to the side of the room.
- Some speakers bring a prop for each and every person in the audience. It could be a piece of candy, a button or lapel pin, a squeeze ball, a printed plaque, or any other memorable knickknack that can be used for an audience exercise, a memory hook, and a long-term reminder of the point(s) you offered.

The more relevant the prop is to you or your message, the higher the probability that the audience will relate to it and retain it.

- Audience props can also take the form of items in the room. A simple thing like a chair could be used as a shield, a mock weapon, a dividing line, or a device for a competitive exercise.
- If people are sitting at tables, they can be asked to duck under them or, based on their sturdiness and people's willingness, stand on top of them.
- If you are speaking after a meal and the table isn't cleared, invite attendees to lightly tap their water glasses with a utensil after you make a point. This can have a unifying, humorous, and even dramatic effect.

As with many other forms of inducing audience involvement, encouraging audience members to draw upon items in the immediate environment is limited only by your imagination, your good taste, room logistics, and your ability to make it all work.

THE PRESENTER AS PROP

Dan Thurmon (see Chapter 11) makes an entrance by somersaulting up the middle aisle, while fully dressed in a business suit. In that sense, Thurmon is his own prop. Many other ways to serve as your own prop in smaller settings carry relatively little risk. All presenters, for example, have the opportunity to serve as a kind of prop depending on how they use their faces and bodies.

- Evangelists are known for moving about the platform and directly addressing specific segments of their audiences.
- Even if you stay behind a podium, the way you use your head and face is a prop of sorts. Looks of surprise, fear, and anxiousness, as well as intentionally rolling your eyes, opening your mouth, or squinting all convey meaning to audience members.

CLOTHING PROPS

Articles of clothing can serve as surprisingly effective props to help increase audience attention and alertness:

- Some speakers use preprinted tee shirts that carry a message they want to reinforce or a gag they wish to employ. Speakers will sometimes don a piece of clothing, a button, or a badge when everyone else in the audience has done so to signify that they are a part of the group and support that group's mission or cause.
- Other speakers bring kooky hats, funny gloves, scarves, coats, and other garments, sometimes wearing them underneath other garments and revealing them only at critical junctures in the presentation. This technique usually gets a laugh.

YOU ASK, I ANSWER

Making time for questions and answers is always an audience pleaser. When you allow audience members to ask questions, you increase the probability that they'll be satisfied with what they hear.

- The question that one person asks may be on the minds of many.
- Often when you're asked a question, you're able to convey information that you wanted to offer but couldn't during the formal part of your presentation. Sometimes the questions are so good that future presentations can be modified to incorporate the essence of the question. (Q&A tips and traps are discussed in Chapter 42).

BRINGING AUDIENCE MEMBERS TO THE STAGE

Enlisting the support of audience members during your presentation by bringing them to the stage or platform is a time-honored technique for encouraging audience participation. Although one or even a handful of people may be participating, virtually everyone in the room identifies with the participant(s). Most audience members are thankful that they are not the ones who are up in front!

When you invite someone from the audience to "come up to the stage," whether such individuals are highly enthusiastic volunteers or were induced by you to do so, there are risks to consider:

- Such participants may become extremely nervous.
- They may blank out.
- You may embarrass them in some way that is then hard to make up for.
- The exercise, skit, or role-play may fall flat.
- The audience may not get your point.
- The selected participant(s) may hog the show and upstage the speaker!

Alert the audience far in advance if you plan to call upon participants. Tell them flat out that you'll be asking for volunteers and then let sufficient time pass so that audience members can ruminate on your offer. Five or ten minutes following your announcement, when you seek participants, some people will jump at the chance. Always avoid coercing someone to participate. It usually backfires big time. Even if someone accedes to your request, he or she may secretly resent being forced to get in front of the room.

To reduce the possibility of selecting some over-eager up-stager, announce in advance your instructions for the person or persons who are selected. This has the effect of altering the mix of those who would serve as volunteers. Usually, this change works in your favor. Once participants have actually been chosen and are assembled in the front of the room, provide your specific instructions.

Always ask for the names of the people who volunteer, and call them by their names a number of times during their tenure on stage. Prior to your exercise, give participants a demonstration—make yourself the first guinea pig. To put participants at ease, intentionally *muff* your demonstration. This will get a laugh from the audience and, by contrast, will make participants look and feel better.

While others are on stage, be empathetic, kind, even generous. You're the one in charge of the show. You have all of the power. It's easy for someone to go astray, especially if your instructions have been unclear or your leadership is lacking.

Of course you don't want to knowingly cause someone embarrassment, but if it happens inadvertently, use all of your skills to ease the situation. A hand on the shoulder, a reminder to the audience that it isn't easy being up there, and lavish praise for having made the effort work wonders.

While the exercise is in motion, go with the flow. Take the attitude that whatever happens is grist for the mill and useful to make a point or generate self-directed humor (humor that pokes fun at *yourself*).

When the exercise is complete, acknowledge the participants again for their involvement and lead the audience in offering them a vigorous round of applause. Later, toward the close of the presentation, thank the participants again and ask the audience to re-acknowledge them with another round of applause. This recognition serves several functions. In the minds of volunteers, it cements how skillful and caring you are as a speaker. It also encourages audience members to heap on applause following your concluding words.

SOLICITING FEEDBACK TO ENCOURAGE INVOLVEMENT

Aspiring public speakers don't often stumble on the technique of soliciting audience feedback in mid-presentation. This technique evolves over time. If you're speaking to a group for 45 minutes, and 5 or 10 minutes into your presentation you lay some heavy point on them, it's perfectly permissible and appropriate to say, "Does this square with your experience?" or "Does this fit in your scheme of things?" While audience members are not likely to answer the question out loud, their body language, such as head shaking and increased eye contact, gives you answers. Gently asking, "Has this been helpful so far?" or "Have I adequately explained it?" helps to keep them involved and offers a form of "space" in your presentation.

HIGHLIGHTING THE KEY POINTS

The longer your presentation, no matter how good you are, the harder it is for people to stay attentive. Based on studies, you have to change your manner of speaking every 7 to 20 minutes or people will start to tune out. Here are some ways to vary your presentation:

- Especially with groups attending conferences during which one presentation follows another, or if you're speaking to a group early in the morning, it's greatly helpful to refocus their attention by exclaiming, "And this is a fundamental point," or, "Here is one of the most important observations I will make."
- Some speakers skillfully say, "If you derive only one benefit from today's presentation, I hope it would be this." You can be sure that, following such an announcement, audience attention levels will be at their highest.
- Doing homework on your audience (see Chapter 43) gives you tremendous leverage when it comes to presenting to them. It is true that scientists, engineers, and people in technical professions are more comfortable with hard data, statistics, and charts. Some actually have a harder time listening to stories and anecdotes.

Because audiences tend to be so overwhelmed by items competing for their time and attention in all aspects of their jobs and lives, you incur little risk of running afoul if you spoon-feed information to them and highlight what you deem important. Rather than being resentful, most audience members will be appreciative.

41

Reading
(and Mis-Reading)
Your Audience

Only the most gifted public speakers develop the capabilities to read their audiences *as* they speak to them. What does it mean to read your audience? It means being attuned to how the audience members perceive you, whether or not they are enjoying themselves, whether the atmosphere of the room is comfortable for them, and, in general, how they would like your presentation to proceed.

Since audiences consist of more than one person, how can you make a sweeping generalization about what is likely to be a group of highly diverse individuals? Think of the situation often depicted in films in which an assembled group gets out of hand. The group becomes a mob and demonstrates behaviors such as rioting and vigilantism. Singularly, no members of the mob would act the way they do in the group.

An audience is not a mob, but it potentially shares some of the same characteristics. The people in your audience are greatly influenced by those around them. If you tell a joke, and no one laughs, even an individual who finds the joke humorous will refrain from laughing. Likewise, if the people surrounding an individual show a strong response, such as laughter, that person is likely to respond in the same way. In other words, when you win over the leaders within the audience, you begin to win over the rest of the audience.

AUDIENCE CUES

The notion of reading your audience implies that your audience sends out messages. As a rule of thumb, the more nervous or ill at ease you are during a presentation, the less likely you are to pick up on the cues offered by the audience. Why? Because your focus is so wrapped up in how you are coming across and what everyone might be thinking of you that you have no faculties left for actually watching the group and receiving its messages.

Audible Responses

If an audience laughs, groans, or sighs directly following a comment, you are in luck—you have immediate feedback. Some people instinctively believe that silence is the hardest type of feedback to read, but there are many types of audience silences that are quite revealing. If the audience makes an unexpected noise, like laughter, note what made the reaction occur and use it to your benefit in another speech. At the time, you can act like you intended to induce laughter, actually show your surprise, or come back with a line that adds to the mirth, such as, "Was it something that I said?"

Movement

The old axiom about people leaning forward in their seats being related to their attentiveness is of questionable value. Some people may lean forward because they prefer to do so; others may lean back because it is comfortable, they have indigestion, they are daydreaming, and so forth. Their actual movement is a more accurate indicator of what the audience is experiencing. People leaving during your presentation is a clear sign, as is people coming into the room to hear you. An attentive audience is quiet when it should be, laughing when appropriate, murmuring when its members are confused or excited, and tearful when the presentation becomes emotional.

You have several options when you "read" such an audience. For one, you can slow down, measure your words, use the most appropriate language, and continually seek agreement. Preface some of your statements with "Don't you find it true that," "Haven't you found it to be so," or "How many of you can relate to this situation?"

POSITIVE MEASURE OF SUPPORT

If you are fortunate enough to be in a position in which someone in the audience makes a remark reflecting a highly favorable reaction to your presentation, by all means, play it up. You could make the argument that one person calling out a highly positive response is not representative of the group. However, my experience indicates that such comments invariably do represent the sentiments of the majority. A person vocalizing such sentiments is merely one of the more outspoken or aggressive souls in the group.

STIRRING AND SHUFFLING PAPERS

In addition to movement cues, general stirring in the room, shuffling of papers, and other sounds of "organizing" indicate that people are ready for you to end. This occurs most often when a speaker has gone past the time originally allotted, it is near the end of the day, or audience members are simply bored. Once such stirring begins, do yourself and the audience a favor by quickly coming to a close. It is nearly impossible to win them over at this point.

When you get a clear signal that you need to end, make some of your best points. You can give a summary, you can close the loop by coming full circle and connecting with what you first said, or you can give a short anecdote, a call for action, or an encouraging or motivating close.

RESISTANT AUDIENCES

Not all audiences are salvageable, but you still give them your best. Dr. Robert Pennington says that when dealing with resistant audiences or resistant individuals take control of the room. If you greet people as they enter and shake hands, as has been suggested, you gain a better sense of who they are and how they are feeling about attending your presentation. If the stage or podium is far from audience seating, move to the floor so that you are close to participants. Physical proximity can reduce resistance.

"When people feel safe to disagree they agree more easily," Dr. Pennington says. So, nurture a climate that allows for opposing opinions. Use language such as, "Most everyone will agree with my view on this issue . . ." If a particular member of the audience is disagreeable, work on keeping calm and maintaining your self-assurance. If you feel threatened by this person you are likely to verbally attack him and then he gains allies. This is never to your advantage. "Most angry or obnoxious people don't expect anyone to care about what they think," says Dr. Pennington. "Being receptive to their attack, actually asking them to express themselves more" can help them to be less aggressive and eventually more cooperative.

HANDLING THE
CHALLENGING AUDIENCE

Sometimes an audience isn't resistant—it is merely "less than ideal." Speaker Francine Berger advises maintaining the expectation that some audience members will be stressed or tired, have unrealistic expectations, or may have a low motivation for attending. If such is the case, you are not their real target.

If you encounter trouble, ask questions "and make sure you understand the answers." Sometimes rephrasing what you have said can work wonders. "Picking up on someone's comment and expanding it to the group," says Berger, may work as well.

Do your best to encourage audiences with gestures, nods and facial expressions, and eye contact. Don't convey that you are stressed or anxious about the reactions you are getting from them. Some audiences may perk up in the presence of a composed speaker.

Learn from each experience. "You won't win them all," she says. Recognize, however, that "people get value from your presentation even if they didn't appear responsive." You may hear afterward from someone whose life you touched.

DEALING WITH HECKLERS

If you are not experienced with dealing with hecklers, they can represent a true thorn in your side and potentially disrupt your presentation and sense of control. Hecklers may not have anything in mind other than to get a laugh and draw attention to themselves for doing so.

While some hecklers may engage in malicious heckling, most hecklers are benign. If you know how to work with them, they may actually help you to enliven your presentation. Most audience members, including hecklers, appreciate a quick wit. If you are able to offer comeback lines directly following a heckler's intrusion, usually you can generate a big laugh from the audience and the heckler. Here are some tried and true comeback lines you might wish to employ:

- So, how long have you been on earth?
- Hey, your part doesn't have any lines!
- First time at a big conference?
- Your taxi is waiting!
- So, they didn't let you talk much in school?
- Here, speak into the mike so you can fail louder!

By the time you have offered a second quip following a heckler's intrusion, most of them will cease and desist.

SPEAKING TO ADULTS

Most public speakers speak to adults in the majority of their presentations. We think intuitively we understand how to speak to fellow adults; however, some unique characteristics of adult learners are worth noting. James Daggett, CAE, CMP, founder of JRDaggett & Associates—strategic consultants and managers of meetings, conventions, tradeshows, and events—observes that adults can differ widely in their learning capacities—you can't make the assumption that everyone learns in the same way.

So, how do adults learn best? Daggett suggests that you let your audiences know what to expect. Given that your environment is comfortable and conducive to learning, use as many sensory channels as you can. In other words, not merely sight and sound but touch and smell and even taste. (This is not as difficult as it seems since you can evoke memories of how things feel, smell, and taste.)

WHEN YOU'VE BEEN ASKED
TO CHOP YOUR SPEECH

1. Well-prepared and seasoned speakers have already timed the different segments of their presentations and know that if the "ABC" story is eliminated they can save five minutes, and if the "DEF" suggestions are pulled, they'll save another three, and so forth. Using this modular approach also enables the veterans to customize for particular groups.

If you're not prepared in this manner, you may decide to simply give broader treatment to all the elements of your speech. In many instances, that will work fine. This situation is tougher, however, if your speech is sequential in nature, that is, the listener has to hear "a" and "b" to get to "c" and "d," and you have a powerful climax based on everything that came before it. This leads us to suggestion number 2.

2. Always carry with you a timer, preferably with a magnetic base, that you can attach to the lectern or table in front of you. I learned the hard way that watches don't do the trick. They are hard to see and it doesn't look good to sneak a peak at them during your speech. Radio Shack, as well as Sharper Image and a host of other vendors, carries large display timers. To avoid the beep, I set my timer for five minutes more than I have, knowing that I need to end at the five-minute mark.

3. Don't make any excuses when you're in front of the group. Don't say, "If I had more time," or "Well, I prepared for 45 minutes," and so on. This doesn't help you, the audience, or your host. Simply use the time allotted in the best manner you can. The pro knows that the show must go on, and that a truncated time frame is more often than not the *norm* in public speaking.

4. During the course of your presentation, tactfully offer to make an additional handout available that will cover the points you have insufficient time to address in detail.

5. Strive to be the one speaker at their meeting or convention who gets the meeting back on schedule. If you were scheduled for 45 minutes and you're given 27, end on the button. Although few speakers are penalized for speaking too little, many are penalized in the minds of their listeners for speaking too long. You can become a hero to the host or meeting planner and possibly the larger group, by getting them back on track. This is valuable, so don't discount it.

6. Think *compassion.* Maybe the president's 18 minutes were boring. Many people may need to get to the restroom. Perhaps the activities of the morning were draining. Your 27 minutes can be the bright spot in a person's day.

SUMMARY VERSUS CLOSING

Summarizing what you said is not the same as actually closing. Your summary can occur from three minutes to 30 seconds prior to your last actual word. Your closing statement follows your summary.

Your summary is not a time for making apologies about what you didn't address. It is a time to reinforce the vital points you made, to acknowledge the audience, and to prepare them for the close. You can initiate a summary in many. While you can simply say, "in summary," strive instead to create a link to your opening statement. When you wrap your speech in a tidy bundle it gives audiences the feeling of having come "full circle." They like this form of closure.

CLOSING: SHORT AND SWEET

Max Dixon says to close your speech you want a "simple idea expressed beautifully and tended to well, very well." He suggests that you end the speech in an uncommon manner. "Audiences are aching to feel that they have been listening to something of importance and relevance," says Dixon.

As with opening a speech, you have many options for closing. You could pose a question to the audience so that they depart with your words still in mind. You could make a call for action. You could tell a brief story, and/or you could give thanks for the opportunity to address the group.

Strive to offer a closing that is as energetic and high-spirited as your opening. As such, the mundane, lame, overused, "thank you" can never be your closing.

You can close with a pledge or promise. Depending on your presentation objective, pledging action or making a promise can leave a strong impression on audience members. You could make a prediction. A positive prediction is preferred but a negative one might be appropriate depending on your topic and your objectives. Near-term predictions can prove memorable; some audience members will recall that they "heard" it first from you.

LAST SENTENCE, LAST WORDS

When you utter your final words, remain steadfast. Don't walk away from the lectern or off of the podium. Hold your place, and gaze out to the audience for a few moments. The gap between your last actual word and the first sound of applause can range from a fraction of second to several seconds. Maintain control of that brief segment as you maintained control during the presentation.

If you delivered an effective presentation and your closing was masterful, the audience may need an extra moment to let those words sink in. When the applause comes, keep your head up, remain buoyant, and nonverbally convey appreciation. Speech trainer Tony Jeary says, "Be gracious at the end and smile. Audiences have a need to give applause. Give them every excuse to offer lavish applause."

ACCESSIBLE AND PROFESSIONAL

Jeary advises remaining accessible until the last person leaves. I modify that to say "until the last rational person leaves." Some individuals want to tug on the speaker's ear for at least the length of the presentation. Nevertheless, adopt the attitude that you are "on" long after you have delivered your closing sentence and everyone has cleared the room.

Traps and Tips

I f your idea of being an effective public speaker is to never stumble over a passage or slur your words, forget it. Even the best public speakers are prone to these types of miscues. As with so many other things in life, it's not what happens that's key, but how you handle what happens. If adroitly or nonchalantly corrected, a minor miscue is quickly forgotten by the audience.

BLANKING OUT

What happens when you blank out and lose your place in front of the audience? Elsewhere, I discuss how Tony Alessandra simply says to the audience in a loud, comical voice, "Now where was I?" Invariably, someone in the audience tells him.

For many aspiring public speakers, the fear of "blanking out" is a great inhibitor that serves to diminish the effectiveness of their presentations. Such speakers can be seen with outlines, notes, PowerPoint slides, and all manner of props to remind them each and every step of the way exactly where they need to be and what they need to be saying. While this practice may ensure that they do not lose their places, it may not be worth it. Being overly protective and overly cautious inhibits natural energies, restricts the presentation flow, diminishes potentially effective gestures, and otherwise makes your presentation less than a pleasure to witness.

Here are a variety of retorts you can use if you do lose your place. Keep in mind that all of them need to be said in an upbeat if not humorous manner for the greatest effect:

- "Okay, now where were we?"
- "Let's see, what number (or passage or page) did we get up to?"
- "Now you've gotten me off track."
- "Okay, who knows where we left off?"
- "I was right in the middle of something . . ." (Then, slightly look up toward the ceiling; invariably, someone will offer the correct answer.)

OUT OF OPTIONS

If you blank out on key names and there are no other options, you're probably better off to skip them. Most members of the audience won't notice. Even if those people who thought you were going to cite them notice that you don't, they'll be forgiving if your presentation is effective.

QUESTIONS AND ANSWERS: TIPS AND TRAPS

Your presentation may include a question and answer session. If so, you often have the wonderful opportunity to address or clarify anything you overlooked. After announcing that you are ready to take questions simply say, "First question." As you listen to questions from audience members remain neutral.

If a question is somewhat negative, then before answering it, reword the question in a more positive manner. Then answer the question by looking directly at the questioner for at least the first minute or two of your response. Don't be afraid to be bold. Sometimes simply say "yes" or "no."

Be gracious as you field questions. If someone asks something previously addressed in your presentation, answer anyway. Others in attendance might better understand the explanation in Q&A than they did during the presentation. On the other hand, if someone poses a question that has already been asked simply say, "I believe that we have already taken that question," and move on.

The best way to handle a rambling question is to simply pick some aspect of it and respond to that. Occasionally, you will encounter a "non-question question." This occurs when someone makes a statement and then waits for you to respond to the statement. Don't take the bait. Simply ask, "What is your question?"

If a series of questions start heading down a path you would prefer not to take, bridge to some other topic, offer a strong observation about the new topic, and then call on someone who hasn't spoken before.

Handle audience questions near the end of a presentation but not as the *last* element. Questions tend to dissipate the power of what you said. Time your presentation so that you can adequately include a Q&A session and still have several minutes to build up to a powerful close. Beyond poor timing, a number of traps during Q&A sessions linger. Here are the most common ones and how to stay clear of them:

- Not repeating the question—Some speakers make the mistake of not repeating the question for people who are out of audible range. It is vital to repeat questions, perhaps paraphrasing them so that the questions will be even clearer to more people in attendance.
- Answering too quickly—Even if you have the precise information the questioner is seeking, pause for a moment before delivering your answer so it seems as if you've contemplated the issue. When you answer too quickly, you run the risk of coming across as a know-it-all. No one will fault you for pausing for a moment, and the results will be to your benefit.
- Guessing when you are unsure of an answer. Audiences quickly spot shaky responses during Q&A sessions. If you don't know the answer to something, plainly say so at the outset. If you prefer to attempt an answer, preface you response by saying,
  —"In my estimation . . ."
  —"I'm not sure, but my guess would be . . ."
  —"I can only take a stab at that . . ."
  —Anything that conveys that you're imparting what you know but that it may not be the most reliable answer is sufficient.
- Over answering. Long-winded responses to questions are the death knell of speakers who otherwise have made a good presentation.

Granted, there are occasions when you need to give background information to adequately answer your question; however, this is the exception and not the norm.

- Letting one person hog the show. Within a large gathering there is invariably someone who has a multipart question or who keeps asking questions. It makes sense for you to follow through on two questions. The third time the same person poses a question or makes a comment, simply respond by saying, "Let's give others a chance to participate," or "Let's hear from those who haven't spoken up yet."

- Looking away from the questioner. When a question is posed, address the questioner directly by looking at him or her. After a minimum of 10 or 15 seconds it's okay to look away to take in the whole audience. Don't address the larger audience, however, without first making sustained eye contact with the questioner. It may seem as if you're belittling the questioner.

- Pointlessly sparring with the questioner. This is not a pitfall—it's a landmine! If you find that a question posed to you somehow converts to a one-on-one dialog, the outcome is often unfavorable. You'll either (1) bore the audience, (2) frustrate them, (3) unduly arouse the questioner, or (4) shortchange your session. The antidote to this situation is to gently invite the questioner to see you after your presentation or during any break time.

- Enduring a long-winded questioner. A long-winded questioner is someone who is speaking to hear his or her own voice and doesn't particularly care about the answer to the question. Brace yourself and attempt to let all questioners finish before you speak.

  If damage may be done to the Q&A session unless you intervene, as politely as possible, say, "In recognition of our time constraints, let me jump in and answer that . . ." While you might turn off the questioner, you'll win points with everyone else in the room who already was fearing that the windbag would never finish.

- Answering without understanding the question. This usually happens because you either did not fully hear the questioner, you cut off the questioner before completion, or the questioner was inarticulate. You can always clarify on the spot by using language such as "Now if I understand your question . . ." At that point, the questioner will either correct you or nod his or her approval. You could also ask the questioner to rephrase the question.

If you keep your answers short and to the point, even if you address the wrong issue, at least you didn't spend a lot of time. Thereafter, the questioner or someone else will speak up again, further clarifying the original question.

- Answering hypothetical questions. This is a judgment call. Some questioners will ask you about situations that have never happened and never are likely to happen. Hence, your answer represents pure conjecture. You can choose to answer hypothetical questions, prefacing your remarks by saying, "In the event that . . ." You can also politely decline to answer hypothetical questions, saying:
  —"I would prefer not to speculate."
  —"Let's leave that to the forecasters."
  —"That merits further exploration, but I will have to pass on it for now."

- Conveying contempt for a question or the questioner. If you speak often enough, it will happen. Someone is going to ask you a hostile question, one that contorts a point in your presentation or is otherwise inappropriate. Use all of your interpersonal skills and remain on an even keel. Attempt to remain empathetic.

Why Speakers
Fail to Hit the Mark

There are many ways to successfully deliver a presentation and, understandably, many more ways to fail, as I've discussed in previous chapters. In addition, here are common mistakes that speakers make, professional speakers included, each of which has to do with a lack of adequate preparation.

1. MISUNDERSTANDING THE ASSIGNMENT

Before ever leaving your own office, it is critical to understand why you have been scheduled to speak to this group at this time. Such understanding necessitates that you read about the organization, get information about the audience's current challenges and hot buttons, and learn what the meeting planner has in mind for the presentation. Five-minute conversations over the phone usually won't supply you with all you need to know in that area.

2. FAILING TO KNOW YOUR AUDIENCE

Beyond understanding the setting and why you are invited to speak, knowing the audience is itself an art and a science. Beyond the information about their job level, salary, and degree of diversity, you will also want to know their age range, educational background, and what this particular meeting has been designed to do for them.

Probe even further. How far have they come? Do they know one another or are they assembling for the first time? What will they hear before and after the presentation? What did they hear last year or at a similar meeting? How would they like to feel and what would they like to get out of your presentation?

Unless you find answers to these types of questions and there isn't much more that you could know, don't accept the presentation. Without this information, your presentation may hit the mark, but chances are that you will simply dance around the periphery of what you need to do and say to be successful.

3. WAITING FOR LATECOMERS

If you're giving a general session or keynote address in a large assembly hall, this is not an issue. If you are giving a breakout session, a workshop, or some other type of training session, often there is discretion as to when you will formally begin the presentation. Do not penalize those who have come on time and are ready to have you start as scheduled.

Only in the case where it is readily apparent that the majority of the attendees are missing are you justified, perhaps, in delaying the start of a presentation. In such cases, you can confer with audience members present and others who may be in the halls to see if something has delayed the bulk of the anticipated audience. Short of that situation, it is your responsibility to start on time. Those who trickle in afterward have the personal responsibility to find out about whatever they missed.

As you become more adept at speaking to groups in various settings, you begin to realize the wisdom of starting with a story or an audience warm-up technique. In such cases, the late arrivals do not miss any of the meat of your presentation and the punctual arrivals feel satisfied that you began on schedule.

4. OFFERING EXCUSES

Perhaps the most pitiful opening a public speaker can make in addressing an audience is stating that he or she is just getting over an illness, or is fatigued because of a heavy workload or travel. Audiences do not care about your personal circumstances en route to your presenting at this particular time—nor should they.

If you are too ill, exhausted, or stressed to make an effective presentation, alert the meeting planner as far in advance as possible so that he or she can find a substitute speaker.

5. SPEAKING WITHOUT A MICROPHONE

As a public speaker you cannot afford to speak without a microphone, even to the smallest of audiences. I have seen speakers time and time again think that they can simply wing it. But, if you are going to speak for more than 20 minutes, do yourself and your audience a favor by using a microphone.

6. TAPPING OR BLOWING INTO THE MICROPHONE TO TEST IT

No public speaker should ever do this. Ideally, you have already checked out the microphone long before your presentation. If, for whatever reason, you don't have the opportunity to test the microphone before going on, you can see if everything seems okay by observing others use it.

The larger the meeting, the greater the probability there will be a "sound person" someplace in or near the room who will be monitoring the equipment. This person will make adjustments on the fly once he or she hears you say anything into the microphone.

Public throat clearing is akin to tapping or blowing into the microphone. It is completely amateurish to get up in front of a group, particularly with a microphone at hand, and clear your throat. We have all seen speakers do this. Why don't they take care of this before they get in front of the group? Public throat clearing is a telltale sign of someone who is uncomfortable in front of a group and is likely to make the group feel uncomfortable as well.

7. SHIFTING YOUR WARDROBE

The time to ensure comfort in what you are wearing is long before the presentation begins. If you're not comfortable speaking with a tie, and the meeting and speaker dress codes allow for you to not wear a tie, don't put one on!

After you've given a number of presentations, notice your instincts when it comes to your speaking wardrobe and mid-speech rearrangements. Then, take charge of the situation before your next presentation. Talk to the meeting planner about the dress code and what makes you most comfortable, and then find the happy middle ground. It may save you from making unnecessary mid-speech wardrobe adjustments.

When is the audience okay with a wardrobe adjustment? When something happens during the presentations such that it is obvious that a change needs to be made. Suppose you're speaking in an air-conditioned room, and the performance of the air conditioner is less than stellar. People are starting to feel uncomfortably warm and notice that you feel uncomfortably warm. Invite them to remove their jackets before announcing that you're going to do so as well. In such cases, you win points with the audience.

8. FIDDLING WITH AV EQUIPMENT IN MIDPRESENTATION

Once you have begun your presentation, it is not the time to determine whether an overhead projector, slide carousel, LCD panel, or other equipment is in working order. It is the height of unprofessionalism to check out your equipment in any way once the presentation has started.

9. USING INAPPROPRIATE AV MATERIALS

People will forgive you for graphics with bad color scheme, corny jokes, or inconsistencies. What riles meeting planners and audience members the most is when a speaker uses minuscule fonts barely readable in the middle of the room, and impossible to discern from the back of the room. Some speakers apologize in advance saying, "Please forgive me for the clarity of this slide," or "I know the print is hard to see, so I will read it for you." These are rather lame apologies since, for a public speaking engagement, presumably you had days, weeks, or months to improve the quality of your AV materials.

10. STEPPING OUT OF SIGHT

No, this doesn't mean becoming invisible to the audience. Many speakers who stay close to the audience make the mistake of wandering past the first few rows of participants. This means that the people in the front seats must literally turn around in order to keep watching you. As a device for generating audience interest, it is perfectly permissible to extend past the first few rows for 10 or 15 seconds at a time. However, if you plant yourself down one of the aisles and force people to turn around and look at you for an extended length of time, you will tax their energies, eventually their patience, and ultimately their attention. Remain visible to all by respecting lines of sight and boundaries.

11. READING FROM NOTES OR A SCRIPT

The audience is in place to hear you speak, not to hear you read, unless, of course, you are simply quoting a relevant passage from a book, article, or other document somewhere in the body of your speech. Regardless of how skilled a reader you are, it is far less interesting for the audience to hear you read than to hear you speak. In academic conferences, presenters often "deliver a paper" and make the dreadful mistake of reading their paper word for word.

12. BUILDING UP TOO SLOWLY

You can tell stories of an extended length that lead up to a point that you want audience members to take home. That is different from what we are discussing here. We have all encountered presenters at one time or another who simply rambled on for minutes at a time not realizing that they were losing the goodwill that most audience members have for speakers at the outset of a presentation.

13. PACING BACK AND FORTH

Dissipating your nervous energy by pacing back and forth adds nothing to your presentation and can detract from it in damaging ways. Any expressions of nervousness you exhibit, pacing being one of the most visible, will be immediately observed by audience members who will individually question your effectiveness, wonder how long this presentation will last, and ask themselves why they are even in attendance.

14. MISMANAGING THE SNIFFLES

Everyone has his or her own pet peeves when it comes to attending a presentation. For me, it is the sniffles. A speaker proceeding along with intermittent sniffles detracts from my ability to stay focused. Some speakers do this out of habit. Others do it because they find that their nose is running and they didn't have the foresight to carry a tissue with them or place one nearby.

If you have a significant problem with sniffles, sneezing, or coughing while on stage, excuse yourself for the time necessary to remedy the situation, and then, when you are ready, turn back to the audience. Here, it is difficult to avoid making reference to what happened so have some comeback lines at your disposal. These could include the following:

- "That wasn't a planned part of the presentation."
- "Well, now that we have that taken care of . . ."
- "I'm glad to be back!"

Do not make specific reference to any of the particulars of the situation. Even in the best case scenario when you're able to get a laugh by referring to your difficulty, it will be the wrong kind of humor. Stick with the relatively clever and safe lines above, and then pick up where you left off.

15. MAKING REPEATED REFERENCES TO SPORTS

Independent of the male-female ratio of the audience, a presentation peppered by sports analogies reflects a weakness in the preparation, background, and perhaps even intellect of the presenter. With all that goes on in the world in political, social, religious, artistic, scientific, and educational arenas, how justifiable is it to have a speaker offer one sports analogy after another?

16. LOOKING AT YOUR WATCH

A quick way to drain all the energy out of the room during your presentation is to take a peek at your watch. It seems harmless enough, but the moment you do it, you convey a message to everyone in the room that you have something other than addressing them on your mind. You also run the risk of having audience members steal a peak at their own watches, which diverts their attention from your presentation and gets them thinking about how much time is left and what they're going to do next.

Fortunately, there are several excellent alternatives to sneaking a peek at or even wearing a watch during your presentation. First, the ideal situation is when there is a clock on the back wall of the conference room and all audience members have their backs to it. In such settings, every time you look at the clock, it will seems as if you are peering out to the back rows of your audience.

If a clock is not available, you have the option of working with the meeting planner to ensure that someone is flashing time cards for you, usually from the first row. For a 60-minute presentation, they may flash the 30-minute card to you, no bigger than an 8- by 11-inch sheet of paper. When handled discreetly, no one else in the audience is aware that you are being offered a time signal. At the 15 minute mark, then 10, 5, 3, 2, and 1 minute marks, you are gently led to your ending time. This strategy can work well with audiences of less than 100 people. In larger halls, you may find it difficult to look for, comprehend, and acknowledge the time cues.

The most effective solution is buying a timer, clock, or travel alarm with large display. Regardless of the meeting room setup, there is always space to position your timepiece. The few audience members who might notice the tiny device have little interest in it. During the course of the presentation, you'll have several opportunities to look in all directions, so sneaking peeks at your timer will not be a challenge.

17. AIRING COMMERCIALS

Whatever your arrangement with the meeting planner regarding the sale of your products, if you make an extended pitch, you can't help but turn off a significant portion of your audience. This occurs regardless of your success up to that point.

Audience members are leery of being "sold" these days—they are already bombarded by commercial messages on television, radio, the Internet, and in print media. The last thing that most audience members want to hear is an extended commercial by a presenter, even among those groups and those audiences who routinely allow presenters to sell their wares. So, if the privilege is extended to you, approach it carefully and tastefully.

18. RUNNING OVERBOARD

Many aspiring public speakers haven't made the effort to time their presentations. As a result, they often run overboard. They realize in, say, a 30-minute speech, that they are only half way through it with five minutes to go. Then, they commit a greater presentation sin: They attempt to rush through all of the points remaining, thereby making audience members ill at ease, giving them the impression that they have been shorthanded, and raising anxiety to an undue level.

19. FINISHING TOO ABRUPTLY

As discussed in Chapter 41, too many public speakers close with a mundane, undramatic, "thank you." Besides signaling that you lack the capability to masterfully draw to a close, you also leave many audience members feeling shortchanged. In a public venue, one for which you were scheduled days, weeks, or months in advance, terminating your speech abruptly is one of the surest indications that you have "miles to go" before becoming a polished public speaker.

20. DISAPPEARING AFTER THE PRESENTATION

Perhaps if you are William F. Buckley, Ted Koppel, or Elizabeth Dole, you can depart right after your presentation, having previously alluded to some other pressing engagement. The audience will grant you the slack afforded to those in position of power, authority, or celebrity. For the rest of public speakers, stand your ground after having delivered your presentation. Likewise, do as much as you can to meet and greet audience members at the start of the presentation (see Chapter 37). Practically speaking, you gain no points for attempting to develop a "mysterious" persona. Stick around and reap all the benefits of having done a great job.

21. NOT THANKING THE MEETING PLANNER

Be sure to directly thank the meeting planner before you leave. I both thank the meeting planner in person and drop a letter in the lobby mailbox that essentially says: "Dear Meeting Planner, I couldn't leave town without thanking you. What a great job you did in putting together the conference. I want you to know that I appreciate your efforts. I wish you well in future programs and all endeavors. Yours truly . . ."

Bibliography and Further Reading

Ailes, Roger, *You Are the Message* (Burr Ridge, IL: BusinessOne Irwin, 1986).

Alessandra, Tony, *The Platinum Rule* (New York: Warner, 1996).

Benson, Herbert, *The Relaxation Response* (New York: Avon, 1990).

Bradford, William, *Managing for Excellence* (New York: Wiley, 1997).

Brooks, Bill, *You're Working Too Hard to Make the Sale* (Burr Ridge, IL: BusinessOne Irwin, 1995).

Brooks, Bill, *Nichemanship* (Burr Ridge, IL: BusinessOne Irwin, 1992).

Burnham, Terry, and Jay Phelan, *Mean Genes* (New York: Penguin, 2001).

Burrus, Dan, *Technotrends* (New York: HarperCollins, 1994).

Carnegie, Dale, *How to Win Friends and Influence People* (New York: Pocket Books, 1994).

Cathcart, Jim, *The Acorn Principle* (New York: St. Martin's, 1998).

Collins, James, and Jerry Poris, *Built to Last: Successful Habits of Visionary Companies* (New York: Harper Business, 1997).

Connor, Richard, and Jeff Davidson, *Getting New Clients* (New York: Wiley, 1993).

Connor, Richard, and Jeff Davidson, *Marketing Your Consulting & Professional Services* (New York: Wiley, 1994).

Cooper, Morton, *Change Your Voice, Change Your Life* (Los Angeles: Wilshire Books, 1996).

Daniels, Aubrey, *Bringing out the Best in People* (New York: McGraw-Hill, 1994).

Davidson, Jeff, *Breathing Space: Living and Working at a Comfortable Pace in a Sped-Up Society* (New York: MasterMedia, 1991).

Davidson, Jeff, *Marketing for the Home-Based Business, 2nd ed.* (Avon, MA: Adams Media, 1999).

Davidson, Jeff, *Marketing Your Career and Yourself* (Avon, MA: Adams Media, 1999).

Davidson, Jeff, *The Complete Idiot's Guide to Assertiveness* (Indianapolis, IN: Alpha Books, 1997).

Davidson, Jeff, *The Complete Idiot's Guide to Managing Stress, 2nd ed.* (Alpha Books, 1999).

Davidson, Jeff, *The Complete Idiot's Guide to Reaching Your Goals* (Alpha Books, 1997).

Davidson, Jeff, *The Joy of Simple Living* (Emmaus, PA: Rodale, 1999).

Dement, William, *The Promise of Sleep* (New York: Delacort, 1999).

Detz, Joan, *How to Write and Give a Speech,* (New York: St. Martin's Press, 1992).

Dyer, Wayne, *You'll See It When You Believe It* (New York: Avon, 1996).

Dychewald, Ken, *Age Wave* (Los Angeles: Tarcher, 1989).

Elsea, Janet G., *First Impression, Best Impression* (New York: Simon & Schuster, 1978).

Gitomer, Jeffrey, *The Sales Bible* (New York: Morrow, 1994).

Hesse, Hermann, *Siddhartha* (New York: Bantam, 1982).

Jampolsky, Gerald, *Love Is Letting Go of Fear* (Berkeley, CA: Celestial Arts, 1988).

Jeary, Tony, *How to Inspire Any Audience* (Berkeley, CA: Publishers' Group West, 1999).

Jeffries, Elizabeth, *The Heart of Leadership* (Dubuque IA: Kendall-Hunt, 1996).

Klein, Allan, *The Courage to Laugh: Humor, Hope, and Healing in the Face of Death and Dying* (Tarcher, 1998).

Levering, Robert, and Milton Moskowitz, *Hundred Best Companies to Work for in America* (Plume, 1994).

Mitford, Jessica, *The American Way of Death* (New York: Simon & Schuster, 1978).

Pascale, Richard, Mark Mallemann, and Linda Gioga, *Surfacing the Edge of Chaos* (New York: Crown, 2000).

Porter, Michael, *Competitive Advantage* (New York: Macmillan, 1985).

Powell, Colin, *My American Journey* (New York: Random House, 1996).

Ries, Al, and Jack Trout, *Positioning: The Battle for Your Mind* (New York: McGraw-Hill, 1981).

RoAne, Susan, *How to Work a Room* (New York: Warner Books, 1994).

RoAne, Susan, *What Do I Say Next?* (New York: Warner Books, 1999).

Salsbury, Glenna, *The Art of the Fresh Start* (Health Communications, 1996).

Silva, Michael, and Craig Hickman, *Creating Excellence* (New York: New American Library Trade, 1984).

Tart, Charles, *States of Consciousness* (New York: E. P. Dutton, 1975).

Toffler, Alvin, *Future Shock* (New York: Random House, 1970).

Vlcek, Don, *The Domino Effect* (New York: McGraw-Hill, 1991).

Wilder, Lilyan, *Seven Steps to Fearless Speaking* (New York: Wiley, 1999).

Yoho, Dave, and Jeff Davidson, *How to Have a Good Year Every Year* (Berkeley, CA: Berkeley Books, 1991).

About the Author

Some people regard Jeff Davidson as the best there is at offering new perspectives and fresh solutions to the career and life balance problems that people face today.

Jeff's speeches have been featured in *Vital Speeches of the Day* on six occasions along with the likes of Dr. Henry Kissinger, Lee Iacocca, George Bush (senior), William Bennett, Michael Eisner, Jimmy Carter, Alan Greenspan, and the Dalai Lama. Members of his nearly 700 audiences know him as a high-content, high-energy speaker who delivers humorous yet compelling presentations.

He has been featured in 68 of the top 75 newspapers in America, based on circulation including *USA Today, The Washington Post, Los Angeles Times,* and *The Chicago Tribune.* As a five-time state winner of the U.S. Small Business Administration's Media Advocate of the Year Award, Jeff has published more than 3,300 articles on the topics of entrepreneurship, management and marketing effectiveness, and life balance.

Jeff has attracted clients such as America Online, Wells Fargo, Nations-Bank, Swissotel, IBM, American Express, Westinghouse, and more than 400 other leading organizations and associations. He is also a founding faculty member of www.MentorU.com. He devised 26 online training programs for MentorU.

For five years running, Jeff's popular books in the fields of self-help and business, such as *Marketing Your Consulting and Professional Services, The Joy of Simple Living, The Complete Idiot's Guide to Time Management,* and other titles in that series, have sold an average of 100,000 books annually.

Jeff can be reached on the web at www.BreathingSpace.com and via email at KeyNoteSpeaker@BreathingSpace.com.

Index

Abbreviations, humorous, 54
Adcock, Sharon, 79, 84, 85, 86
Adult learners, characteristics of, 292–293
Agreements/contracts, 173
  audiovisual needs, 197
  cancellation, 197, 206–208
  deposit due, 196
  educational materials, 197–198
  fees/travel expenses, 196
  getting paid, 196, 206–212
  instructions to clients, 198, 208–209
  location, 195
  number of attendees, 195
  preparing for and negotiating, 173
  ready availability of forms, 118
  refund sliding scale, 207–208
  sample form, 194–195
  variations on product sales, 199–205
  what is covered in, 193–198
  what meeting planners seek, 175–183
Ailes, Roger, 57
Airline travel/reservations, 247–248
Alessandra, Tony, 210, 279, 296
American Society of Association Executives
  (ASAE), 218
American Society of Composers, Authors,
  and Publishers (ASCAP), 234
American Society of Training and
  Development, 117
Antion, Tom, 53
Articles, converting transcripts into, 131–132
Asaenet.org, 218
Association executives (as source of topics),
  25
Audience:
  audible responses from, 289
  befriending, 262
  bringing members to the stage, 285–286
  compassion for, 294
  cues from, 289

exercises for, 275–276
gathering information about specific
  members, 235
greeting members (before/after
  presentation), 119, 258, 265–267, 295,
  309
incorporating observations, 236
influences on listening experience (story
  telling), 104–105
involving, 230–234, 275–280
knowledge of, 53, 302
movement/noise in, 289–290
participation packets, 8, 177–178, 183,
  230, 279
playing along with member of, 279–280
positive measure of support from, 290
preparation techniques, 230–233
props, 282–283
questions from, 284, 297–300
reading/mis-reading, 288–295
resistant/challenging, 290–291
respect for, 119
responsiveness, 281–287
secondary, 8–9
size (in speaker agreement), 195
soliciting feedback (mid-presentation),
  286–287
surveys/quizzes, 231–232
using member names, 277
wanting you to succeed, 262
Audiovisual considerations. *See also* Taping
  presentation; Videos; Visuals
  assisting meeting planners, 188
  fiddling with equipment midpresentation,
    304–305
  needs (in speaker agreement), 197
  rights (meeting planner concerns), 176
  using low-quality inappropriate materials,
    305
Austin, Emory, 93

Bender, Peter Urs, 243
Benny, Jack, 112
Berger, Francine, 291
BFI method (Brute Force and Ignorance),
　54
Billings-Harris, Lenora, 223–224, 225
Biographical information (on one-sheet), 143
Blackwell, Joel, 8
Blanking out or stumbling, 111–112,
　261–262, 296–297
Bookman, Robert, 75
Brainstorming guidelines, 32–33
Branding, 121
Breathing exercise, 261
Briles, Judith, 130
Buckley, William F., 309
Bureaus, speakers, 164, 211
Burg, Bob, 121
Burrus, Dan, 201–204
Bush, George W., 112–113
Buzzwords, 6–7, 237

Calloway, Joe, 205
Cancellations, protection against, 197,
　206–209
Cathcart, Jim, 135, 179
Change (as topic), 21, 34–38
Clark, Dan, 72, 96, 273–274
Clients/meeting planners:
　assisting/consulting to, 188
　communication with, 215–216, 226–229
　concerns/desires of, 117–119, 175–176
　contracts with (see Agreements/contracts)
　current challenges for, 23–24
　liaison, one-person, 177
　satisfied (using in marketing efforts):
　　on one-sheet, 143
　　testimonials from (see Kudo letters)
　selection committees, 182–183
　serving (even when not booked), 221
　as source for topics, 22–24
　what speakers want from, 176–179
Clipping file, 46
Closed circuit television, 89–90
Closing:
　common mistakes, 309
　ending your speech, 294–295, 309
　remaining accessible and professional after
　　speech, 295, 309
　vs. summary, 294
Clothing/wardrobe:
　fiddling with/shifting during speech, 304
　packing/travel tips, 246

props, 284
recommendations, 58–59
Coach, speech, 62–66
Comeback lines (when nobody laughs), 53
Conferences (meeting type), 40
Connor, Richard, 24
Consultant, acting as, 122, 188
Contact information, 141–142, 193
Contact management software, 217–218
Contracts. See Agreements/contracts
Control, anticipated loss of, 260–261
Conventions (meeting type), 39–40
Copyrights, 149–150, 176, 205, 233–234
Corporate sponsors, 130
Corporations/companies (as host), 44
Cost (meeting planner concerns), 175. See
　also Fee(s)
Cultural change, 35
Cuomo, Mario, 273
Cyclical topics, 4–5

Daggett, James, 292
Daniloff, Nicholas, 211
Dark zone, 257
Davidson, Jeff:
　model (four mega-realities), 29
　sample humorous introduction of, 240
　sample marketing document called "What
　　Is It Like to Work with Jeff
　　Davidson?," 179–181
　sample one-sheet, 144–145
　sample serious introduction of, 241
　signature story, 97–98
　strategic URLs, 139–140
Dawson, Roger, 265, 266
Deficiencies approach (finding topics),
　15–16
Deposit, 196
Desires, seven subtle unconscious, 12–13
Detz, Joan, 60
Diction, 59–60
Digart, Charles, 6
Directories, national, 219–220
Discounts and favors, 137–138, 189–190
Diversity issues, 36, 222–225
Dixon, Max, 294
Dole, Elizabeth, 309
Domain registrations, 139–140
"Domestic partner," 225
Dramatic, flair for the, 273
Dual presenters, 55
Dual purpose engagements, 190
Dychtwald, Ken, 4

Editorial coordination (publications/
　marketing), 128–129
Educational institutions, 45
Educational materials (in speaker
　agreement), 197–198. *See also*
　Participation packets, audience
Elasticity calculations, 136–137
E-mailing photos, 154
Embarrassments (source of stories), 95
Emerson, Ralph Waldo, 215
Emotion(s):
　appealing to, 10–17
　　inspirational presentations, 11
　　motivational presentations, 11
　　seven subtle unconscious desires,
　　　12–13
　conveying, 273–274
Employee stock operating plans (ESOPs),
　37
Ending your speech. *See* Closing
Enjoyment, 66–68, 261
Ethnic/minorities (diversity issues), 36,
　222–225
Evangelists, 284
Eventplanner.com, 218
Exaggeration, 148
Excuses, offering, 303
Extracting data from other sources (*vs.*
　original material), 70

Family/relatives (source of stories), 94
Federal Directory (Carroll Publishing), 220
Fee(s), 133–140, 206–212
　cancellation, and partial payment, 197,
　　206–208
　consistency with materials, 210
　discounts, 137–138, 189–191
　dual purpose engagements, 190
　establishing, 135
　guidance on, 211
　increasing, 138–140, 212
　keys to earning big checks, 209–210
　multiple engagements, 189–190
　negotiating, 189–190
　peer comparisons, 136–137
　prompt payment, 178–179
　ruling your niche (industry specialist),
　　211
　scale of, 133–135
　shared speaker, 190
　taking payment in product/services *vs.*
　　money, 190
　for taping presentation, 201–205

　upgrading materials when increasing,
　　138–140
Feedback:
　mid-presentation (soliciting to encourage
　　involvement), 286–287
　requesting on evaluation/marketing form,
　　159, 160
Fisher, Roger, 189
Flexibility, 176, 228
Fonts, 85, 243
Forums (meeting type), 41
Freezing the moment, 74–76, 272–273
Friedman, Francis, 123
Friedman, Scott, 52, 54
Fripp, Patricia, 101, 259, 260
Fujioka, Ray, 84
Funeral industry, 31

Gay, lesbian, bisexual, and transgender
　(GLBT) community, 225
Gillebaard, Lola, 51
Gitomer, Jeffrey, 233
Giuliani, Rudy, 75
Goal setting, 126–132
Government agencies, 45, 190
Grove, Andrew, 34
Gurus (as source of topics), 26

Hands-on speakers (meeting planner
　concerns), 176
Headsets, telephone, 88, 217
Heckler(s), dealing with, 292
Heckler, Lou, 101
Hennig, Jim, 189
Hensley, Dennis, 54
Hepburn, Katharine (author's signature
　story), 97–98
Hickey, Margaret, 27
Horizontal opportunities, 129–130
Host organizations, types of:
　educational institutions, 45
　government agencies, 45
　large corporations, 44
　local groups, 45
　mid-sized companies, 44
　professional associations, 45
　professional societies, 44–45
　small businesses, 44
　trade associations, 45
Hotel(s). *See also* Travel
　glitches, 87
　mailing packages to, 245
　noise-reduction technology, 248

Hotel(s) *(Continued)*
  preventative measures while checking in, 248
  proper packing, 246
  working with audiovisual staff, 86–88
"Hot" topics, 4
How-to presentations, tips, 279
Humor, 49–56
  abbreviations as, 54
  comeback lines when nobody laughs, 53
  by duos (team speakers), 55
  handling attack of sniffles with, 307
  interactive, 52, 279–280
  in introductions, 50, 240
  knowing audience, 53
  opening lines, 50
  pauses enhancing, 112
  reading jokes, 51–52
  reasons for, 49–50, 56
  story listening trance and, 105
  tips on, 51
  using everyday experience, 52–53
Humorists, 54
Hutson, Don, 146–147

IDIOS syndrome (I'll do it in Saturday), 54
Image magnification technology (I-Mag screens), 82–83
Inclusive language, 224–225
Industry:
  background in (meeting planner concerns), 175
  collecting statistics, 125
  researching, 22–23
  ruling your niche, 211
  seminars, conducting, 124–125
  specializing/targeting single, 123, 211
  writing newsletter for, 123–124
Insensitive terms, 179, 222
Inspirational presentations, 11
Intellectual property rights (copyright), 149–150, 176, 205, 233–234
Interactive humor, 52
International Association for Exposition Management (iaeme.org), 218–219
Internet/Web sites:
  benefits to public speakers, 140
  fee guidance Web sites, 211
  having all functions Web-ready, 139
  for marketing, 142, 149
  meeting industry Web sites, 218–220
  online presentations, 88–89, 139

quality of your Web site reflecting fee level, 210
  securing strategic URLs (domain registrations), 139–140
  selling products on, 140
Introduction (of speaker), 239–244
  humorous, 50, 240
  preparing introducer, 242, 243–244
  to be read or not to be read, 243–244
  sample humorous introduction (of author), 240
  sample serious introduction (of author), 241
  submitting text for, 242–243
  transition: shaking hands with and thanking introducer, 244, 267–268
  writing it yourself, 239–242
Invitations to presentations, 130
Irritations approach (finding topics), 15
Irvin, Dale, 50
Isomer, Jeffrey, 190

Jackson, Jesse, 273
James, William, 272
Jeary, Tony, 12–13, 60, 295
Jeffries, Elizabeth, 200
Jitters, avoiding/dealing with, 259–262

Karr, Ron, 189
Kennedy, John F., 111, 273
Kessell, Louise Omoto, 99–100
Keyboard, no-click, 216
Kilpatrick, Kurt, 53
Klein, Allen, 276
Koppel, Ted, 309
Kudo letters, 132, 156–162
  formats for use of, 158–159
  highlighting (making easy on receiver), 159–161
  "iffy," 161
  long-term contact, maintaining (with senders), 161–162
  obtaining, 132
  permission required to use, 158
  in perspective, 162
  self-generated (evaluation/marketing form), 159, 160
  why people write, 156–157

Latecomers, waiting for, 302–303
Learning organization (as topic), 21
Lecruises.com, 218
Lectures (meeting type), 43

Lee, Bill, 123–125
Letters. *See* Kudo letters
Liaison, one-person, 177
Librarians (as source of topics), 26–27
Life's gambles (source of stories), 95
Lighting/glare, 249, 257
Literature, meeting/conference (quality of;
    client factor), 178
Local groups, 45
Location (in speaker agreement), 195
Logos, 143
Lohan, Kevin, 74–75
Love/affection/empathy, conveying (to
    audience), 271–272

Mailing list, building, 130–131
Mailing packages to yourself, 245
Mapes, Mary Jane, 96
Mapping (in story telling), 100
Marketing, 115–172
    becoming industry specialists, 211
    client's mind-set, 117–119
    corporate sponsors, 130
    evaluation/marketing form, 159
    getting paid and selling your services,
        133–140
    goal setting, 126–132
    horizontal opportunities, 129–130
    invitations to presentations, 130
    mailing list, developing your, 130–131
    measuring progress, 126–132
    meeting other speakers at conventions, 132
    niche, 211
    opportunities for (at every presentation),
        132
    persistence in, 191
    positioning, 120–125
    preempting/closing the deal, 184–192
    publications, editorial coordination,
        128–129
    revenue opportunities, 128
    selling services, 128, 187–188
    selling true impact of a presentation (four
        levels), 186–187
    setting fees (*see* Fee(s))
    vertical opportunities, 129
    what if you lose the booking, 191–192, 221
    when they can't afford you, 189–190
Marketing materials:
    collecting and using kudo letters, 132,
        156–162
    consistency, importance of, 210
    "one-sheet," 141–154

copyright, 149–150
    as door opener and closer, 149
    lower cost alternative to, 149
    proper information for, 141–148
    samples, 144–145, 146–147
preassembled packets, 220
ready availability of, 118
sample document "What Is It Like to Work
    with Jeff Davidson?," 179–181
upgrading with fee upgrades, 138–140
video demonstration tape, 131–132,
        163–172 (*see also* Taping presentation)
    credentials bolstering, 210
    customizing with interview of yourself
        by video crew, 205
    how used by meeting planners and
        speaker's bureaus, 164
    industry professionals' advice, 166–170
    production strategies for, 164–166
    purpose of, 163
    veteran speakers' strategies, 170–172
May, Rollo, 260
Mayer, Lyle, 60
Measuring progress toward goals, 126–132
Meeting planners. *See* Clients/meeting
    planners
Meeting Professionals International, 22
Meeting room(s):
    client arranging as requested, 178
    consulting on setup of, 188
    layouts, 249–257
        classroom style, 251–252
        closed boardroom seating, 254–255
        crescent theatre seating with side aisles,
            250–251
        facing parallel tables, 256
        herringbone classroom style, 252
        hollow square, 253–254
        O-type setup, 255
        in the rounds, 256–257
        standard U-shaped seating, 252–253
        theatre-style seating, 250
        T-shaped setup, 255–256
    prepresentation walk of, 249
Meeting types/variations, 39–46. *See also*
    Host organizations, types of
conference, 40
convention, 39–40
forum, 41
lecture, 43
retreat, 43–44
seminar, 41–42
symposium, 41

Meeting types/variations *(Continued)*
  training, 42–43
  workshop, 42
Microphones, 205, 303–304
Mistakes, common (in public speaking),
    301–310
  disappearing after presentation, 309
  failing to know audience, 302
  fiddling with AV equipment in
    midpresentation, 304–305
  finishing too abruptly, 309
  inappropriate, low quality AV materials,
    305
  looking at watch, 307–308
  making repeated reference to sports (sports
    analogies), 307
  mismanaging sniffles, 306–307
  misunderstanding assignment, 301
  not using microphone, 303
  offering excuses, 303
  pacing back and forth, 306
  public throat clearing, 304
  reading from notes or a script, 305–306
  running overtime, 309
  selling (extended pitches in speeches), 308
  shifting wardrobe, 304
  stepping out of sight (moving behind front
    rows), 305
  in story telling (building up too slowly),
    306
  tapping/blowing into microphone, 303–304
  waiting for latecomers, 302–303
Mitford, Jessica, 31
Model, creating, 29
Most memorable character (story telling), 95
Motivation, speaker's, 18–21, 98–99
Motivational presentations, 11
Moving on the platform. *See* Physical
    activity/movement
Mpiweb.org (Meeting Professionals
    International), 219
Mpnetwork.com, 218
Multimedia, 84
Multiple engagements, 189–190
Music, using, 233–234

National Speakers Association's directory
    (*Who's Who in Professional Speaking*),
    117
*National Trade and Professional Associations
    of the United States,* 219
Newsletter, providing, 123–124
Newspapers (as source of topics), 25

Nightingale, Earl, 33
Nine-eleven terrorist attack, impact of, 179
Nonprofit organizations, 190

One-sheet. *See* Marketing materials
Online presentations, 88–89, 139. *See also*
    Internet/Web sites
Opening your presentation, 269–274
  conveying emotion, 273–274
  conveying sense of love, 271–272
  with dramatic flair, 273
  gambits, 230–233
  starting your speech, 50, 269–271
  surveys, 230–233
Opinion leaders (as source of topics), 23–25
Other speakers:
  avoiding hearing those before you,
    258–259
  comparing yourself with peers, 136–137
  emulating one-sheet of, 149–150
  exchanging materials/videos with, 136
  getting tapes of, 237
  meeting at conventions, 132
  recommending/suggesting, for desired fee,
    221
  working off of, 236
Overhead transparencies, 81–82
Ownership, instilling sense of, 37–38

Pain, listeners', 10, 279
Painting, word, 100, 102
Pancero, Jim, 192
Paradigm shift (topic type), 5
Participation packets, audience, 8, 177–178,
    183, 230, 279
Pauses/silences:
  effective uses of, 108–114
  enhancing humor, 112
  historical examples, 111
  in midsentence, 110–111
  not wasted time, 108–109
  for powerful climax, 110
  practicing, 113–114
  seeming longer to speaker than audience,
    109
  seriousness conveyed by, 112–113
  before starting speech, 110–111
  stumbling/blanking out, 111–112,
    261–262, 296–297
Peers. *See* Other speakers
Pennington, Robert, 290–291
Perez, Rosita, 205
Peters, Tom, 26

Photograph, professional, 150–154
Physical activity/movement, 76–77, 283–284
  common mistakes:
    pacing back and forth, 306
    stepping out of sight (moving behind
      front rows), 305
  expansive, 73
Physical comfort (audience), 104
Pocket dictators, 217–218
Porter, Michael, 35
Positioning in marketing, 120–125
Pre-presentation:
  arriving well in advance, 118
  breathing exercise, 261
  client factors (giving speaker "space" prior
    to presentation), 178
  control factor, 260–261
  creating fail safe environment, 261–262
  greeting members, 119, 258, 265–267
  jitters/anxiety, dealing with, 259–261
  shielding yourself from other speakers,
    258–259
  taping key words to floor or podium, 261
  transition: approaching showtime, 267–268
Presentation(s):
  audience (see Audience)
  common mistakes, 301–310
  customized, 176
  ending/closing (see Closing)
  high-content, 69–72
  impact of (four levels), 186–187
  introduction to (see Introduction (of
    speaker))
  opening (see Opening your presentation)
  opportunities for marketing at, 132
  perceived value, 72
  taping (see Taping presentation)
  topics for (see Topics)
  trouble (see Problems/challenges)
Presentation materials:
  GET audience participation packets, 8,
    177–178, 230, 279
  kit, 182
  props, 282–284
  visuals (see Visuals)
Presentation tips: developing/enlivening,
    47–114
  assignment expectations, 71–72
  audience involvement/responsiveness (see
    Audience)
  body and movement, 73–77
  deep-seated appeal, 61
  diction, 59–60

freezing the moment, 74–76
fresh, keeping material, 45–46
humor (see Humor)
logical sequence at right time, 70–71
mixed volumes and tones, 74
pauses/silences, 108–114
presenting best of you, 57–68
seamless, 235–238
stimulating/enervating audience, 71
story telling (see Story telling)
trilogistic speech, 61
visuals, 78–90
Problems/challenges:
  audience, 291
  being asked to shorten your presentation,
    293–294
  blanking out or stumbling, 111–112,
    261–262, 296–297
  equipment glitches, 83, 87
  hecklers, 292
  jitters (pre-speech), 259–262
  questions from audience, 284, 297–300
  working with hotel audiovisual staff,
    86–88
Products/services, selling, 128, 140,
    144–145, 190, 199–205, 308
Professional associations/societies, 44–45
Professional Convention Management
    Association (PCMA), 219
Prop(s):
  audience, 282–283
  clothing, 284
  presenter as, 283–284
Publications, editorial coordination, 128–129

Question/answer session, 284, 297–300
Questionnaire, pre-speech, 119
Quiz exercise card, sample, 232

Reading:
  by introducer, of your introduction speech,
    243–244
  jokes, 51–52
  from notes/script, 305–306
Reagan, Ronald, 49, 75, 273
Register.com, 139
Religion, 224
Restructuring/downsizing, 35–36
Retreats (meeting type), 43–44
Robbins, Tony, 10
Roberts, Julia, 67
Robertson, Jean, 96–97
Robinson, Grady Jim, 95

Room layouts. *See* Meeting room(s), layouts
Roosevelt, Franklin Delano, 111
Rumsfeld, Donald, 273
Rylatt, Alistair, 74–75

Salsbury, Glenna, 150
Santos, Tricia, 122–123
Schwarzkopf, Norman, 273
Seasonal topics, 4
Seating arrangements. *See* Meeting room(s), layouts
Secondary audiences, identifying, 8–9
Selection committees, winning over, 182–183
Selling products/services, 128, 140, 190, 199–205, 308
Seminars:
    conducting your own, 124–125
    speaking at, 41–42
Sexual references, 225
Shared speaker, 190
Shortening presentations, 293–294
Six-Three-Six Rule, 84
Slides, 82
Small businesses, 44
Sniffles, managing, 306–307
Speaker(s):
    always being at your best, 57–68, 237–238
    athletic skill, 76
    contracts (*see* Agreements/contracts)
    enjoyment (secret to effective speaking), 66–67
    marketing (*see* Marketing; Marketing materials)
    as the message, 57
    motivation, 18–21, 98–99
    responsiveness, 119
    style (meeting planner concerns), 176
    wardrobe tips, 58–59
    what meeting planners want from, 117–119, 175–176
Speaking topics. *See* Topics
Speech coach, using, 62–66
Sponsors, corporate, 130
Spoon feeding audience, 279
Sports analogies, overusing, 307
Sports/hobbies (source of stories), 94
Stallings, Fran, 102–103
Starsite.com, 218
State and Regional Associations of the United States, 219
Statistics, industry (collecting), 125

Story telling, 91–97, 98–107, 306
    bringing audience along, 91–92
    fitting into speech, 102
    listening experience (audience factors), 102–105
    mapping, 100
    mistakes in, 92, 306
    MIT (most important thing), 99–100
    motives and, 98–99
    painting a picture, 102
    perfecting your story, 99–100
    practicing, 105–107
    reconstructing setting (going to story location), 100–101
    signature story, finding/developing, 91–97
    word painting, 100
    words/expressions, choosing carefully, 101
Sturm, Brian, 103
Summary *vs.* closing, 294
Surveys/questionnaire/quizzes, 119, 177, 230–233
Symposium (meeting type), 41

Taping coaching session, 64–65
Taping presentation:
    discount for organization that does this, 137
    issues, when taping requested by client, 201–205
        copyright, 205
        fee, 204–205
        microphone in audience, 205
        sample taping agreement, 202–203
    opportunities for onsite testimonials, 131–132
    reasons to tape yourself, 131–132
    reviewing tapes of yourself, 46, 131, 272–273
    salvaging, 87
Technology, incorporating new, 37
Telephone:
    conference call, 184
    headsets, 88, 217
    leaving messages, 228
    no-click keyboard for using during conversation, 216
    recording conversations, 32, 216–217
    toll-free and fax numbers, need for, 118
Television, closed circuit, 89–90
10 Percent Rule, 84–85
Terminology, sensitivity/awareness in:
    inclusive language, 224–225
    insensitive terms, 222

religious views, 224
  sexual references, 225
  war and attack metaphors, 179
Thatcher, Margaret, 273
Thinking *vs.* speech (speed of), 108
Thomas, Carol Copeland, 224
Throwaways, saving, 28–29
Thurmon, Dan, 76, 283
Time factors:
  avoiding looking at your watch, 307–308
  being asked to shorten your presentation, 293–294
  running overtime, 309
  techniques for keeping track of time, 293, 308
  using a timer, 293, 308
  waiting for latecomers, 302–303
Topics, 1–46
  association executives as sources for, 25
  brainstorming guidelines, 32–33
  buzzword approach to selecting, 6–7
  change as, 34–38
  commentary sections of newspapers as sources for, 25
  creativity in finding, 33–34
  cyclical, 4–5
  deficiencies approach to finding, 15–16
  emotions, appealing to, 10–17
  exercises to stimulate thought, 16–17
  expanding on what you're already saying, 29–30
  gaps in other people's presentations, 31
  gurus as sources, 26
  "hot," 4
  ideal, 19
  inspirational presentations, 11
  irritations approach to finding, 15
  librarians as sources for, 26–27
  list generation, 14
  long-term, 4–5, 7–8
  meeting planners as sources for, 22–24
  meeting types and, 39–46
  model for generating, 29
  motivational presentations, 11
  opinion leaders as sources for, 23–25
  paradigm shift, 5
  recording telephone conversations, 32
  researching, 22–27
  seasonal, 4
  serious/humorous versions, 8
  seven subtle unconscious desires, 12–13
  variety of, 3–9
  what people traditionally want, 13–14
  your driving forces (topics of passion) and, 19–20
  your hidden strengths, 28–33
  your intriguing subjects, 31
  your motives for speaking and, 18–21
  your throwaways as, 28–29
Trade associations, 45
Trade Show Exhibitors Association, 219
Trading services with clients, 190
Trailblazers (change as topic), 36–37
Training (meeting type), 42–43
Travel:
  airline travel/reservations, 247–248
  efficient use of time, 246–247
  expenses, 196
  glitches, 87
  impact of 9/11 terrorist attacks, 179
  mailing packages to yourself, 245
  preventative measures while checking in, 248
  proper packing, 246
  tips, 245–248
Trends, spotting, 5
Trilogistic speech, 61
Trudeau, Garry, 270
Tunney, Jim, 110–111
Turisi, Judy, 58

Ury, William, 189

Vertical opportunities, 129
Videos:
  demonstration tape (*see* Marketing materials, video demonstration tape)
  as part of presentation, 83–84
  taping your presentation (*see* Taping presentation)
Viewcharts/flipcharts, 80–81
Visuals, 78–90. *See also* Audiovisual considerations
  10 Percent Rule, 84–85
  benefits, 78–79
  closed-circuit television, 89–90
  color combinations, 85–86
  fonts, 85
  general principles for using, 84–85
  importance of quality of, 118–119
  key considerations, 79
  online presentations, 88–89
  shapes, 85
  Six-Three-Six Rule, 84

Visuals *(Continued)*
  types of:
    image magnification technology (I-Mag
      screens), 82–83
    multimedia, 84
    overhead transparencies, 81–82
    printed materials, 79–80
    slides, 82
    videos, 83–84
    viewcharts/flipcharts, 80–81
  working with hotel audiovisual staff,
    86–88
Voice:
  improving diction, 59–60
  mixed volumes and tones, 74, 281
  using speech coach, 62–66
Voice and Speech Trainers Association
  (VASTA), 63
Volunteering to serve in an additional
  capacity, 188

Walker, Al, 239
Walters, Barbara, 281
Wardrobe. *See* Clothing/wardrobe
Washington (directory), 219
Waterman, Robert, 26
Web sites. *See* Internet/Web sites
Wexler, Phil, 43
"What it means to you" (use of phrase),
  277–278
Wilder, Lilian, 60
Wilkinson, Bruce, 7, 96
Word list, 59–60
Word painting, 100
Workshops, 42

Yoho, David Alan, 95–96, 109–110, 185
Yudkin, Marcia, 148